PRAISE F...

*Beating Depression and Bipolar Disorder Without Drugs: A
Memoir of Survival in a Male-Dominated World*

This is an outstanding memoir by a brilliant Clinical Psychologist, Dr. Julia Sherman. It is beautifully written, scientifically
sound, and easily understood by the thoughtful reader. I recommend this book to everyone interested in learning how to overcome life obstacles successfully.

> Florence L. Denmark, PhD, Distinguished Research
> Professor, Pace University, New York, Former President of the
> American Psychological Association

Julia Sherman is an illustrious psychologist and important fore-
mother in feminist psychology. This is her story, a tale of survival and resilience in her battle with depression in the context
of a male-dominated, medicalized mental health profession. The
description of her battles—with her illness and also with dismissive medical providers insisting on drugs for her treatment—is
a cautionary tale. Her call for women to work together and use
their combined political power is timely; I hope this book will
serve as a catalyst for action.

> Nancy Russo, PhD, Regents Professor of Psychology
> and Women and Gender Studies—Emeritus, Arizona State
> University

This memoir is quite extraordinary since it is written by a sophisticated researcher and clinical psychologist who bravely,
frankly, reveals her own struggles with mental illness—even as
she finds psychiatrists lacking, even dangerous. Sherman also
creates a new kind of memoir, one that brings research studies
to bear on her own personal and professional experiences as a
daughter, a graduate student, and a working professional. She
reveals the extent to which she and most of us were subjected

to misogynist contempt by our teachers and to outright sexual harassment and assault. This work documents an era that, alas, has not entirely passed. Brava, Julia!

Phyllis Chesler, PhD, Emeritus Professor of Psychology and Women's Studies at City University of New York

This engaging, honest tale was written by a distinguished clinical psychologist who did seminal work in the psychology of women and contributed with her impressive evolutionary theory on the origins of bipolar disorder, both of which were intertwined with her personal life. The book is worthwhile for several audiences: those who practice psychotherapy, those who care to vicariously experience the social changes of America during the mid-to-late Twentieth Century, those who are distressed by the over-reliance on drugs and the medical model in modern psychiatry, and those particularly interested in the psychology of women. There are other sources on all of these topics, but Sherman's autobiographical story stands out for its ability to weave together the professional and scientific with the personal.

Fred Previc, PhD, University of Texas at San Antonio, author of *The Dopaminergic Mind in Human Evolution and History* (2009) MIT Press

Beating Depression and Bipolar Disorder Without Drugs

A Memoir of Survival in a Male-Dominated World

Beating Depression and Bipolar Disorder Without Drugs

A Memoir of Survival in a Male-Dominated World

Julia A. Sherman, PhD, ABPP

Persephone Publications
Madison, Wisconsin

Cover design by Susan Wenger, Cover to Cover LLC, Tucson, AZ.

ISBN: 978-0-9899987-7-2 (Print Edition)

ISBN: 978-0-9899987-8-9 (Digital Edition)

This book is a work of memoir; it is a true story based on the author's best recollections of various events in her life. The names and identifying characteristics of certain people mentioned in the book have been changed to protect their privacy. In some cases, the author has compressed events and time periods in service of the narrative, and dialogue has been re-created to match the author's best recollections of those exchanges.

Dedication

*To my parents: Roy V Sherman, PhD
and Edna Schultz Sherman
and
The Good Samaritan*

Acknowledgments

My thanks to editor Sharon Miller and Larry Bodine, Esq., for their help and advice, and to those who read and criticized parts or all of the text: colleagues Larry Cahill, PhD, Phyllis Chesler, PhD, Barry R. Komisaruk, PhD, Fred Previc, PhD, Nancy Russo, PhD, and friends Casey Baldus, Joan Jensen, Sondra Match, MSW, and Mark Stinsky, PhD.

Contents

Foreword

I originally wanted to title this book *The Personal is Political*, a feminist rallying phrase from the 1970's (Hanisch, 1970), but alas and alack, few people knew what it meant. It means that women, including me, have been moved to action, and political action, out of the realization of the hurt, bias, and injustice wrought upon us simply because we're female.

Part memoir, part history, part science, and part a call to action, *Beating Depression and Bipolar Disorder Without Drugs: A Memoir of Survival in a Male-Dominated World* provides intellectual and emotional focus on specific feminist issues with an emphasis on the fraudulent hype of psychiatric drugs, the problems of depression and bipolar disorder, a new theory, and a drugless treatment born in the crucible of scientific knowledge and desperation. Moreover, there are other things you should know, and I don't know who'll tell you if I don't. This is a story from the "Dark Ages" of the 20th century, and it is my hope that you'll learn something of use.

My name is Julia Sherman, and I have a PhD in clinical psychology. I earned that PhD in 1957 when not many women were getting PhDs. I am a Diplomate of the American Board of Examiners in Professional Psychology, and I was elected Fellow of both the American Psychological Association and the Association of Psychological Science. I was awarded these recognitions of excellence even though I've never held a regular academic position.

We are at a turning point: Millions of women have legal protection against physical injury, abuse, and forced pregnancy from husbands or stray males for the first time in all of history. These changes have happened during my lifetime. Over two hundred years ago, our nation began with the principle that all men are created equal, and ever since we've been moving toward better fulfillment of this ideal and the full inclusion of women. But one swallow doesn't make a summer, and one Year of the Woman is just a great beginning.

In the old days when I grew up, lots of girls didn't get the same education as their brothers. Some of us didn't even get to choose who we married or if we married. Many of us weren't told the facts of life and had to find out the hard way. Divorce was difficult to get and the terms were often unfair. Child support was a joke. Things have changed, but rights on paper are often not rights in fact. Women aren't equally paid and equally represented in positions of status. Power is still overwhelmingly held by men who aren't always just and ethical, and women are often intimidated into foregoing their rights. Women have been oppressed since the beginning of recorded history, and the methods to oppress them have often been subtle. That's what the consciousness raising groups of the last century were all about. This memoir will alert you to some ways oppression was and is achieved.

In 1971, I wrote *On the Psychology of Women: A Survey of Empirical Studies,* the first scientific book on the topic, superseded this year by a handbook twice its size (Travis & White, 2018). Now, almost fifty years later, I am addressing the topic again. This time, the account enlightens personal experiences with the insights of science.

My life story is a harrowing one of surviving sexual abuse, #MeToo experiences, dosage with psychiatric drugs until I was a hulk of my former self, and the malignant vengeance of men who sought to punish me because I dared to be a witness against one of their own who had sexually abused a patient.

However, with a vital urge for survival, I've sought answers: Why was I so depressed and miserable? From years of thinking and research into the scientific literature came a new understanding of depression and bipolar disorder involving chronobiology: a new frontier in neuroscience. I went off the psychiatric drugs, and, using the results of my research involving light and dark treatments, I've led a healthy drug-free life for nearly twenty years. The rigors of life have pulled much from me but left me with a pen. As Clifford Beers (1908/1981) said in the title of his memoir, I am truly A *Mind that Found Itself.*

Chapter 1

The Effects of Childhood Traumatic Experiences

Iwas born in 1934 when Shirley Temple was everyone's darling. Like her, I had blonde hair and big eyes, though her eyes were brown, not blue like mine. When I was not yet five, Dr. Simmons, president of Akron University, a big tall man with blue twinkly eyes, tossed me in the air after the Sunday church service at the Universalist Church (similar to the Unitarian Church). I squealed with delight. When he set me down, I gazed up at him and solemnly declared to the resounding laughter of the surrounding adults, "I'm going to marry you when I grow up." I was dismayed by the laughter. What was the joke? What did I do? As an adult watching *Heidi,* an old Shirley Temple movie, I realized that I'd seen it before, and I was startled to find how much I'd identified with little Shirley and her precocious, pert manner. My behavior with Dr. Simmons could have come right out of a Shirley Temple movie.

That Shirley Temple became my ego ideal may seem strange, but there were a series of incidents that helped make it so. When I was three years old, a deputation of my mother's sisters and friends came from Iowa to visit us in Ohio, and they brought me a beautiful, expensive Shirley Temple doll, the kind of doll a girl should treasure. I, myself, had been dolled up for the occasion in a flounced, lemon-yellow muslin dress. I was ceremoniously presented with the doll, and then the ladies became absorbed in their own conversation and paid no more attention to me. There was no one for me to play with or talk to.

It was a lovely, warm sunny day, and I wandered outside. The backyard was idyllic, surrounded by a carefully trimmed privet hedge; the interior was rimmed with glorious, blooming flowers planted by my father. In one corner there was a spot reserved for my turtle. Dad had sunk my old white, enamel baby bath tub in the ground, filled it with water, and put a rock in it so that the turtle had a place to rest. Here my turtle lived, and I was happy to see it stretch out its little neck as though in greeting. "Wouldn't it be a good idea to give dolly a bath?" In she went. In the process of bathing her, I must admit that I may have gotten a little muddy, and dolly didn't come clean easily. Puzzled, I dunked her again—and again. "Hmm, not a very good result." As I surveyed the disaster, my mother and the horrified ladies arrived. Aunt Teen was still tut-tutting about it some thirty years later.

There are other memories less benign.

"Don't go outside," Mother called from upstairs. About four years old, I was alone downstairs and supposed to get my own breakfast. Opening the cupboard door, I put one foot on the shelf and hoisted myself onto the kitchen counter. From here I could stand and reach the bright orange Wheaties box and get a bowl. I placed them on the counter and carefully climbed down. Then, I went to the ice box for a quart of milk and poured myself some cereal and milk.

"Remember now. Don't go outside," Mother called again from upstairs.

"I won't," I shouted and ate my cereal. The sun glowed through the window; the house was quiet, and I forgot what Mother said. It was summer and I was bare-foot, dressed in shorts and a halter. I left the house, crossed the street, and began playing in the sandbox of our neighbor where I sometimes stayed when Mother was sick. She'd been sick a lot. The father at this house was the county sheriff, highly respected and important in the community. I hadn't been there long when my mother came flying up in a rage, gowned in her long, navy blue housecoat with the beautiful red hibiscus flowers on it. For a sick woman, she was mighty swift. Glowering with iridescent fury, she yelled, "I told you not to leave the house." She grabbed me by the arm and began dragging me home. I howled in pain, "Stop, stop, you're hurting me." She paid no attention. The pain was excruciating; she'd dislocated my shoulder; I passed out.

As I grew up, I couldn't throw a ball, swim normally, or hit a golf ball any distance. But I didn't understand there was anything seriously wrong with my shoulder until I was in my fifties and it became painful. After spending fruitless weeks in physical therapy, I went to a new doctor who x-rayed the shoulder and told me it'd been seriously injured before the age of five.

In retrospect, I realize why my mother was so angry that I'd disobeyed her and left the house. Her reputation as a mother was on the line. I couldn't be seen wandering off by myself to the sheriff's house. He had twin boys about ten years old, Billy and Jim (pseudonyms). They and the rest of the boys in the neighborhood played football in the street outside our house, or sometimes all of us played Kick-the-Can. One day, before the dragging incident with my mother, when I was still four, I found myself on the cold cement floor in the basement of the sheriff's house, with my arms and legs held down, yelling my head off. Lots of boys were there. Billy and Jim had their father's gun and threatened me with it if I continued to make noise. They put the gun to my head and pulled the trigger. It clicked. I was terrified and fell silent. Billy and Jim told the boys to form a line, and, one by one, they approached me. My legs were held down, spread apart so the boys could see my vagina, and some of them touched it. They were quiet, almost reverential. I kept struggling and trying to see, but Billy held my arms down, my angry little fists pressed against my neck; another boy kept covering my eyes. Suddenly Billy's mother appeared on the steps coming down into the basement. "What are you boys doing?" she shouted. I don't remember any more.

Later, there was an "inquiry." Even though the boys' mother had seen me held down, genitals displayed, with their father's gun to my head, I don't know what she told my mother or what she told her husband. There was a public image problem. The facts were unpalatable and begged to be replaced; hence, the inquiry.

As it commenced, I was ceremoniously presented to the sheriff while he sat at the kitchen table eating his breakfast, his big gun strapped to his ample waist. He was a tall, heavy-set, jovial man who didn't seem much interested in the proceedings, steadily shoveling in the bacon and eggs. My mother hovered in the background, along with a host of boys and their mothers who suddenly appeared out of nowhere, crowding the edge of the small room. The sheriff started talking to me about Negroes, but I didn't know what he meant. (Very young children don't notice racial differences.)

"What are Negroes," I asked.

"They're black people," he said.

"What do you mean, black?"

"They're black," he repeated.

I was puzzled, "You mean black all over?"

"Yes, black all over."

"You mean even their teeth are black?"

The sheriff boomed with laughter and the interview came to an end. I don't know why he was talking to me about Negroes. Apparently, the plan was to summon the neighborhood to a "hearing" in which it would be demonstrated that my allegations implicating his sons in misbehavior were groundless. There were lots of talkative little boys who knew the truth, but it didn't matter. This was a show trial for adults. The sheriff probably planned to lead me into some kind of testimony that would implicate a Negro. Much later, my aunt told me that a Negro man who cleaned for us lost his job although he was in no way responsible for what happened in the basement. To top off the ludicrous injustice of the situation, my mother later reproached me because she had to let him go. "He was such a good worker," she said plaintively.

Like many a mother confronted with a daughter's sexual abuse, she found my story about the events in the basement hard to believe. Her line of thinking went something like this: "How could those nice boys, the sheriff's sons, do such things?" She ended up believing I was a liar, and though she was erratic in her child rearing practices, she impressed on me the importance of being honest. As a result of her admonishments, I became honest to a fault.

Still months later, when I was walking home from school, a boy I didn't recognize came up to me and hissed in my ear, "Don't tell, or your mother will die." His threat paralyzed me with fear. How cunning he was. How did he know that it'd be more effective to threaten me with my mother's death than my own? My mother had been seriously ill with separate surgeries for gallstones and kidney stones, and I feared for her. Now "telling" became associated with traumatic stress. I wasn't even sure what I wasn't supposed to tell, but the message was clear: Watch your mouth or bad things will happen. How many girls and women are intimidated not to "tell"?

Notice how early the boys were forming into a tight-knit cooperative band for sexual exploitation. The behavior involved threats of violence and cover-ups, a situation we'll see repeated among adults in the epidemic of psychiatrist sexual misconduct in Madison, to be described later.

However, those rowdy boys weren't through with me. A year or so later, Billy and several of his now early teenage buddies formed a circle near my house. I was surprised; I'd never seen them do anything like that before. When they beckoned me to join them, I was puzzled, but flattered. After I entered their circle, Billy asked, "Who has the biggest one?" It seemed I was to be the judge in a penis contest. I had never even seen a big, erect penis and really didn't understand what they were, but the boys kept urging me to make a judgment. It seemed important to them, and I resolved to do my best. Their penises were all erect, and I went around the circle inspecting, trying to decide which one was the biggest. When I reached the end of the circle, I couldn't contain my curiosity, and I touched the proffered penis. It disappeared. What happened? I turned around. All the penises were gone. "Where did they go?" I asked. They didn't answer; I was quickly ushered away and "forgot" all about it.

Traumatic experiences adversely affect mental health (Thurston et al., 2018), a fact that came out in the testimony of Dr. Christine Blasey Ford during the 2018 Brett Kavanaugh Supreme Court Confirmation hearings. In my case, during a period of severe stress as an adult, these early traumas revived, and for months I had recurring nightmares in which I awakened to find my fists painfully pressed against my neck as they were that day on the cold, cement floor. I was puzzled. Was something wrong with my throat? I went to a doctor who told me that there was nothing physically wrong. It took me awhile to figure out what was going on.

Traumatic memories from the past were coming back, expressing themselves in my dreams and even in my art. I had taken up watercolor painting and was so taken with the tiny image of a tiger found in an oil company ad that I made a painting of it. Of all the things I could have painted, why this image? This is an example of what Freud called the "return of the repressed." When I free-associated to the tiger, the first thing that came to mind was Billy, who became a star for the Detroit Lions. My attraction to the tiger logo is an example of what psychologists call stimulus generalization. Lions and tigers are closely associated. (There'll be more about stimulus generalization later.)

Next, I spent hours copying a picture of a hibiscus, though it was orange, not red, like the flower on my mother's robe. The power of those events to force their way into awareness after more than fifty years is amazing. I also painted a pink bittersweet flower surrounded by much too much barren ground to be an effectively balanced painting. I was inspired by a bittersweet I'd seen in the west, amazed how it could pop out of that cold, empty springtime ground. The repressed memory?

As a child, I took it for granted that my mother loved me and that she would protect me and provide for me. It took a long time for me to understand how much she resented me. When I was about six, an incident occurred that began to register the truth. I was waiting with her while my father backed the car out of the garage. She was holding my hand. I said something she didn't like, and she began to squeeze my hand in the most intense, painful manner. I protested, "Mother, you're hurting me." She only squeezed harder. I was shocked, and my mind snapped back to the time she dislocated my shoulder. As I struggled to bear the pain, I saw a brilliant, pink portulaca, blooming in the space between the cement sidewalk squares. It was a stray flower, growing all by itself, far away from the other plants. Despite the fact that it had only the dirt between the squares of sidewalk, it bloomed.

My mother and I were different. She had brown eyes and dark brown, straight hair, often worn in a braid wound about her head while I had blue eyes and blonde hair. My mother had been good looking, a popular, outstanding student in high school. My father had been smitten with her, and they married after a brief courtship. However, she hated being a mother and resented us children. As an adult, I once phoned her long distance from Wisconsin to wish her a happy Mother's Day. In reply, she said, sobbing, "I never wanted to be a mother. I wanted to have a career. I had a chance to go to Washington and work at the Library of Congress."

She regretted marrying my father who never lived up to her expectations. Before marriage, she briefly worked at the Muscatine Public Library and did some research for Dr. Benjamin F. Shambaugh, an eminent early twentieth-century historian and prolific author. My mother expected my father (and, later, me) to be like Dr. Shambaugh, producing distinguished publications.

She, herself, aspired to be a writer, publishing short articles and poetry.

She was an unending source of disappointment. Near the end of my sixth decade, I read Joanne Harris's novel, *Five Quarters of the Orange* (2001). The venomous mother-daughter relationship leaped from the pages, and I celebrated with shocked empathy as Boise, the rebellious daughter, battled her mother. I was a wimp in comparison; I had lived in the hope of a different mother. When I was a teenager, the novel that captured my heart was Jean Stratton-Porter's *Girl of the Limberlost* (1909). In this story the daughter, like me, has a mean mother, and she finds solace by wandering in the deep woods. In the novel, though, the mean mother changes, and there's a happy ending. My hope for a different mother was not to be. Despite calculated interludes of niceness, she never changed.

My mother suffered from an undiagnosed rare neurological disorder, which I, too, inherited. She spent much of her time lying in bed, reading magazines. This was still the era when doctors prescribed rest for everything. She rarely went outside; never went for walks; engaged in no exercise, and moped in the dark interior of the home. No wonder she was "poorly." At some point later on, she was prescribed phenobarbital, which made the neurological disorder worse, and, like one of the characters in Helen Santmyer's novel, *And Ladies of the Club* (1982), who became addicted to laudanum, she later became addicted.

I was always frightened that my mother would die, and from early on I felt responsible for her. I remember my father giving me the job of carrying a bowl of soup up the stairs to her bedroom. The soup jostled back and forth in the shallow bowl. What could I do? Try as I might, each step made it worse. I was horrified as I saw my mother's soup slop over the sides, first one side and then the other each time my short little legs climbed another step. By the time I reached my mother's room, there was almost no soup left and I was hysterically crying. Surprisingly, she took pity on me, and my father came quickly to my rescue when he heard me crying.

My father was a just and kindly man who loved my mother and his family. He was head of the political science department at Akron University and hardworking both in his profession and at home. He often scrubbed the kitchen floor, improved our homes, and gardened with great success. He had worked his way through college and graduate school as a chef at Reich's Café in Iowa City, receiving his PhD in political science in 1927. He often cooked for us and rarely complained about my mother, but she often disparaged him behind his back. My father was a great, positive influence in my life. It was he who one day pulled Darwin's *On the Origin of Species* (1859) from the bookcase in the hallway outside my bedroom. He abjured me: "Remember this book." I was far too young to read the book, but I did remember.

I absorbed other of my father's values as well. The Universalist Church we attended had a creed which began, "We believe in the truth, known or to be known." What a powerful guiding principle for life. I was brought up in a home of liberal values with a strong awareness of advocacy for civil rights for women, Jews, and Negroes, the 1950s name for African-Americans. My mother was the first president of League of Women Voters in Akron; my father advocated for the right of Negroes to buy property in white neighborhoods, and he spoke out about discrimination against Jews at the university. When, at age thirteen, I was chosen to give the eighth-grade valedictorian speech, it was natural for me to speak on civil rights for Negroes. I have been a feminist all my life, a product of an earlier wave of feminism.

Dad was also a devoted Mason. I never understood what this meant until late in life when I ran across a book that described Masonic beliefs, normally kept secret. Then I realized that he conveyed some of these values to me: love of nature, responsibility to contribute to the community, and the courage to face death, which he did with exemplary stoicism. However, the great debt I owe my father is his protective care. It's entirely possible that I wouldn't have survived without it.

During the summer of the incident in the basement, the public relations campaign to demonstrate that "there is nothing to see here" continued. The sheriff, his wife and sons; my father, the professor, and my mother had proper images to uphold. My mother was unusually conscious of her reputation. She came from a small town in Iowa, and she was German, not so popular during World Wars I and II. Moreover, she hid a big secret all her life: She was actually the illegitimate child of my grandfather and an unknown Chippewa woman (ascertained by DNA testing). Like Mrs. Bucket in the PBS series, *Keeping Up Appearances*, her public image was extremely important to her. In any case, probably through the sheriff, it was arranged for a reporter from the Akron Beacon Journal to come to our house to take a picture of my mother and me making baking powder biscuits. Mother hated to cook and frequently ruined the food. On this occasion, she forgot to list the baking powder among the ingredients for the recipe, an omission she found highly amusing.

To get me ready for the photographer, she put some gooey, green wave set on my hair and tediously formed Shirley Temple corkscrew curls. I didn't want that green stuff on my hair, and I squirmed and complained. In order to get me to cooperate, she kept telling me that she was going to make me beautiful. At the end, she gave me a mirror to look at myself. I burst into tears. The wet hair hung down, scraggly, framing my sour face. I didn't look beautiful at all. However, I quickly forgot about it and behaved on cue when the photographer came.

Looking into a mirror came to have special significance for me. Mother took me to see *Snow White and the Seven Dwarfs*. "Mirror, mirror on the wall, who is the fairest of them all?" asked the stepmother. Alas, the mirror didn't give the right answer, and the stepmother flew into a rage and turned into a witch. Then she took a poisonous green apple, and, with great aplomb, dropped it into a bubbling cauldron, from which it emerged as a shiny red apple. Later, she conned Snow White into eating the apple, and then Snow White seemed to die. At that point in the movie, I began wildly screaming, and Mother had to take me out.

Subsequently, I never liked that shade of green. The reaction wasn't as strong as a phobia, but it was definite. The movie crystallized the negative experiences I associated with my mother because she, too, could turn into a witch. I suffered from a broad traumatic reaction that included maternal abuse that occurred so early that I didn't consciously remember it. For example, she boxed my ears as a method of punishment. The hands are simultaneously clapped over the ears, which is extremely painful, but leaves no mark. She'd threaten, "Be quiet, or I'll box your ears." Like a dog, even a child too young to talk remembers such pain and its source.

These traumatic events showed up again a few years later when I was perhaps seven years old. My father brought home a live lobster for dinner. I had never seen a lobster before and was fascinated. He told me to watch to see what happened, and I looked on intently as the creature, which was green, was lowered into a bubbling pot of boiling water, like the witch's cauldron. In a few minutes, I was horrified to see it turn bright red. Green to red, live to dead. I became hysterical. I don't remember what the occasion was, but we were eating in the dining room instead of around the kitchen table. Although my father commanded me to sit at the table, I covered my eyes with a napkin and refused to eat. No way would I take a single bite of that lobster.

My reaction illustrates the spread of post-traumatic stress from mother, to movie, to green, to cooking lobster. This is another example of stimulus generalization. The classic historic scientific demonstration of this phenomenon was often presented in psychology textbooks: A child, who was conditioned to be afraid of a white rabbit, subsequently also became afraid of other white objects. The fear had *generalized*.

In my case, the original trauma had to do with memories of my mother turning into a mean, punishing person—a witch. This brought on a post-traumatic stress reaction in the movie when Snow White's stepmother changes into a witch; the green apple turns red; the witch turns back into the wheedling stepmother and poisons Snow White, putting her in a death-like state. Bottom line: Mother kills daughter.

A sympathetic sibling could have cushioned the effects of my mother's abuse, but my brother John, nearly three years older, delighted in picking on me. When I was five, my brother and I were playing on the floor at my mother's feet while she sewed. For no reason, John hauled off and slugged me, knocking the breath out of me. My mother didn't even stop stitching. "Now, John, don't do that," she said benignly. I was furious. She was just going to let him get away with that. John was rolling on the floor laughing, and I saw my chance. Seized by righteous rage, smaller though I was, I hauled off and punched him. To my amazement, I hit the right spot and soon he was writhing in agony. That was a rare and satisfying moment.

John had multiple ways to make me miserable. He'd pull on my fingers saying, "Now your hands will look really ugly."

"No, they won't. No, they won't," I'd say, struggling to get away.

"Yes, they will," he'd say, pulling again on my fingers. "You're going to have big, big, ugly knuckles."

Or, he'd grab my arm and hit me with it, saying, "You're hitting yourself. You're hitting yourself."

One time, he and a neighbor boy tied me in a chair, and they wouldn't let me go. They kept shoving a picture of Gene Autry in my face saying, "Kiss him. Kiss him."

Even in high school, when I asked his advice about calling a friend of his to invite him to a dance, he didn't tell me that the guy was going steady. He let me call him, only to receive a humiliating refusal. Although lots of brothers pick on their sisters, they ultimately develop a firm loving relationship as adults. For John and me that never happened.

I wonder how many girls are conditioned to their lesser role in life by the way they're treated in comparison to their brothers and the way they are allowed to be treated by their brothers. He got new furniture; I got cast offs. I was required to clean my own room, but also his, which I deeply resented. When it came to college, I knew that money for his education came first. This I accepted and understood that I would have to make my own way.

To her credit, Mother *was* attentive to my intellectual development. My parents were best friends with Dr. Howard Evans and his wife, Maud. He was Dean of Education at Akron University, and she was a grade school teacher. They were childless, and my intellectual development often benefited from their advice to my parents. At night before we went to sleep, Mother would read Mother Goose rhymes to us. That is a practice that helps develop children's literacy, but she also read us Grimm's dark fairy tales. She seemed to delight in impressing upon us how harsh life could be and how cruel adults could be to children. I identified with Hansel and Gretel, Snow White, and Cinderella.

I was well fed and clothed, though not always appropriately. For example, I remember walking miles out of my way because I didn't want to be seen in my brother's oversized hand-me-down rubber boots that buckled up the front. At the other extreme, for my entrance into the first grade at Firestone Park School, Mother sewed me a blue velveteen, princess-style dress with hand-embroidered designs down the front. I guess she wanted to impress upon the teachers what an extraordinary child I was.

Starting school had been a momentous event, and I vividly remember getting my small pox vaccination. During the summer, before school started, my mother obtained the first-grade reader. It was bound in a red cover and had many pictures and few words. Mother slowly read each page to me, showing me the words as she read them. It was a snap. "See Jerry run." I easily learned to read the book. For a couple of days, I attended kindergarten where we sang and where there was a sliding board, which fascinated me. But Mother thought kindergarten was beneath me, so she arranged to have me tested by a psychologist to see if I could qualify for early admittance to first grade. I remember solemnly putting together the foal and mare puzzle, the preschool intelligence test used at that time.

I passed the test and, now, here I was, in my blue velveteen dress, entering the first-grade class after the semester had begun, and after the class had started. The students were all seated in neat rows; I knew no one there. They all knew one another from kindergarten. The teacher impatiently waved me to a desk in the back, and I sat down in my seat, but, after a while, I had to go to the bathroom. I didn't know what to do and wet my pants. Next thing I remember was walking home alone many, many blocks, crossing a main city artery, Market Street. The dress was ruined, and Mother never made me another one.

As a child, I gradually began to understand that something was wrong with my relationship with my mother. I heard schoolmates say they knew some people who took in an orphan to do the work around the house. "Aha," I thought. "That's it. I'm an orphan." The idea festered in my mind, and one day the thought grieved me so much that I began to sob. Mother wanted to know what was wrong, and I struggled to speak the terrible words, "I'm an orphan," and continued to sob. Finally, I got it out. For a short time, she seemed to take pity on me and things were better, but it didn't last.

When I was about eight, I told her that I was going to run away from home. She was amused. With a straight face, she declared that if I was running away, I'd better take a sandwich with me. We went to the kitchen where I watched intently while she ostentatiously fixed a sandwich. I was puzzled that she seemed to be enjoying herself, and I became suspicious. What was she up to? With a flourish, she carefully placed the sandwich in a wax paper bag, and then into a brown paper sack. She handed me the sack, accompanied me to the front door, and waved me goodbye. After a few blocks, I turned back, conscious of the futility of the plan. My mother greeted me matter-of-factly, and I didn't even cry. The experience had a strong effect: It persuaded me that my mother didn't care how I felt.

My mother thought herself extremely clever in the way she handled my running away, and I heard her laughingly tell the story to a friend on the telephone. I'm sure she repeated the story to my father, but I doubt that he was amused because the next day she belatedly inquired as to the reason for my leaving, which I explained was abuse from my brother. She said nothing in reply.

John was special to her because he replaced her first, still-born son, as well as her cherished brother, only slightly younger than she, who drowned in the Mississippi River when she was a teenager. Moreover, John was sickly like her, which made her solicitous of his needs. John had dark brown hair and brown eyes like her. He was mischievous, cute, and could do no wrong. However, twice he broke his arm by running it up the wringer of the washing machine, and one time he set a fire in the basement. Even though I was much younger, I knew it was wrong to start a fire and told him not to do it. Luckily, it was quickly discovered and put out.

I was a much better student than my brother, and the difference in our intellectual abilities quickly became apparent. When I was five, we were driving in our Ford automobile, and Dad was trying to drill John on arithmetic. John and I were in the back seat, and Mother was in front with Dad.

"What is three minus three," Dad asked John.

No answer. I had also been listening to the drills and knew the answer. "Zero," I said.

Dad chortled; he was pleased with himself that the child who took after his side of the family outsmarted her older brother. My Dad and I both had blue eyes and light hair. I was a good student, and more reliable and obedient than my brother. I wouldn't say I was my father's favorite, but he saw the need to protect me, and I was considered a gifted child, though by today's standards, I wasn't that exceptional. Since I looked like my Dad, he claimed me as a feather in his cap; I reflected well on him and his side of the family.

So far, I've told you how my life began, but this material also illustrates important psychological concepts having to do with repression and the unconscious. These are concepts from Freud's theory, most of which I reject (Sherman, 1971). However, the unconscious *is* a repository for traumatic memories which can influence our behavior without our conscious awareness or intent. These memories are said to be repressed, that is, excluded from conscious awareness because of their traumatic content. This also means they're outside the brain's system of rational thought. Unfortunately, a repressed memory doesn't always stay quietly hidden, sparing its owner a reminder of a painful, awful experience; the repressed material sometimes tries to force its way into consciousness. Since it comes from a primitive, pre-verbal part of the brain, the memory may be expressed in an aberrant form and identified as a symptom. Sigmund Freud called this "the return of the repressed." During a classical psychoanalysis, the patient lies on a couch with the therapist sitting behind, listening as the patient talks about whatever comes to mind. The idea is that repressed material will come to the surface and, with the help of the therapist, be integrated into conscious awareness, leading to reduction of symptoms. To learn more about psychoanalysis and contemporary psychoanalytic therapy, now called psychodynamic therapy, see Novotney (2017).

Freud's book, *Psychopathology of Everyday Life* (1951), gave numerous examples of how the unconscious expresses itself in behavior. Some of the examples were from his personal experience, but not labeled as such. However, going back to Freud's book some fifty years after I first read it, I found it hard to understand. I hope the more contemporary examples I've given from my American experiences will clarify the processes involved. Notice the detail in the experiences I recounted; these are actual memories, not fabrications. You've heard the claim, "I remember that as clearly as though it were yesterday." Ironically, emotional memories can be remembered more clearly than the events of yesterday.

The repressed material I reported was of different types: recurring nightmares, recovered memories, and the expression of traumatic memories occurring in my paintings. However, they all illustrate the deep memory impression of traumatic events and the urge of the repressed to come forward, "to speak out."

(The meaning of these experiences I figured out myself using the technique of free association.)

New research supports the validity of repressed memories and Freud's expectation that they would eventually be anchored in specific anatomical structures in the brain. (Freud had begun his career as a neurologist.) Studies by Professor James Cahill and his colleagues (1998, 2001) report a second memory system that encodes emotional information more sharply than is the case with the ordinary memory system. The stronger the emotion, the more sharply the memory is encoded. Unlike ordinary memories, which are consolidated in the hippocampus and later transferred to the neocortex where they become part of our general knowledge, emotional memories are stored in the amygdala, a part of the limbic system, which is the oldest part of the brain and wired for survival. There is a sex difference in the emotional memory system. Women's memories are stored in the left amygdala and men's in the right. Moreover, women's emotional memory system is stronger than men's. Women take note: You may clearly remember a past traumatic event that your male partner genuinely has no memory of.

Because emotional (traumatic) memories are stored in the old brain, they're not easily accessed or understood by the conscious mind like ordinary memories. The old brain differs from the neocortex, which is the result of later evolution and thinks in a different verbal, sequential, logical way while the old brain thinks in a primitive, nonverbal way, guided by basic instincts. The old brain and the emotional memory system have a bottom line dedicated to our survival; they try to warn us about potential dangers.

It may be helpful to view repressed memories and the unconscious in an evolutionary context. When we humans were in an earlier stage of evolution, we didn't have a neocortex, a sophisticated, thinking brain. At that time emotional memories had a more clear-cut survival value. Suppose that as a simple primate, you were in a terrible earthquake, and the experience was so traumatic that you "forgot" (repressed) it. Years later, when small earth rumbles occurred, they would trigger the emotional memory system, which would bring back the memory of the earthquake, and you would know what's happening. Consequently, you'd have a better chance of protecting yourself and surviving the quake. In the meantime, since the memory was "forgotten," you weren't consciously troubled by it.

The old brain and emotional memory system may still serve their function. On three occasions, I developed a strong antipathy and avoidance feelings toward three well-liked, ostensibly respectable men who were later revealed as predators of women. This puzzled me. Was it female intuition? Yes, but was it based on repressed traumatic memories? The men were Bill Cosby, Charlie Rose (observed on television), and the sinister Dr. Yallow (pseudonym), whom you'll meet later.

On the other hand, repressed memories may cause problems, such as in the case of post-traumatic stress disorder (PTSD). The old brain's primitive thinking style sometimes causes it to overreact or give a false alarm. For example, in war veterans, it may unleash a flashback of combat in reaction to a harmless loud noise. Or, the old brain and emotional memory system may intrude on consciousness in a disruptive way. Because it's dedicated to our survival, under conditions of threat, the old brain may override the left hemisphere to deliver its message, which may manifest itself in a bizarre symptom as will be illustrated in a later chapter with examples from my patients. Information from the unconscious must be interpreted to be useful to conscious thought.

This view of the unconscious and repressed memories explains many long-standing observations: Timely opportunity to talk about traumatic events may prevent repression because talking is a left hemisphere activity that encodes traumatic information in the conscious left hemisphere. *Unspeakable* occurrences, such as incest or secret crimes, are more likely to be associated with repression since, by definition, they're rarely spoken about and are stored where they're not easily accessed. Therapeutic techniques to retrieve repressed information—

amytal (truth serum) interviews, hypnosis, speeded responses, free association, automatic writing, dream analysis, drawing or writing with the left hand—are successful because they permit access to the old brain by evading the left hemisphere's control. Talking therapy may help individuals integrate repressed memories; in other words, talking about the memories with an empathetic listener defuses traumatic emotions and encodes them in the conscious left hemisphere.

Although emotional memories are now established factually on a sound scientific basis (Cahill et al., 1998; 2001), "forgotten" memories have been a controversial subject. Professor Elizabeth Loftus (2003) demonstrated that it's possible to suggest false memories of sexual abuse, and it's important to evaluate this point in legal proceedings. On the other hand, the research of Loftus does not discredit the potential serious traumatic effects of childhood sexual abuse. Traumatic events can have serious adverse effects on behavior.

Chapter 2

When Girls Were Girls

In the United States during the 1940s and 50s, girls were less sexually active, and some forms of sexual expression, like oral sex, were practically unknown. Today more girls are sexually active at younger ages, and they even menstruate earlier. I'm sure they're better informed, but making self-directed decisions about sexual engagement may still be a challenge. Today's freedom represents a strong cultural shift, especially compared to a hundred years ago. Girlish innocence no longer commands admiration as it once did.

Growing up during the Depression, I was largely sheltered from its effects, but when World War II broke out, everything changed. We lived on Archwood Avenue in Akron, Ohio, and heavy traffic pounded past our house night and day, bringing war matériel back and forth from the factories—rubber tires, aircraft. Moreover, that wonder of wonders, the Goodyear blimp, was located in Akron.

My father was intensely patriotic, and to my horror, he tried to enlist in the Navy. He became seriously dejected when even the Seabees refused him. They claimed there was something wrong with his back, but he never had a back ache in his life. When others tried to escape the draft by claiming to have a bad back, it was ironic that my father was rejected because of a back problem he didn't have. This anomalous event was my great, good fortune. I don't know how I would have gotten along without my father.

There was a labor shortage, and Mother saw her opportunity. Recovered from her surgeries, she quickly talked her way into a job as head of employment counseling for the handicapped at the local government employment office. I was now nine years old, and after she started work, it was my responsibility to get dinner started. Mashed potatoes were a staple of our diet, and I peeled the potatoes and got them on to cook. As we sat around the kitchen table eating dinner, Mom would talk about her experiences with clients. I was fascinated, and the idea of helping other people appealed to me. Later she took a correspondence course in abnormal psychology from the University of Chicago, and I looked at her text book. I wasn't mature enough to understand it, but her counseling stories and interest in psychology encouraged me toward a career in psychology. She enjoyed the job and performed it with success.

Because my mother was working, the summer of my ninth year my parents decided that my brother and I would go to live with my paternal grandparents on their Iowa farm, but our departure was abrupt. I was asleep when my father packed me into the car, and when I woke up, we were at my grandparents' farm. My father spent one night and left the next morning without even saying "goodbye."

My grandmother quieted my sobs, explaining that John and I were to spend the summer on their small farm in southwestern Iowa. Although I was initially dismayed, it turned out well. The farm had no indoor plumbing and John and I pumped water from the well and carried the buckets to the house. The outhouse was equipped with a Sears Roebuck catalogue, which was an endless source of amusement. My weekly bath was taken in a galvanized metal tub with water Grandma heated on her prized gas stove.

Lacking electricity, at night we played board games gathered around the kerosene lamp that Grandma carefully cleaned and adjusted each morning.

I spent a lot of time with my grandmother who had always wanted a daughter, and John and I actually got along fairly well. Each morning we fed the orphan lambs with a green coke bottle filled with milk and topped with a rubber nipple. John and I took turns holding the bottle as the lambs greedily sucked up the milk. I was surprised when Grandma wouldn't let John bully me out of my turn. Grandma had been a schoolteacher and knew a thing or two about children.

She showed us how to collect eggs. However, try as I might, I couldn't get the eggs without a painful peck on the hand. Those Rhode Island Red hens would cock their heads, give me a beady eye, and get me every time. I cried, but Grandma didn't make fun of me or insist. Instead, John was given the job of plucking out the eggs, and Grandma tactfully allocated to me the task of carrying the shiny tin egg bucket.

There were also hordes of kittens to play with. I named and tamed them all. (My first literary success occurred that fall when we returned to Akron. The teacher sent me to the blackboard to write a story about my summer, and I wrote about the kittens. The teacher thought so well of the story that she had me copy it on paper and take it to the principal.)

Every evening, John and I fetched the cows from the pasture. On Saturdays, we went to the nearby town of Tingley, and, on our first Saturday, I was stunned when Grandma ordered us sundaes. I had no idea such delights existed. Earlier, Grandma let me pick out the cloth bags of chicken feed with the best designs on them. I was thrilled to be given this responsibility. (She made dresses from the cloth of the sacks.) Grandma taught me to sew, and I sewed a little doll quilt. Under her instruction, I also wove a small rug. One time she bought me a coloring book and a box of sixty-four Crayolas, which became one of my prized possessions. Grandma sewed extraordinary quilts. She was an outstanding cook and a methodical, clean, even-tempered, and highly intelligent woman. She ran a successful chicken business, and it was understood that this money was her own.

Although my brother and I got along well during the day, he'd pester me at night, and we fought. We both slept on a blanket on the floor in the living room outside my grandparents' bedroom where it was cooler. One night apparently there was one fight too many, and I awakened the next morning to find myself alone in a big bed in an upstairs room. What had happened? I began calling for my grandmother. She quickly arrived and told me that I would be sleeping up there from then on. She showed me the potty under the bed and somehow made it seem that sleeping up there wasn't so scary and lonely. The bed was high off the floor, and it was a bit of a struggle to get into, but it was comfortable and covered with attractive quilts that Grandma had made.

My grandfather was a kindly man and tolerant of our misbehavior: When we got into a forbidden pasture with a fierce billy goat, he yelled at us, vaulting over the fence and holding the goat at bay with his pitchfork until we got out. On another occasion, he had to yell us out of the wheat bin where we weren't supposed to be. John knew better, but coaxed me to get in, gleefully getting in himself. Grandpa was alarmed because you could sink in the wheat and smother to death. But most of the time we were good.

One day, my father arrived at the farm. Overwhelmed, I didn't want to let him out of sight, but he summoned my brother to accompany him behind the barn, and I wasn't allowed to go. I began to cry, wild with a sense of exclusion and rejection. "Why can't I go with them? What are they doing? Why can't I go with them?" Returning, my brother's face shone with smug satisfaction. They'd gone to relieve themselves, but such was the suppression of knowledge about sexuality and bodily functions that I had no idea what they were doing. No one said, "They've gone to piss," which would have settled the matter. Finally, my grandmother gave me a sketchy explanation that satisfied me more because of its empathy than its cognitive content.

I remember nothing of the trip home. Again, there were no explanations or goodbyes. Dad carried me asleep into the car and drove all night till we got home. The next thing I knew, my father awakened me—John was gone. Dad gave me a brusque order, "Go upstairs and see your mother." Dazed, I realized I was back in Akron. I got out of the car, went into the house, climbed the stairs, and stood awkwardly in the door of their bedroom, slowly gathering courage to approach my mother. She remained seated at her vanity, facing the mirror; she was getting ready to go to work. I first saw her face reflected in the mirror. Without rising, she summarily greeted and dismissed me. It was a chilling experience—like an eclipse of the sun. She was clearly furious. Apparently, Dad had conveyed criticism from his mother about how she raised us, perhaps concerning my brother and somehow involving me, and they had had a fight. She was still put out the next day when she angrily groused to me about grandma's criticism of the shoes she'd sent with me—huaraches and a pair of new saddle shoes that I never wore.

Compared to my childhood, Dad had grown up in a much more loving environment on his parents' farm. Grandparents can be a great source of good in a child's life. That brief summer with my father's parents taught me that I could be special, and it provided a template of a pleasant, industrious, orderly, clean way of living devoid of excessive emotionality. Unfortunately, after that summer on the farm, I had little contact with my grandparents, even by mail.

The summer before sixth grade marked a big change in my life: Our family moved from the part of town where the factory workers lived to West Hill where the owners of the rubber factories lived. At my new school, I was confronted with the meaning of class differences. King School had superior teachers and a cafeteria that served hot lunches for a nominal fee. Having absorbed the idealistic, democratic principles of my father, I was startled that another public school would be so different from Firestone Park. I was awed by the huge mansions and my contacts with wealthy classmates. Trinka Davis, who later became a successful entrepreneur and philanthropist, told about flying to Chicago for dinner. For eighth-grade graduation, she received the gift of a car and chauffeur. I keenly felt the rejection of the moneyed when the invitations to Mrs. King's dancing school were sent out and I didn't get one. Moreover, our house on Malvern Road was a mile from King School, and half the distance was up a steep hill. In addition to the barriers of wealth and class, the physical location of our home formed a social impediment since bus service was irregular and at the top of the hill.

However, I didn't miss the old neighborhood; I'd already lost my best friends there. My first best friend, when I was four, had moved away. Juanita Mick was younger than me, and we always played at her house down the block. This probably suited her mother fine, since Juanita was an only child then. I was a good girl, and we played well together. Once I fell down the cellar stairs and she caught me, cushioning my head so I wouldn't be injured. I was surprised to realize that she cared about me—my first valuable experience with friendship.

My next best friend, Phyllis Figard, was about my age. Again, we always played at her house. We both were studying piano, but the main thing we liked to do was play paper dolls. We would lie sprawled on the floor and outline the doll on a piece of paper and create our own new dresses. It was great fun, but then her family also moved away. I was invited to visit them at their new property out in the country. They had a big back lot, and Phyllis took me out into the field and said we were to catch snakes. At first, I didn't want to, but she told me that people even held poisonous snakes to their faces to prove their faith in God, and these were only garter snakes. She grabbed one and popped it into a bushel basket. Seeing how easy it was, I joined in. There were a lot of snakes. All went well until that evening. We had dinner and then her father conducted a Bible lesson around the dinner table. Mr. Figard was an extremely religious man, and he no doubt thought he was doing the right thing, but his evangelical approach was sadly misguided. At the end of the lesson, he looked at me straight on and said, "Your parents are going to Hell."

I was startled. "No, they're not," I protested.

"Yes, they are. They're going to burn in Hell," he roared.

I became hysterical. I had already lived for years in mortal fear that my mother would die, and now Mr. Figard was consigning her to the fires of Hell. Somehow Mrs. Figard got me quieted and to sleep. Early the next morning, my parents came and got me. After getting the story out of me, which set off more tears, they convinced me that it was all nonsense and that they weren't going to Hell.

It took a while to make friends in my new location, but I wasn't unhappy until my relationship with my mother took a turn for the worse. My hair was worn in pigtails, and my mother braided my hair every morning before she left for work, but this became my daily torture session. With each cross of the hair as she plaited the strands, she pulled painfully tight. I could see her grim face in the mirror, unmoved by my cries of protest. Why? What had I done?

But my pigtails came to an untimely end. By the next year, I had a new best friend, and while I was playing at her house, Barbara suggested that we cut off my pigtails. Although I was the only girl in my class with pigtails, I wasn't sure this was a wise idea. Barbara tried to convince me, taking me to her mother. Mrs. Turbeville was a wonderful woman and a great cook— generous—not a mean bone in her body. When she agreed with Barbara, I was persuaded that the pigtails should go, and Barbara's mother proceeded to cut them off. They were excited and assured me that I was going to look really great. Then they gave me a mirror to look at myself. I looked into the mirror. I felt horrified and deceived. I didn't think I looked nice at all. I began to sob hysterically. The incident revived the memories of the witch looking in the mirror in the Snow White movie and looking into the mirror after my mother promised me I'd look beautiful in the Shirley Temple curls. An inappropriate overreaction was the result. Barbara's parents hastily packed me off home where my mother was none too pleased to find me without braids.

My mother hadn't prepared me, but when my menstrual periods began at age twelve, I wasn't surprised because I knew from the other girls that I too would start "bleeding." During eighth grade more and more of us sat along the side during gym class because it was deemed unwise for girls to participate while menstruating (which is nonsense). I was amazed that the other girls were so unembarrassed, and taking heart by their example, I bravely took my place sitting along the side of the gym when it was my time.

I knew almost nothing about the facts of life and neither did many other girls. Charlotte, who lived up the street, told me, "See that little line of hairs that goes from your belly button down? Well, when it comes time to have a baby, this line splits open and the baby pops out." Another friend told me that she figured out what her older sister's Kotex pads were for: She used them to stuff her bra. I kid you not. She didn't realize that her own older sister had breasts.

Luckily, I was home when I got my first period. As I undressed for bed, I was surprised to see spots of blood on the crotch of my panties, but then I realized what was happening. I told my mother; she came into my room and in a special low growl said, "Let me see." I pulled down my panties; she saw the blood and said she'd get me a Kotex. That was it—no explanations or further discussion, ever.

That growl was special. I'd never heard it before and never heard it again until she mentioned Simone de Beauvoir's book, *The Second Sex* (1949/1952), an equally forbidden and taboo topic. She was apparently discussing the book with her women friends; I begged her to tell me about it, but not a word. She was theoretically a feminist, but it wasn't a consistent point of view.

I did well in the new grade school and was chosen valedictorian of my eighth-grade class, which required me to give a speech at the graduation ceremony. I had absorbed the idealism of my family and church and got the idea to speak on the topic of civil rights for Negroes without realizing that I was presenting highly controversial ideas to this wealthy, solidly white audience in 1947. After the speech, except for a brief word of praise from my English teacher, Mrs. Ault, I was snubbed, totally ignored. My parents didn't attend the ceremony because my mother was recovering from my sister Patty's birth. Although I was deposited at the school by my father, no arrangements were made to bring me home and there was nothing for me to do but walk the mile home alone in the dark. I cried all the way.

Everyone was in bed asleep when I got home so I went to bed. Off and on, even now, I have nightmares of being alone, trying to find my way. I wasn't lost that night, but perhaps, as Gestalt psychologists suggest, the nightmare is simply a metaphor for my life.

The next day no one in my family asked me how my speech went or how I got home. I guess my parents eventually figured out that I walked home alone because arrangements were made for me to go with a neighbor to the final event of the graduation celebrations, an up-scale dinner at a downtown hotel where we were served Baked Alaska for dessert.

My sister Patty had been born shortly after my thirteenth birthday, and I felt responsible to care for both the baby and my mother who called me, "Mother's little helper," and sought to butter me up. I felt sorry for my mother and did everything I could to help her. One night shortly after my sister was born, I heard her cry and cry. I couldn't figure out why my mother didn't get up to take care of her. (I'm sure my father never heard a thing.) After a while, I felt sorry for my little sister. I got up, went downstairs, and heated up a bottle for her. Without anything being said, I understood that this was now my job. I didn't mind helping and adored my little sister. During high school, I played a major role in doing the housework, laundry, ironing (my mother did teach me how to iron my father's shirts), cooking, and child care. My father did all the food shopping.

As my high school years progressed, I began to hate my mother. From what I've recounted already, it's obvious that I didn't feel loved and felt that she favored my brother, but she became downright mean: She took my cage of pet mice and put it in the garage where they froze to death. "Isn't that too bad," she said. She grabbed our pet cat, threw him in the car, and roared away, dropping off the cat miles into the countryside. You should have seen her face when she saw him strolling up the driveway a few weeks later. "Hurrah, hurrah, hurrah for the cat!" Not that I said a word or betrayed my glee.

She told me I could go to Alabama with Barbara, her Mom, and sister, but at the last minute she, with triumphant satisfaction, refused to give me the $35 I needed for the bus fare. I was eventually given the money, probably because my father intervened.

When my three-year-old sister got into my room, ruined my lipsticks, and made a mess that it must have taken hours to create, I angrily reproached my mother for not watching her. She became furious. "Get in the bathroom!" she commanded. She soon joined me with one of my father's belts. "I couldn't find a razor strap," she said. "I guess this will have to do. Take off your clothes!" She lay on the blows but quit before she drew blood. I guess she thought better of it; beating her daughter wouldn't look good to my father or her liberal friends. I told no one, but it was a decisive turning point in our relationship: I never loved her again.

In the 1950s, girls were expected to get married and have children. A college degree was nice, but then you got married. Many girls were conflicted about achieving intellectually because they felt it damaged their chances in the marriage marketplace. In the psychological literature, this attitude was called fear of success, but when I later tried to research the phenomenon, it proved difficult to demonstrate empirically. Perhaps, as in my case, girls also recognized the counter pressure to do well in order to succeed in the broader context, and the two pressures fought it out. At the level of emotional experience, fear of success was real enough to me. For example, I came in first in the state Latin contest, and my teacher openly praised me in class.

I was so embarrassed that I dropped Latin as soon as I could. I didn't want to be known as a brain.

Prevailing cultural attitudes also put a premature end to my study of mathematics in high school. I didn't know anything about analytical geometry, but it was the next mathematics course offered after the second year of algebra, and I thought I should take it. I liked the intellectual challenge of mathematics and did well enough with it. However, when I walked into the room on the first day of class, there were only three other students, all Jewish boys, including Charlie, who was acknowledged to be a genius. I felt out of place.

Charlie's presence was especially awkward. He'd been attracted to me: One day after school he invited me for a ride and took me to his house where he tried to explain Judaism to me and gave me a taste of matzo. I was puzzled by this dry, tasteless food and wasn't getting his explanation of its significance. I did get the bottom line: He couldn't date me because I wasn't Jewish. I felt affronted but accepted that well enough. However, now I was to be in a class with three boys, including Charlie, the genius I couldn't date.

Moreover, although it was only the first day of class, the boys were way ahead of me. They were excitedly grouped in front of a large, strange geometrical model they'd put together over the summer to illustrate a mathematical concept.

"What's that?" I inquired. They tried to explain it to me, but I didn't understand. Then the teacher, Mr. Kinny, entered the room. Pointing to the model, I asked him, "What's that?"

Mr. Kinny replied, "That's a _____." He said something I'd never heard of.

"I don't understand," I said.

"Of course you don't understand," he said. "You're a girl."

"Well," I said, "If I wasn't supposed to be in this class, why didn't someone tell me before this?"

I turned on my heel and headed for the principal's office. The boys trailed after me protesting. They wanted me in the class, but I was having none of it and promptly dropped the class. It's too bad I didn't take analytical geometry because it meant I couldn't take calculus. However, I still mastered the required minor in statistics in graduate school.

Unfortunately, traumatic sexual experiences continued during my adolescence. As I was leaving King School, a man called me to his car. He was the father of a friend of mine, naked from the waist down. When I was at this friend's house, he sometimes grabbed me and tried to tickle me or make me give him a kiss. I'd struggle and scream until he let me go. I was stunned that he exposed himself to me. I told no one and pretended that it never happened.

Another time when I was about fourteen and on the bus trip to Alabama with my friend Barbara, her mother and sister, I was sexually molested. The trip took about twenty-four hours, and we were dozing in a bus station, waiting for our next bus. I awakened to see a disgusting glob of pink flesh next to my pretty, white straw purse, now with gooey white stuff all over it. The man next to me rose quickly and moved away. I woke up Barbara and dragged her with me to the bathroom where I washed off my purse, and indignantly explained what happened. I still didn't understand the idea of sexual arousal, penile erection, masturbation, emission of semen. It didn't even consciously register that the pink glob was a penis. I only knew it was something dirty. We never told her mother or discussed it again.

After school started in the fall, I was hoofing it up the hill to catch the bus when a car stopped. The man inside offered me a ride. I thought the driver was a neighbor and gratefully got in the car, but I was mistaken. "Oh," I said, "I thought you were my neighbor." The door remained shut, and he drove away. I was hugely alarmed, but I thought it best to act as normally as possible and presume that he would drive me to school. He began asking me lots of questions, and I chatted with him while he drove. Before he let me out of the car, he said, "You know, I could've done anything I wanted to you." Again, I told no one, but I began to feel like a hunted animal.

My mother's motto was, "If you don't work, you don't eat," and during my sixteenth summer she obtained jobs for me. One of these was across the city in a small factory that made fireworks. I walked the half mile up the hill to catch the bus and traveled for over an hour before reaching the factory. There I sat with several women around a table, each of us silently putting five little pellets in tiny envelopes eight hours a day. When lit, the pellets unfurled as "snakes;" however, they exuded fumes of mercury, which was hazardous for us. The owner hovered over us, telling us to hurry, and showing us faster ways to do the work. Breaks for lunch and the bathroom were strictly supervised. It was a sweatshop, and I was humiliated when the owner's daughter, a high school classmate, saw me working there.

One day as I walked in the rain down the street to the factory, a car door opened; I was grabbed and pushed inside. Behind the wheel of the car was an enormous woman, one of the workers.

"Are you going to work?" she demanded.

"Yes, that's where I was headed," I replied.

She turned around. Her huge, blubbery face stared at me full on, "You go to work and we'll tear off all your clothes and throw you in the street." She gestured to the two big men standing outside the car in their raincoats, hats slouched against the rain. The man who grabbed me was a labor organizer; they had called a strike. Given my liberal background, I knew about strikes and labor rights, and, once the reasons for the strike were explained, I willingly joined the picket line. We took a welcome break for a hot lunch in a nearby café, and then returned to the picket line. However, as it became dark, I began to worry. The men wouldn't let me leave.

The day hadn't started in the most reassuring manner with the threat to tear off my clothing and throw me in the street, but all had been peaches and cream since then. At lunch I'd been joined by the men, and one of them had been particularly friendly and nice, maybe too nice? Were they going to picket in the dark? Surely it was time to go home. I became suspicious. Would they hold me against my will? Desperate, I thought fast.

Okay," I said, "I'll stay, but I think I'd better call my father and let him know that I'm going to be late."

"Your father? Who's your father?"

"He's head of the Political Science department at the university," I said.

This guy and his buddies held a hurried conference—I could go! I finally arrived home long after dark and told my parents what happened. My father didn't say much, but I was no longer sent out on these jobs. What would have happened if my father hadn't been a person with status in the community?

It was about this time, or maybe a year earlier, when I looked at my body and noticed that my stomach stuck way out. I remembered being laughed at: "Julia, you look like you're pregnant!" The remark had deeply wounded me. I didn't want to look like I was pregnant. I decided to stop eating. At the time, it seemed like a sensible decision. I didn't eat breakfast or lunch, and I ate only a little supper when we all gathered around the kitchen table for the evening meal. (I didn't want my parents to catch on to what I was doing.) I wasn't hungry. I felt fine, but I started to get extremely thin, and for two mornings in a row Mother roused herself to make me breakfast. On the third morning, she made me breakfast so late that I couldn't eat it and walk the half mile up the hill to get the bus, and I couldn't take the sunny-side-up eggs with me. I had started to think that my mother cared about me, but when I didn't eat that last breakfast, she never got up again, and I never heard another word about it.

Anorexia nervosa is thirteen times more common among females (McCarthy et al., 2012), but I don't know if my weight loss was sufficient for the diagnosis. No one commented about it, and I kept getting thinner. With satisfaction, I noticed that when I was lying down, my hip bones jutted up over the cavity where my stomach used to be. No one would think I was pregnant now. Toward the end of the school year, they took a picture of our choir class and posted it on the school bulletin board. I looked at the picture to find myself. I looked and looked. Finally, I found me, a scrawny hag at the end of the row. That was the end of the diet. Guess I should have looked in the mirror more often.

That summer Dad magically appeared every morning when I came downstairs. "What would you like for breakfast?" was his cheerful greeting, and we shared a companionable meal of grapefruit, fried eggs, bacon, toast, butter, and home-made jam. I soon returned to normal weight and no longer concerned myself about my weight.

Although I'd been having scary experiences with older men, boys my own age were nice to me. We'd kiss and pet, but they never went too far. I enjoyed their attentions. The next year, I met a boy named Chuck, and he and I became more intimate. Unfortunately, my mother came out and spied on us as we were parked outside our house. This she did while not giving me any information about boys, men, and sex (or birth control). She accused me of having intercourse with him, which I denied, and which wasn't true. She obviously didn't believe me because she called his mother, and I never saw him again. He was gone, in the Marine Corps. I got a few letters from Paris Island, but then she saw to it that I wouldn't get any more. Chuck was Catholic and poor, and my mother was prejudiced against Catholics. I was bitter and heartbroken.

Was it about that time that I attempted suicide? No, I don't think so. It must have been earlier, perhaps after reading *Romeo and Juliet.* I had no idea how to kill myself; information about such things was practically nonexistent. But I reached into the medicine cabinet for the bottle of aspirin. "How many should I take? How many would it take to kill me?" I thought to myself, "Ten seems about right."

A surprised, but wiser, girl awakened the next morning.

What brought me to this moment on the knife-edge of life? Does it seem strange that I don't remember more exactly? Contrary to common sense, adolescents may impulsively attempt suicide for the most trivial reasons, but can I remember what was going on at the time? I allowed thoughts and images to come to mind without judgment or inhibition—the technique of free association. I saw myself in front of the medicine cabinet. What rivets me there? A partially used packet of quinine came to mind, a packet so old that it's brown with age. Who would be taking quinine? Wasn't that for malaria? Later, I learned that quinine was also used for abortions, and I wondered. Well, if it was me she was trying to abort, it didn't work.

My words shock me; the summoned memories reawaken an anger I had long since put to rest. I'd recently published a tribute to my mother, remembering only the positive aspects of our relationship. It seemed the right thing to do, but how will we understand my life if we fail to examine the fullness of my experiences with her? I don't blame her for the mental problems that were to plague my later life. These have a neurophysiological basis and a strong hereditary component. Her poor mothering didn't help, but much of what I achieved in life is because of her.

I am Edna's daughter.

Chapter 3

Leaving Home

During my sixteenth year, an incident occurred that made me doubt my self-image as a strong, healthy person. My girlfriends and I attended a Presbyterian youth group, and it was there I met Bruce. He was the sweetest, nicest young man, and I quickly became totally enamored, but he was planning to become a minister and I was an agnostic. How could an agnostic be a minister's wife?

The church sponsored a summer camp, and we all trundled off for a week of religious study and fun. The Universalist Church, which I attended, wasn't a Christian church: We didn't believe in the Trinity or the divinity of Christ. But I was taught to be open-minded, so I saw no problem in hearing what the Presbyterians had to say. When it came to taking communion, however, I wasn't sure it was the right thing to do, and this question became the focus of painful agonizing. We were all standing in a circle to take communion, and I was next to Bruce, still trying to decide what to do. When it came my turn, I heard a voice say, "Go ahead, Julie. Go ahead." So, I took communion.

The voice wasn't loud, and I knew it could be in my own head, but it was profoundly unsettling. Either I had an auditory hallucination, or God spoke to me, which seemed improbable. I wasn't eager to share this experience with others, but I did go to the camp physician to get my ears checked, and I told my parents about it when I got home. We decided I had something wrong with my ears. Nonetheless, the event made me uneasy.

As I neared the end of high school, I applied to various colleges for scholarships. My mother wanted me to become a doctor, and, as part of her campaign, when I was ten, she had given me a toy doctor's kit to encourage my interest in medicine. I was initially puzzled and wary since a gift from her was decidedly out of character. The kit had a little cardboard carrying case, with toy pills, a stethoscope, and other toy tools of the physician. Playing doctor was fun, and I decided that being one when I grew up was all right with me. In retrospect, it is apparent that my mother's thwarted ambitions were laser-focused on me. I was to achieve; I was to succeed; I was to be a vindication for her sacrifices.

My becoming a physician was also agreeable to my father. When he was a boy, he thought of becoming either a physician or a minister. I never saw him pray or read the Bible, but unlike my mother, he was a spiritual person in his own way. On one of my visits home from school, he took me to lunch at the Akron City Club, which my parents had joined as part of their growing financial success in real estate. (My parents had taken up selling real estate to supplement my father's income as a professor.) I was pleased and flattered. I'd never been taken out to eat before, but I was surprised when my father turned the topic to religion. "Julia, you need to believe in God," he said.

"What do you mean?" I asked. Religion had remained a worrisome topic for me. I'd already read the entire Bible on my own and found it totally incomprehensible. Dad tried to explain God to me, but I didn't understand what he was trying to say. "What is God?" I asked.

Finally, he said, "God created the world. He wound it up like a clock, set it in motion, and it's been running ever since."

This was the deist view of many of our founding fathers, but I'd never heard of it. The idea struck me as silly and of no use. I felt badly; here was my poor, beloved father urging me to believe in an idea that seemed preposterous. I dismissed the whole wound-up-clock deal but remembered that I should believe in God. What God and how, I had no idea. It would be years before I had a coherent world view. When I converted to Lutheranism in my late twenties, I thought my father would be pleased, but to my disappointment, he was dismayed instead. He had wanted me to become a deist, like him.

My father's interest in becoming a physician had developed during the influenza epidemic of World War I. Although a boy, he'd been the only one in the family to remain well, and it was he who took care of the rest. During World War II, when he raised rabbits and chickens to ease the food shortage, he prided himself on his ability to take care of the sick animals. He, himself, was almost never ill, nor did he have cavities in his teeth—an amazingly healthy man.

As my parents planned my future, they focused on the nearest medical school, Western Reserve University in Cleveland. As head of the Political Science Department at Akron University, my father had hired one of their graduates, Dr. Betty Danneman, to teach political science. Betty had attended Flora Stone Mather College, the "girls' school" that was part of Western Reserve University, and doubtless at my parents' behest, she took an interest in me, giving me an "in" with the alumni association, which sponsored a scholarship. Betty drove me to Cleveland to see the university and for a required interview for the scholarship.

On the way to Cleveland, Betty lost control of the car on the icy bridge crossing the Cuyahoga River. First, I saw the bridge railing approach and the enormous chasm; I expected to plunge to the valley below. Miraculously, Betty managed to turn the wheel. Now, we careened into oncoming traffic. Again, I expected to die. Then, finally, back in our lane.

We arrived on time for the interview, which went all right. Afterward, I was ready to go home, but Betty wanted to treat me to lunch and shopping. It was all too much for me, and I fainted in the store. On the way back to Akron, I vomited in the car. Not surprisingly, Betty didn't volunteer to drive me to the final scholarship interview. I would be on my own. My father deposited me at the bus depot in Akron and told me to get off the bus at 105th and Euclid in Cleveland. The university, I was told, was a simple walk up Euclid Avenue from there, but this, I was to discover, was a dangerous area.

When I got off the bus, it was as though a pack of dogs had been presented with a piece of fresh meat. I was immediately accosted by a group of teenage boys. I dodged around in the bus station, hiding in various spots, finally crouching down in the phone booth. When I came out, my pursuers were gone, and I walked the several blocks to the university without incident. Later, when I was at the university, I learned to navigate the neighborhood successfully, even at night. It was a matter of watching out the corner of my eye and proceeding with purpose.

I had wanted to go to Wooster College where Bruce was planning to go, but I received only a half-tuition scholarship there while Flora Stone Mather awarded me a full tuition scholarship. Bruce thought we should date other people, and distance and new boyfriends took their toll; the relationship broke off. I wasn't ready to make a mature commitment to marriage. Although Bruce was a wonderful person, I was so intellectually focused and driven by my mother's ambitions that it's hard to see how our marriage would have worked.

Although I had a scholarship to attend Flora Stone Mather, my parents still had to come up with money for my room and board, and my brother was attending Miami University of Ohio. I didn't ask them for extra money; my clothes and spending money came from my own earnings. Nonetheless, during the first year's spring break, my mother carried on and bitterly complained about the money they were spending on me. That did it. I said nothing, but my spine stiffened. I determined to get through college as soon as possible so I wouldn't have to listen to her complaints. As a result, I finished college in three years going to school during the summers and taking extra classes.

The first summer, I worked as a waitress at a Cleveland restaurant, and I began to learn about sexual harassment. The hostess was the mistress of the owner, and Danny, the dishwasher, would come up behind us to feel our breasts when we were at the coffee urn and had our hands full with cups and saucers of hot coffee. Betty, our top waitress, showed me how to handle Danny: Turning quickly, she dumped the hot coffee all over him. Another summer I worked in a doctor's office where the executive secretary sternly warned me about potential sexual advances from one of the doctors. Sexual harassment was an expected part of life.

I loved college. I had always loved learning things, the intellectual challenge. However, I didn't like memorization, and I had no ear for languages. Nonetheless, despite a heavy schedule of mathematics, chemistry, and a double major in psychology and literature, I received only two Cs, and graduated Phi Beta Kappa. One of my Cs was in comparative anatomy which effectively killed my chances for getting into medical school because I needed a scholarship. Furthermore, at that time almost no women were admitted to medical school. I hated memorizing all those bones, and I found that I was at a severe disadvantage. The boys in the medical fraternity were far better prepared than I. They studied together, had copies of prior tests, and knew what to expect. I decided that my becoming a physician wasn't a functional plan. It had always been my parents' idea anyway.

Meanwhile psychology grabbed my interest. Of all I learned in college, the ideas that most captured my imagination were from psychoanalysis. My professor, Calvin Hall, was an expert on Freud's theory and actively engaged in research on the analysis of dreams. I gained an understanding of psychoanalytic theory, insight into my own psyche, and an ability to understand not only my own dreams, but those of others. This knowledge was useful personally and professionally throughout my life.

Dr. Hall offered his students the opportunity to participate in a special project for extra credit. We were to record our dreams for a week and analyze them according to objective standards of rating laid out in his book on the topic. This sounded like a snap. I had only a couple dreams a week—or, so I thought. As it turned out, I dreamed every night, often more than one dream a night, and the dreams were sometimes long and complex. We were instructed to record our dreams as soon as possible after dreaming them, which meant that I had to get up frequently during the night to write them down. (Recording dreams as soon as possible is essential because memory of dreams fades rapidly.) I filled pages with my handwritten records. Then I had to rate the material and prepare a coherent report about the findings in accordance to Dr. Hall's dream analysis manual. I got an A in the course.

I quickly developed a knack for analyzing dreams. One day, a group of us were sitting in the corner drugstore on Euclid Avenue talking about dreams. The waitress overheard us and challenged us to tell her the meaning of her dream that her boyfriend was dead—commonly interpreted as an indication of hostility. I immediately asked, "Did you have a fight with your boyfriend?"

Paling, she exclaimed, "How did you know that?" She turned and hurried away muttering, "Sweet Lord Jesus. Sweet Lord Jesus."

Another time, I was sitting with a friend in her dorm room when she told me a dream—she was riding a horse, only she was underneath the horse. I pounced on her, "You've had intercourse. What was it like?" I bombarded her with questions but got only vague replies. She was embarrassed and hadn't wanted me to know about it.

In considering how to describe my college years, the alliteration "boys, books, and booze," came to mind, but, fortunately, I had far too little money and was working far too hard to consume much booze. I had no conception of the possible problems connected with alcohol use. My mother never drank alcohol, and my father didn't drink regularly until after I left for college. I wasn't accustomed to the idea of drinking. In the 1950s, alcohol wasn't permitted in the Mather dormitories, and as freshmen, we had to be in by ten p.m.; even as upperclassmen, we were rarely allowed out past midnight.

However, liquor always flowed at the fraternity houses and on the weekends. Drinking was considered a normal part of having a good time. Since my dates were honorable young men who had to pay for the drinks, I never got drunk. However, on one occasion several of us from Mather House went to a fraternity party beer bust. I don't know what they gave us, but Marilyn and I quickly passed out and had to be carried back to the dorm. It was humiliating, but also something of a lark. It was still daylight, and my dorm mates saw to it that we weren't harmed. In retrospect, I wonder if all the girls were so lucky.

During the first two years of college, I had a splendid time and a distracting number of suitors. I finally became pinned to an engineering student with whom I'd begun a sexual relationship. I was totally thrilled the night I was pinned, but a few months later, he dropped me for another woman. I felt soiled, used, and discarded. Why was I dropped? I suspect he found a woman more sexually appreciative. After our first brief coital experience in the darkened back seat of his car, I said, "Is that all?" I'd been expecting something great—or at least something.

My third year of college was dreary, and during the spring semester of that year I was sexually assaulted, ironically on the occasion of my election to the psychology honorary society, Psi Chi. Invited to a party given by the psychology graduate students to celebrate our election to Psi Chi, I was pleased and excited. I expected a dignified event attended by faculty. Instead, I was taken to a small, dark apartment crowded with morose, smoking young men. My fellow graduate, Gordon Bower, was there. He later became an eminent professor of psychology at Stanford University. At some point, someone got up and said some official words, but there was nothing to do but drink. I was disappointed that there were no memorable conversations, something I had expected of a graduate student gathering. At the end of the party, one of the young men offered to drive me back to the dorm. I was unsuspecting and certainly needed a ride. When he parked in the lot behind the church next to the Mather dorm, he assaulted me. He began to kiss me violently and thrust his body atop mine—pressing painfully hard.

"Stop, stop," I yelled when I could get my mouth free from his.

He said not a word, and I continued to fight. Suddenly he stopped, straightened his clothes, and the incident ended in an incongruous manner. He came around, opened the door on my side of the car, and without a word, he walked me to the door of the dormitory. I thanked him as though I'd had a nice date.

Subsequently, I learned that rape situations create a kind of mental numbness, and there's always that huge lurking terror— what else is this man capable of doing? Women fear for their lives. No, I wasn't going to risk offending this man. However, once the door to the dormitory closed, I became hysterical. I was bruised on my body, but especially on my face and lips, which were rapidly swelling. My dorm mates quickly gathered with ice and sympathy. They gave me their full support and passed a warning word about this man throughout the campus. It was a terrible experience, but nothing compared to the experiences of many, many other women.

During the last summer in Cleveland, my work as a receptionist in a doctor's office turned out to be a blessing for a friend who'd become pregnant out-of-wedlock. Like my mother, she hadn't realized she was pregnant until she was well along. One day when we were in her room, I noticed it and blurted out, "You're pregnant." The tell-tale bulge was plain to see, but like my mother, my friend, who was a brilliant woman, hadn't wanted to see it.

Through the doctors I worked with, I was able to get her discreetly placed in the Florence Crittenden Home where she had the baby and placed it for adoption. Each week on my day off, I took the bus across town, bringing her the books she requested. She was amazingly stoic. I felt lucky that it was her and not me who was pregnant, not that I drew any practical conclusions from her plight. I still had no knowledge of contraception. If I'd spent more time talking with the other girls in the "Smoker" at Mather House, I probably would've found out, but I didn't smoke, and I was buried in my books.

Given my mother's ambitions for me and her ostensibly liberal, feminist ideas, it's truly remarkable that she left me so ignorant of sexuality. Moreover, did she ever wonder if I could manage pre-med coursework while carrying extra credits, working on the side, and attending summer school? My parents had developed a totally unrealistic idea about what I could do. It was frightening and sometimes embarrassing as I heard them exaggerate my accomplishments to their friends.

So far, I'd successfully navigated college, but I screwed up at the last minute. In the 1950s in the Midwest, the drug culture was virtually nonexistent, but amphetamines were popular among students to keep us awake. At that time, they were cheap and easy to buy in the local drug store. Fortunately, I never thought to use them until the end of my college career when my girlfriends wanted to have a party for me before I left town. The only problem was that I had my final exam in trigonometry the next day. What to do? Miss a party? I decided to go to the party and take an amphetamine tablet to keep me awake for the exam, which worked fine. I was wide awake for the exam. The problems were a snap. All was well until I got the results. I failed the exam and came out with a C in the course. I had an A going into the exam; otherwise I would have received an overall failing grade. I was stunned. In retrospect, I had experienced an abnormal mood elevation from a single amphetamine. It destroyed my judgment and created a false sense of confidence. I never took them again.

At that time, amphetamines were regarded as harmless, and it wasn't until much later that their potentially devastating effects became widely known. My officemate in graduate school, like many others, ended up in a psychiatric hospital as a result of popping amphetamines. In recent years, illicit use of an amphetamine called Adderall, prescribed for treatment of attention deficit disorder, has resurfaced as a problem. Fortunately, I learned from the amphetamine experience and wouldn't use any recreational drugs, despite social pressure. If I didn't fit in, I didn't fit in.

After all my hard work, I was graduating from college. Now what? It became suddenly and painfully apparent that I had neglected the obvious: I hadn't thought through my future, and I wasn't prepared for any kind of job that would support me. My dominant thought had been to get my mother off my back. Guided by my gonads, I had come close to marriage and I was dazzled and distracted by many young men. Almost all the girls I knew were getting married. What was I prepared to do? Not much. I had adamantly refused to take teacher education. The education courses seemed puerile, and I don't think I was conventional enough to do well as a teacher. My mother wouldn't hear of my becoming a nurse. At home, sitting at the kitchen table, I sent up a trial balloon allowing as how I might become a reporter. My mother became furious.

"Oh, no you're not," she yelled. "You're not yet twenty-one, and until you're twenty-one, you'll do as I say."

The thought of her high-handed attitude made me livid for years. I don't know if she was legally correct, but I was in no position to challenge her. It was decided that I would apply for the psychology PhD program at Western Reserve University. When I finally got their reply to my application, the answer was "No." Upon further inquiry, I learned that they thought I was too immature. I should do something else for a while and apply to graduate school later.

For a long time, I was disturbed that the Western Reserve faculty thought I was too immature to study psychology. What caused them to reject my application? Was it Dr. Wallin who taught social psychology? He opened his lecture one day with remarks about the results of the midterm exam, "Someone in

this class is either a goddamn genius or a goddamn book worm."
With a shock, I realized he was talking about me. His hostile,
contemptuous tone made it clear that he didn't think I was a
genius. I had aced his test, but I was neither a genius nor a book
worm. We had one text for the class, and I used a new method
of study, which worked well. First, I read the material quickly.
Then I studied it, and right before the test, I quickly read it again.
I was flabbergasted that a professor would make such a foolish
statement. I didn't even discuss it with him.

I remembered a run-in with the undergraduate dean of Flora
Stone Mather, Dean Walker. She came by one day while I was
sitting on the grass watching a tennis game.

"Mather girls don't sit on the grass," she said.

"What?" I said. (It never occurred to me to rise to my feet
with a courteous salutation such as, "Good morning, Dean
Walker.")

"Mather girls don't sit on the grass," she repeated. I could
hardly believe my ears, but obviously she wanted me off the
grass, and I got up. In retrospect, I should've apologized, but I'd
never heard of anyone being criticized for sitting on the grass.

Another time, I thoroughly upset her. Desperate for money,
I'd gone to the college placement office for assistance in getting
a job so that I could stay in Cleveland and take courses during
the summer. From my talk with the counselor, we figured out
that the best way for me to make money was waitressing, so
that's what I did.

During my mandatory meeting with Dean Walker in the
fall before the semester began, I regaled her with stories of my
adventures as a waitress, for example, the paranoid black chef,
recently discharged from a mental hospital, who got so mad he
sent a butcher knife zinging into the wall. Did I also tell her
about being groped at the coffee machine? Dean Walker was a
great audience and listened intently. I babbled on and on, happily sharing what, to me, had been a great experience. When I
finished, she sternly announced that I had no business taking
employment as a waitress. Oops. Later, I learned that the place-

ment bureau caught Hell. Mather girls weren't to be referred to jobs as waitresses.

There were other things that might have suggested that I wasn't serious enough for graduate school. Maybe it was the time my roommate Dru and I rode the dumbwaiter up and down from the fourth floor to the basement. The housemother's face was white when she ordered us out of it. Seems we could have been killed.

Ours was a scholarship dorm and, in exchange for work, we paid a lower fee. My job at the dorm was to wait tables. During my summer of work at the restaurant, I had become highly skilled in carrying a string of plates, coffee cups, and glasses balanced on my two arms, mimicking the ways of the top-notch restaurant waitresses. I was proud of my new skill, and when classes started in the fall, I reveled in showing off, delighting to see how much I could carry at one time. I never dropped anything. I had no idea I was offending the sensibilities of Mrs. Trautman, our housemother, though I was hugely amused as I saw her hold her breath while I juggled myriad plates, glasses, and cups of hot coffee. Nonetheless, I was genuinely puzzled when, after a couple weeks, she called me aside and primly informed me that I was to carry the plates one at a time. She patiently explained that my style of service wasn't suitable for the decorum of their dining room.

Then there was the time I caught a mouse in a quart jar and kept it in my room. She came storming to my room, furious that I should be keeping a mouse there. "Why, Mrs. Trautman," I said, "That mouse was running around loose in the dorm until *I* caught it."

The rejection of my application for graduate school at Western Reserve continued to upset and worry me. Did they think I was mentally unstable? Unhappy and concerned, I went to the student counseling center where I was assigned a therapist who followed the ideas of Carl Rogers of the University of Chicago. Rogers thought that clients (his term for patients) would figure out their own problems if you reflected back to them what they said. I found the counseling session frustrating, useless, and puzzling.

"What brings you to counseling?" she asked.

"I'm upset that I was rejected for the psychology graduate school program here," I replied.

"You were rejected for entry into the graduate program," she said.

"Yes, they said I was too immature."

"They said you were too immature," she replied.

"What did they mean—I'm too immature?" I asked.

"You don't understand what they meant by saying that you're too immature," she said.

"No, I don't get it. I had good grades. Nobody's ever told me I was too immature before," I replied.

"You're at a loss to understand why you were rejected," she said.

It went on like this for fifty minutes. It was surreal—like a Beckett play. I had no idea she was even interested in what I was saying. Rogers emphasized that the therapist must convey deep concern for the client in voice and manner. This she failed to do, and I was surprised and heartened when I ran into her in the library and she asked me how things were going. Later, in graduate school, I was also taught Rogerian therapy, with a similar negative outcome.

Actually, my rejection at Western Reserve was fortuitous because I later heard their graduate psychology program described as a "snake pit." I was told that the faculty was arbitrary with students, and sometimes blocked their graduation for unfair reasons. Also, their program didn't emphasize scientific method as did the one at the University of Iowa in Iowa City, where my parents decided I should next apply. Dad drove me out there for an interview, and I talked to Dr. Arthur Benton, who was head of the clinical program. He told me on the spot that I was admitted to the program. I couldn't believe my good fortune, yet I was frightened.

"But, Dr. Benton," I said, "At Western Reserve, they said I was too immature."

Dr. Benton chuckled. "We'll mature you here," he said.

Years later, my mother told me that she had greased the way for my admission to graduate school in Iowa. Secretly, she took the bus to Cleveland to meet with Dr. Elizabeth Hastings, Dean of the Graduate School at Flora Stone Mather College. From my mother's account, she was in a fighting mood when she saw the dean. In essence, here is what she said: "My daughter was a scholarship student at Flora Stone Mather. She was Phi Beta Kappa. What do you mean she's not admitted to graduate school?" Mom beamed with pleasure as she related her successful interview with Dean Hastings. They decided that the dean would send a glowing letter of recommendation to the Iowa program. I was extremely touched that my mother had done this. I later learned that the Iowa faculty was impressed that I took such difficult courses and graduated in three years. They weren't bothered by the two Cs. They had studied the variables that predict success as a psychologist and found that a C here and there showed an independent spirit that boded well. I'm sure Dr. Hastings' letter didn't hurt, and it helped me get a position as counselor in the girls' dormitory, which eased my financial problems.

Chapter 4

Graduate School – Iowa City

As the train chugged closer to Iowa City through miles and miles of cornfields, I felt disoriented, like I was lost in cornfields. I carried one suitcase given to me by my Aunt Esther, and I made my way to Currier Hall where I would earn my keep as a counselor at the dormitory. The dorm was a brisk fifteen-minute walk to the psychology building, and that fall I lost fifteen pounds with a little discipline at the table and walking back and forth.

Morality reigned strong at Currier Hall, and one of my duties was to see that the girls were in their rooms at night; bed check was at ten o'clock. At the end of the semester, two young women in another section of the dorm were thrown out of the dorm and out of graduate school because they'd been found in bed together.

"So what's wrong with that?" I asked.

"Well, they were, you know."

No, I didn't know, but the evasions made me realize that sex was involved. I had no clear idea of lesbianism, but I was horrified that they had been surveilled and that such personal behavior could be a career-wrecking event. My job as enforcer of morality made me uncomfortable, and I was relieved to be offered a psychology assistantship for the next semester.

As I got oriented to the psychology department, I was chagrined to discover that none of my academic professors credited any of Freud's ideas; they didn't even consider them worth discussing. Professor Don Lewis simply called them "bullshit." In the 1950s, there were various schools of thought in psychology; one was psychoanalysis, but the one ascendant at the University of Iowa was learning theory and what was called Dust Bowl Empiricism. Psychological concepts had to be clearly defined by observable, objective criteria that could be agreed upon. Ideas, in the form of theories or hypotheses, had to be tested according to scientific methods and the results shown to be statistically significant by use of the correct statistics. Then, in order to be accepted as scientific fact, the experiment needed to be replicated by an independent researcher.

The Iowa academic psychology department sought to extend a rigorous scientific methodology to behavioral science, and scientific method as taught to me in graduate school (especially by Kenneth Spence, I. E. Farber, and Arthur Benton) helped ground me. Their teachings remain the bedrock of my mental processes. They and psychologists at the University of Minnesota (Starke Hathaway and Paul Meehl, my later therapist) advocated theory tested by fact. The dots need to be connected, but they must be correctly connected on the basis of factual information.

The academic psychology department was on one side of the Iowa River, and the medical school where I received practical training in clinical psychology was on the other. At what was then called Iowa Psychopathic Hospital, one of my clinical supervisors, Dr. Paul Baer, was a devotee of psychoanalysis, and I looked to him for clinical expertise. It was he who suggested that I learn about the psychology of women from the book, *The Psychology of Women* (1944), by psychoanalyst Helene Deutsche. I found the book on a dusty shelf at the hospital and began to read. She averred that the three essential traits of femininity are narcissism, passivity, and masochism. Her speculative observations went on and on and on; I found it amazing that anyone would take her views seriously. I didn't even finish the book; I returned it to its dusty shelf.

Years later I threw down the gauntlet with my book, *On the Psychology of Women: A Survey of Empirical Studies* (1971), a scientific approach to the psychology of women. The book was considered and rejected for publication by Stanford University Press. Professor Sanford Dornbusch thought it was biased against psychoanalysis. He was particularly critical that I failed to underscore what he deemed the defining characteristic of women: their dependency. However, the book was published by Charles C Thomas, received an excellent review, and was used in the developing Women's Studies programs across the country. However, my career would have benefited greatly from publication by the more prestigious Stanford University Press.

During my first year of graduate school, all of us were assigned to study in one big room; the faculty wanted to be able to see at a glance who was diligently studying. When I left Akron for graduate school, my mother came out on the back porch to bid me farewell (having secretly engineered all this). "Goodbye, dear," she said. "Have a nice time." The contrast between her unrealistic expectations and reality struck me as totally incongruous and hilarious.

Late nights before exams, when we were all cooped up together in our study hall, tired and grungy, I'd call out in a saccharine voice, "Goodbye, dear. Have a nice time." It never failed to crack everyone up. I was a bit of a class clown. My classmates probably remember me best for the day we were all lined up to proceed for the first day of our preliminary examinations. If we failed the exams, we were out of graduate school. We were all quiet and tense. Then I burst out, "Wait. I have to go to the bathroom." I flew away before anyone could object, leaving behind a roar of raucous laughter.

The academic load in graduate school was killing. All of us were taking a course in learning theory from Kenneth Spence, head of the department. He had received his PhD from Yale and was honored by an invitation to return to deliver the prestigious Silliman lectures on his learning theory of classical conditioning. Rats running mazes weren't my thing, but I was intrigued by his process of thinking and how he tried to pin down the variables involved in learning. He tested his forthcoming lectures by delivering them to our class. As he talked, I realized that something he said didn't check out. Up popped my hand, little smarty Julie, and I posed my question. He looked thoughtful and said, "Let's discuss this after class."

After class, I explained what I thought was a flaw in his reasoning, and he said, "You're right." He altered his lectures as a result of my criticism. From that day forward, I was marked okay in Spence's mind, which was definitely fortunate.

Even so, my path to success in graduate school was by no means smooth. One of my imbroglios was curiously linked to my Shirley Temple fixation. Home for a short time from graduate school, I went to a sale in the basement of Polsky's, a local department store. As I rummaged through a pile of clothing, I pulled out a special Lanz dress. It had a white, eyelet short-sleeved blouse under a jumper with a tight-fitting bodice and a gathered skirt of black cotton fabric strewn with tiny alpine flowers, like the one Shirley Temple wore in the movie *Heidi*. To my mind, it was that dress that nearly got me thrown out of graduate school.

I had an early morning class with Dr. Gustav Bergman, a logical positivist from Vienna who taught philosophy of science. An internationally famous scholar and a star of the psychology department, Gustav was short, fat, and balding, with protruding teeth. Nonetheless, in addition to his attractive wife, I later learned that Gustav carried on an affair with the local poetess. Notoriously self-centered, Gustav was frequently seen shuffling about the psychology building, puffing on a big cigar, heedless of everyone.

Anyway, I was one of the few girls in Bergman's class—it was before Women's Liberation. I always sat in the front row since I couldn't understand Bergman's thick German accent. The one and only day I wore the little Heidi dress, the famous professor suddenly stopped in mid-lecture and demanded, "Miss Sherman, vhy do you hank (hang) on my lips?" I had, unfortunately, drawn the great man's attention. Had I reminded him of the alpine maidens of his youth? Startled, it took me a while to understand what he was saying, and by then he had gone on with his lecture. Puzzled and dismayed, at the end of class, I quickly left the room. I never wore the Heidi dress again and tried to place myself inconspicuously in the classroom.

An eight o'clock class was beastly early during the dark, bitter cold Iowa City winters; I began missing his lectures; I couldn't drag myself out of bed. (This was the first sign of the winter depression that strongly affected me later.) The next thing I knew, I received a summons from the head of the clinical psychology program, Dr. Benton. He minced no words. Once I was seated in his office, he announced, "Miss one more of Bergman's classes and you're out of graduate school." I could scarcely believe my ears, but he confirmed that he meant exactly what he said. Shocked, I nodded my understanding and escaped his office. Sometimes being an attractive young woman was an advantage, but dismissal from graduate school was a heavy-handed testimony to Gustav's vanity.

I didn't realize it, but it was the faculty's intention to wash out the inferior students at the end of the first year. Unlike other graduate schools that kept students around for years, they thought it was unfair to waste the time of students who didn't have the right stuff. As far as I could tell the process was fair, but then I made the cut. My assistantship was with Dr. Walsh (pseudonym) at Iowa Psychopathic Hospital, the main psychiatric training center in the state of Iowa. It was he who told me that I made the cut. I was shaken, like a person who just missed being hit by a bus. I had no idea that we were being evaluated in this way and that I could be terminated just like that.

Dr. Walsh supervised my practicum, that is, my work with patients. In 1955, before psychiatric medications, two treatments for mental illness were in effect that later drew harsh public rejection: electroshock and prefrontal lobotomy. Electroshock was the main treatment for all serious mental illnesses and was frequently prescribed. Later, the movie, *One Flew Over the Cuckoo's Nest*, made these treatments infamous. As part of my training, Dr. Walsh arranged that I learn about both treatments, and he insisted that I directly observe electroshock.

Electroshock was given first thing in the morning in a small treatment room on the first floor of the hospital. The patients who were to receive electroshock that day were lined up in a silent dreary, droopy row, dressed in hospital gowns, sitting in straight-back chairs outside the treatment room. I walked by them into the room where a patient was already being prepared. She was lying down, strapped to a gurney. Although she'd been sedated, she was still awake, quietly waiting. There was a doctor, a nurse, and two orderlies, plus me in the small room. The doctor signaled the nurse who handed him a hypodermic needle.

"He's giving her a drug to temporarily paralyze her," the nurse whispered to me.

"Paralyze her," I thought. "My god, paralyze!"

"Why are they paralyzing her?" I asked.

"So her bones won't break," was the not-so-reassuring reply.

"Oh."

The nurse applied gel on each side of the patient's temples, and the doctor attached electrodes on each side of her head. Then he called for a tongue depressor.

"Open your mouth," he told the patient.

The doctor then placed a gauze-wrapped wooden tongue depressor between the patient's teeth.

"That's to keep her from biting her tongue," the nurse whispered.

"Are you ready?" the doctor asked.

As the doctor flipped the switch, to my surprise, the staff immediately flung themselves over the patient, a further precaution against broken bones. The patient's body convulsed wildly as the staff struggled to hold her down; then she was still, and they wheeled her away to recovery. That was it. Thankfully, I only had to watch electroshock once. However, I was required to come back later to observe her after she recovered consciousness.

There she was—no broken bones—sitting in a chair, slumped over, drooling—totally out of it—a heart-rending sight. When I made my report to Dr. Walsh, he said, "Don't worry. Go back tomorrow, and you'll see an entirely different person."

He was right. The following day, to my great relief, I observed her eating lunch on the ward, talking to the others in an entirely normal manner.

Although electroshock remains a controversial treatment, it's still in use. However, accumulated scientific evidence completely failed to support the value of prefrontal lobotomy. Many unfortunate individuals had this damaging operation, including a sister of President John F. Kennedy. A transorbital lobotomy is performed by entering the brain between the eyeball and the nose in order to slice connections between the two hemispheres of the brain. I interviewed and tested a woman scheduled for the operation. She was severely obsessive compulsive. She washed her hands continually and was orderly to an extreme. Her husband decreed that she be cured or she'd go into an institution for the rest of her life. What a choice. Under this duress, the patient signed the papers for the operation. I examined her intellectual functioning before and after the surgery. Amazingly, there was no change in her Wechsler Intelligence IQ. Does this mean the Wechsler is no good? No. It means that there are specific abilities that the Wechsler doesn't measure: one of them is the ability to plan, and this had been severely impaired. The patient's performance on the Porteus Maze Test, a specialized test that measures foresight and ability to plan, showed a marked deficit. She was no longer compulsive or overly plan-oriented; now she couldn't plan at all. She would be incapable of planning even a simple meal. Would her husband be happy with her now? I was sickened by what had happened to her.

Dr. Walsh was to supervise my Master's thesis. He'd been interested in such questions as differences between psychiatric diagnostic groups in their Rorschach Inkblot Test scores. In this test, patients looked at ambiguous inkblot images describing what they saw. The responses were scored to indicate personality characteristics relevant to diagnosis. I dutifully recorded scores on data sheets, but I couldn't see how he'd get a worthwhile scientific study from this approach. Apparently, he came to the same conclusion and struck out in a new direction. He was new at Iowa, and as a beginning assistant professor in the medical school, he needed to publish in order to get ahead. The idea and the design for my Master's thesis experiment were his, which meant that he could share in publication of the research, which I hadn't realized. The technical staff and I built the necessary pieces of research apparatus for the study (a stimulus generalization task in both the visual and auditory spatial dimensions). However, Walsh hadn't properly thought through the research design, which required a soundproof room. Consequently, the results from the auditory part of the study couldn't be published. The psychology department accepted my thesis; I wrote the article, and we published the part involving visual stimuli, but Walsh had screwed up. I didn't think any more about it, but it was a blow to his ego that festered.

Dr. Walsh and I had gotten along extremely well for months, but one day his attitude abruptly changed. I was called into his office. He was visibly angry and charged me with regarding him "too much like a father." I couldn't understand what he meant, but he was so angry that I didn't dare ask.

I later learned that a sexual misconduct investigation of the head of the hospital had been going on. Perhaps Walsh had been warned against hanky panky. We may have been observed having too good a time in the hospital snack bar. But why was he angry with me? What had I done? What was wrong with me regarding him as a father? I ran this past a male friend. His face lit up. He said, "Perhaps the problem was that you regarded him as a father and he had something else in mind." Hmm. Perhaps his motivation had been perceived; he'd been called on the carpet, and he was blaming me. Male irrational attitudes toward women are a hazard. This wasn't a case of my being pressured for sex, not an explicit #MeToo situation, but it illustrates how a female student could be disadvantaged by social interactions that wouldn't arise with a male student (usually). Walsh became increasingly distant and finally hostile.

Professor-student affairs weren't unknown. My own father told me that he always kept his office door open while talking to a female student. I respected my father's moral scruples. Getting sexually entangled with a professor was dangerous for female students. I was lucky during graduate school; except for one pinch on the behind at a drunken party, I escaped unscathed. However, harassment of women students and researchers was, and is, a serious problem in universities, especially at the graduate level (Abrams, 2018). A student or junior researcher's whole life and career can be ruined by those in power, and what does the university do when one of their top grant-getters is accused of sexual misconduct?

Walsh's next research project involved looking for differences between psychiatric diagnostic groups in their responses to the same research set-up I used for my Master's thesis. I found the research simplistic and couldn't get interested in it. He still didn't pay attention to the research design and left uncontrolled the variable of medications. Patients included in the study were on varied psychiatric medications while others weren't on any. How could we tell whether differences in performance could be attributed solely to their diagnosis? Someone pointed this out to Walsh, and we had to throw out all the data and start over. Walsh had screwed up again, but he still didn't adopt correct procedures to be sure we were testing patients before they started medications. He and I got into a fuss about this, and our relationship deteriorated further.

However, Walsh was still my major advisor. When I went to him with my idea for a dissertation topic, he turned on me in a big way, blocking my research idea on specious grounds. Furthermore, he said, "If you go ahead with this idea, I'll see to it that you never get a job anywhere." Whether you're a female student or male, professors have a lot of power. However, because I was female, it was likely that he'd never have to face me in the future as an important professional capable of retaliating against him. By his actions, he was greatly reducing any chance I'd ever have for an academic career.

Had I been able to pursue my research idea, I would have had a publishable dissertation and accomplished pioneering work in a new, important area of research: the placebo response, now known more precisely as placebo effects (Benedetti, 2014). When patients are given an inert substance instead of a true medication, they often respond as well as if they'd been given the actual medication. This happens because of their belief that they're supposed to get better. I thought it was a fascinating topic, but Dr. Walsh adamantly refused to allow me to proceed with the plan. He made it clear that his threat held whether I did the research at Iowa Psychopathic Hospital or anywhere else. He claimed I would be violating ethics that forbade psychologists to administer medications. However, I had already obtained the co-operation of a psychiatric resident who was going to administer the placebo. I wasn't going to administer any drugs. Dr. Walsh blustered on. *No. No. No.*

Walsh put me in a terrible position. I had to ditch my research plan and come up with a wholly different idea at the last minute in order to graduate on time. The Iowa Psychology Department expected us to complete our degrees in three years. I was between a rock and a hard place. The faculty had announced that no female student could take a psychology degree oriented only toward an academic position. In 1956, the department couldn't place female students in academic jobs; universities wouldn't hire female professors. I would have to get a clinical job, and Dr. Walsh was my major clinical professor. No matter how interested

I might be in research, or how wonderful my dissertation was, it wouldn't make any difference. If he blackballed me, I might not be able to get any job. I was in no position to take that chance. Did Dr. Walsh think that in desperation I would turn to him for a research idea? If so, he was sadly mistaken. It never occurred to me. I'd lost all respect for him and his research capabilities, and, if I felt badly treated before, now I was furious.

I went to Dr. Benton who heard me out. But, in his smooth way, he made it clear to me that he couldn't do anything about Dr. Walsh, and I'd have to give up my idea. The department arranged for Dr. Al Heilbrun, a new member of the faculty, to supervise my dissertation. The idea for the research wasn't mine. Apparently, it was something someone on the faculty wanted done, possibly Spence, himself. The study was about verbal learning and the interaction of achievement imaging, motivational instructions, and the complexity of the learning task. It wasn't much of a clinical topic, and it wasn't flashy, but the psychology department would furnish a room, equipment, and the research subjects. Vastly relieved, I set to work immediately. I ran subjects hour after hour, working intensively. The statistical calculations were laborious, and to check the accuracy of my results, I had to add one to each datum and do the entire analysis over again. (No computers in those days.) Alas, all the effects were negative.

There is controversy about negative results, but in general, such a study can't be published. Normally, an experiment is designed to demonstrate an effect. Well, the research didn't demonstrate anything. Was disaster in the offing? Would I graduate? Would Professor Spence be angry that my results didn't support the predictions?

Before I could receive my doctoral degree, I had to defend the research, which meant going into a conference room to face the faculty, all men. I had to answer all their questions and objections. To my great relief, Spence looked thoughtful but didn't give me a hard time. I later learned that the Iowa Psychology Department thought that it was unrealistic to expect students to demonstrate a great new finding. They were primarily interested in graduating students who showed that they had the basic requisite knowledge, which they decided I had achieved. I would be awarded a PhD. If an academic position had been possible, neither they nor I would have settled for a null result dissertation that couldn't be published. I was impressed by Spence's fair-minded behavior, which I consider a mark of a true scientist. During my career, I tried to follow his example.

Now I was about to graduate with my PhD in psychology, and as happened when I graduated from Mather, marriages began to appear like daffodils in springtime. I was at another turning point. During my first two years of graduate school, I'd had various liaisons. One of my more serious boyfriends occasioned my first visit to a psychiatrist.

Bob was six feet-six, unusual at the time, and a graduate student in Spanish literature. He was an amiable person, and we got along well, but he was impotent. He wanted me to take off the summer and travel with him, expecting that he'd work out his sexual problem during the trip.

For me, this would be a huge commitment since it meant disrupting my graduate studies. I decided to go to a psychiatrist at the student health center for advice. This guy was easy to talk to. He sat with his foot up on the desk, paring his toe nails. How's that for putting a girl at ease? I got a direct answer and good advice: Don't count on summer travels to cure an impotence problem. I broke off with Bob.

Then, there was Jim. I was living in an apartment with two other girls: Ethel Karcag from New York City, and Janet Smith, also from Akron. They shared the only bedroom, and I slept on a couch in the living room. It was all the same to me. In those days, I slept like a log. Ethel, who was studying preschool education, was the leader of our little group. She devised the plan of a weekly shopping trip to the supermarket by taxi, and organized us to divide the expenses and responsibilities, which worked well. She was dating a graduate student in the chemistry department and fixed me up with Jim, also a chemistry graduate student, and a good-looking young man.

As the summer term ended that year, we decided to have a party. We each invited all our friends, and all of them came. Unfortunately, this amounted to far more people than we expected; the apartment was full and the party spilled outside. Jim and his chemistry buddies brewed up plenty of pure alcohol—man that stuff was strong—it hurt even to taste it. They made it into a punch, and we had one wild, roaring party.

Among the chemistry grad students was a black guy, but so what? This didn't register as a problem, until the party crashers arrived—great, big racist brutes. Before I knew what was happening, a fight broke out. Ethel's nice boyfriend, also from New York City, broke a bottle over the bath tub and emerged from the bathroom brandishing the jagged glass, hate beaming from his eyes like searchlights.

Ethel, used to dealing daily with preschool children, started yelling at them, "Stop! Calm down! Stop it!"

Some sense returned to the group, but soon the police arrived. Several of us were taken to the police station. For graduate students, an arrest could be serious, resulting in dismissal from graduate school. At that time, it was the routine discipline for a drunken driving charge. I was surprised that they hauled us down to the police station. We hadn't broken any laws—maybe too much noise. Why didn't they just bawl us out? No one was hurt. No property was destroyed.

One of the policemen began asking us questions. "What time is it?" he asked me.

"Hmm," I thought. "That's a good question." My answer was so far off that it drew a look of scorn. Now I was more worried than ever.

We saw the thugs who'd crashed the party talking to a policeman in the next room, and then leaving by a back door—they were hometown boys. Now the real agenda: The policeman behind the desk said, "My grandpappy fought in the Civil War, but not so as blacks could mix with whites."

"Oh, no," I thought. "What's next?" Fortunately, none of us was charged, but our landlord served us an eviction notice, and I had to find a new place to live. I moved in with two new roommates into another one-bedroom apartment. Again, I slept on the couch. There was no privacy, and Jim soon found himself another girlfriend. These roommates graduated, and my living arrangements went from bad to grim. I took a tiny two-room, share-the-bath place close to the psychology building. The bedroom had been added to the building later and its floor sloped to something close to a twenty-degree angle. Nonetheless, I was perfectly happy until an amorous couple moved in next door. Then, I began to feel morbidly alone, but I soon hit on a solution. As soon as I entered the apartment, I turned on the radio and left it on until I left.

The next year, Don, a fellow student, conned me into moving into his old place, selling me the furniture. It turned out there was no heat at all in the bedroom, and the place was infested with ants. But, the final kicker came when I discovered that Don had sold me furniture he didn't own. When I was ready to move out, I thought I had to leave the apartment vacant, and I was in the process of selling the stuff when the landlord informed me that it wasn't mine to sell. What if I'd sold everything and been charged with theft right before graduation?

All this poverty and instability made me yearn for a more settled life, and I began to think I should get married, which brings up the subject of sex. Unfortunately, when it came to sex, my father had unwittingly given me a bum steer. One night when he'd had too much wine, he said that he regretted the wild oats he'd never sown: "I sure would do things differently if I knew then what I know now," he said.

I took that as advice for how I should conduct my life. It didn't turn out well. My first experience with intercourse at age seventeen was nothing like what Dad had led me to expect. I was disappointed, but above all, puzzled and curious. I kept trying new partners hoping for a better result. Sex was nice, but nothing great. I kept thinking there must be something more;

however, I couldn't be sure. I finally decided that was all there was to it. I was lucky that I never got pregnant. I decided that casual sex wasn't for me, and I should settle down.

During my last year of graduate school, I acquired a serious suitor who wanted to marry me. I hadn't been so wined and dined for years, and I decided, in what I thought was a rational way, that I should get married. The decision was unwise, and apparently my mother knew it. On the occasion of my engagement, she ran out to the back porch and burst into tears. Why didn't she talk to me about it? She'd gone behind the scenes to manipulate my life, but she wasn't capable of talking to me straight out. My fiancé, Jon, was Jewish, and given my low opinion of my mother, I angrily thought, "You hypocrite. You call yourself a Universalist and now I'm marrying a Jew and you're crying." In retrospect, his being Jewish wasn't the reason; she correctly perceived that we were mismatched.

After the honeymoon, we returned to Iowa City because Jon had to finish his final year of graduate school. I was isolated with the creeping recognition that I'd made a mistake in my marriage. Up until now, I'd had close female friends, but during graduate school, women friends came and went from my life. Now I had no close friends, and I wasn't close to my family. I had no one to turn to.

Sometimes it's a small incident that epitomizes a relationship. With my husband, this event occurred one night when he invited some of his friends over to play bridge. I didn't feel well and told him that I was going to bed. He and his friends played bridge in the living room while I lay in bed in the next room. I had the Asian flu and was running a fever of 104 degrees. We shared the same bed. Surely, he should have realized that I was extremely ill, but he showed no solicitude. An alarm bell went off in my psyche, though I never verbalized to myself the fact that he was abnormally self-absorbed and indifferent to my needs.

The next day, the fever was gone, and with the typical disregard for life and limb of young people, I went to work, which was a great mistake because I developed a neurological complication: postural hypotension. (It's necessary to stay in bed for at least twenty-four hours after such a high fever.) If I stood in one spot for any length of time, I passed out. This I learned when I was in downtown Iowa City waiting for service in a jewelry store. I fainted, luckily missing the glass showcase. A nurse, a total stranger, called a cab, put me in it, and took me home. I was so far out of it that I didn't even get her name. Stranger kindness is one of life's great restorative gifts, and memories such as this have helped sustain my faith in human nature, which has sometimes been severely tested.

During my final year in Iowa City, I was on a United States Public Health Post-Doctoral Fellowship at Iowa Psychopathic Hospital, largely under the direction of Dr. Paul Baer, who specialized in child psychology. I was puzzled when I perceived that Dr. Baer was guiding me away from interaction with Dr. Walsh. I think he knew that Walsh had it in for me. I didn't have a clue. During the preceding year I'd worked at the VA Hospital, and Walsh had called me in, strongly encouraging me to apply for the Post-Doc. I'd supposed that bygones were bygones. However, he was still nursing a wounded ego.

The fellowship year started off with high hopes. The head of the hospital was a psychiatrist named Dr. Wilbur Miller, and every week an educational conference was held. Dr. Miller was an expert hypnotist, and one week he put on a fascinating demonstration.

It was a warm autumn day, and the conference room was filled to capacity. I noticed that Dr. Miller went to the back of the room to open a window; he was preparing for a demonstration of post-hypnotic suggestion. After some preliminary demonstrations and explanations, he called for a volunteer from the group, choosing one of the nurses. He hypnotized her with surprising speed and told her that exactly five minutes after "awakening," she would close the open window. Then, he told her that she would remember nothing of what occurred during hypnosis and brought her out of the trance. Without comment, she returned to her seat. Suspense hung in the air. What would happen next?

Amazingly, in exactly five minutes, the nurse rose and walked to the back of the room and closed the window as we sat transfixed in awed silence. Dr. Miller asked her why she closed the window—her ready rationalization really struck me. "It was getting too cold in here," she said. (Actually, the packed conference room was warm.) When questioned, she had no memory of what happened during hypnosis.

This kind of demonstration has been performed many times by different hypnotists and subjects. Though nothing highly unusual, it made a strong impression on me as a student and helped convince me that there was something to the ideas of the unconscious, repression, and psychoanalysis, despite the contrary opinion of my professors.

It seemed to me that hypnosis produced an effect similar to repression: The nurse initiated behavior (closing the window) on the basis of information unavailable to her conscious mind. Moreover, because she was unaware of the real reason she closed the window, her conscious mind in the brain's dominant left hemisphere (left-brain interpreter) made up a reason for shutting the window: a false, but logical explanation. The hypnosis demonstration showed that information could leave conscious memory and affect behavior in precise ways, without conscious awareness. The nurse had, indeed, moved directly to close the window in exactly five minutes. Her experience was like that of patients I describe later, in that unconscious memories affected behavior without conscious awareness.

Unfortunately, during the spring semester, Dr. Miller was relieved of his position; he was accused of having sexual relations with a patient while she was hypnotized. Apparently, he had abused other women, but he overstepped himself when he took advantage of a local physician's daughter. This was my first introduction to a problem that would change my life: the sexual abuse of women psychiatric patients. Unfortunately, I drew the wrong conclusion from this experience. Justice had been meted out, but notice that Dr. Miller wasn't caught until he abused the daughter of someone known and respected in the community, a physician's daughter. The medical community turned decisively against him; this was not always going to be the case.

I was distressed by the news about Dr. Miller. I greatly admired this psychiatrist's skill as a hypnotist, and I'd read several books on hypnosis that he'd left behind in the office I was assigned. Moreover, I was creeped out—taking sexual advantage of a hypnotized woman? Was that possible? Yes, contrary to frequent denials, individuals hypnotized can be induced to do things they ordinarily wouldn't do. To add to the drama, rumor had it that the head of the social work department at the hospital was his mistress, and it is a fact that his wife soon committed suicide. Joan, a fellow psychology intern at the hospital, had been doing psychotherapy with the patient Dr. Miller had abused. We'd had a long talk about the case, and she told me that she thought something fishy was going on, but she didn't know what to do about it. A few days after our conversation, Joan, who had a chronic kidney problem, died of kidney failure. These experiences were vicariously traumatic for me.

The biggest problem, however, came from my psychotherapy case. Dr. Baer wanted me to gain experience in intensive, long-term psychotherapy, an exciting prospect. I was drawn to the role of psychotherapist even though I didn't understand it. What did psychotherapists do that made people better? How did they do it? Could I do it? It was all a mystery. I'd had didactic instruction about psychotherapy and some experience at the student counseling center and the VA hospital, but now I felt that with Dr. Baer's knowledge of psychoanalysis, I'd develop expertise and an in-depth understanding. Dr. Baer selected as my patient a fourteen-year-old boy. Jimmy (pseudonym) was a good-looking, intelligent teenager with dark wavy hair and brown eyes, admitted to the hospital because of widely fluctuating emotions and ulcers. (At that time, it was incorrectly believed that ulcers were caused by emotional conflict.) I met with Jimmy as frequently as three times a week over a period of months, and once a week I met with Dr. Baer, who supervised my work.

From the beginning, Jimmy was tempestuous and obsessed with his hatred of the head psychiatrist of the children's unit. Though a kindly man, Dr. Barnes followed the theory of Dr. Otto Rank, and he believed in no-nonsense authority. He gave Jimmy periodic talks of the "young man, shape up" variety. Jimmy spent hours brooding about Dr. Barnes. In a favorite fantasy, Jimmy drove a chariot, dragging Dr. Barnes behind. (Jimmy was studying Latin: hence, the chariot.) I was bewildered. Why the obsession? This was more than adolescent rebellion. Had Dr. Barnes done something awful to Jimmy? I inquired but uncovered nothing. Dr. Barnes' lectures to Jimmy were no different than to the other children.

Jimmy's attitudes made more sense when I learned details of his history from our social worker's interview with his mother. Jimmy had been born while his father was serving in World War II, and he had been the center of his mother and grandmother's attention. When his father returned, Jimmy, then age five, resented him. He also rejected his brother, born a year later. I considered this. Was his hatred of Dr. Barnes related to his resentment of his father? This idea was plausible, but fit only partially, and even though I was closely supervised, therapy floundered. Jimmy was as disturbed as ever, even suicidal at times. Then, after weeks of interviews, Jimmy confessed his guilt about masturbation. A Catholic, he considered masturbation a mortal sin and was convinced that he would burn in Hell. Despite my reassurances, Jimmy continued to believe that he was beyond redemption. This was a job for a priest, not a psychotherapist, and I arranged for Jimmy to have some sessions with a Catholic priest and soon Jimmy began to cope better with his conflicts about masturbation.

A few weeks later, Jimmy dropped a bombshell—he'd been sexually molested. Once he said this, he refused to discuss the matter further—no details about what happened or how he felt about it. The simple admission of the abuse brought no relief; Jimmy's intense suffering continued, and my doubts about the efficacy of psychotherapy escalated. Meanwhile, without consulting me, the hospital discharged Jimmy and he returned home.

There was one positive development from Jimmy's therapy: He cured me of using the techniques of Carl Rogers. One day, Jimmy came into the therapy hour again furious with Dr. Barnes. As a dutiful student of Rogerian therapy, I reflected back his feelings.

"You feel angry."

"What do you mean I *feel* angry? *Of course*, I feel angry." His voice was heavy with sarcasm. It then rose explosively, "What kind of a stupid remark is that?"

I never used Rogerian therapy again.

In order to become a proper psychotherapist, students were expected to go through psychotherapy themselves. As a result, I started psychotherapy with Dr. Baer, who generously offered to see me for free. During the last three months of the year, however, I rotated to the adult service for an obligatory three months under the supervision of Dr. Walsh. He coldly informed me that my dress was inappropriate. (I had been wearing dresses, no hose, and flat shoes.) He insisted that I wear nylon hose and high-heeled shoes, which was impractical in a hospital with three floors and no elevator, but I knew better than to protest. Isn't it interesting that this requirement wasn't placed on three other women under his direct authority?

Staff meetings were held in Dr. Walsh's office, and I arrived a little late for the final meeting of my time in Iowa City. The office was crowded, and there was no chair for me. Dr. Baer rose to get me a chair. From his position of authority behind his desk at the end of the room, Dr. Walsh said, "No, let her get her own chair." Then he said to me, "If you're going to work in a man's world, you'd better get used to getting your own chair." There was stunned silence in the room. I gulped and headed down the hall to find a chair. In my high heeled shoes, there was no way I could carry it, and I had to drag the heavy, wooden institutional chair clattering down the hall, a profoundly humiliating experience.

I couldn't understand his hostility. I later learned that my letters of recommendation from the academic faculty for a job at the Minneapolis VA Hospital were glowing. My excellent new job and the knowledge of the Iowa academic faculty's good opinion of me must have infuriated him.

The crowning trauma of the year was yet to come, however. On one of my last days at the hospital, Jimmy returned for a follow-up visit. It was a lazy, sizzling August day. The Iowa countryside was so busy growing that it seemed to sap the energy from the air itself. There was no air conditioning. The big screened window in my office was open, but even seated next to the window, there was no breeze. That afternoon, there was no one but Jimmy and me on the second floor of the hospital. Jimmy came in and sat down. He looked okay, but it wasn't long before he became unreasonable.

"You and Dr. Barnes are planning to send me away," he said.

"No, of course not," I replied.

"Yes, you are. I know you are."

"No, Jimmy. What makes you think that?"

"You're planning to send me away."

"Jimmy, what do you mean, 'send you away'?"

"You and Dr. Barnes are planning to send me to prison."

"No, no, Jimmy. We're not planning to send you to prison."

"Yes, you are."

Jimmy's face went through a terrible transformation such as I've never seen before or since. His face became monstrously red and swollen with rage, and he forced out the words, "Don't lie to me. I know you and Dr. Barnes are planning to send me to prison. I'm going to push you out the window."

With a start, I realized that my child patient was much stronger than me, and that he could indeed push me out the window. I thought fast. According to Freud's theory, paranoia results from guilt feelings, particularly about sexuality.

"Jimmy, have you done something you feel guilty about?"

It was the right interpretation. Jimmy's face deflated like a balloon.

"I did the same thing to my brother," he said.

I didn't grasp what he meant at first. He was telling me that he'd seduced his younger brother. In my inexperience, I'd never heard of such a thing. His reply was consistent with Freud's theory, but I had no formal training in psychoanalysis, and I was surprised when my interpretation worked. Moreover, I was frightened, shocked, and horrified. Part of my psychotherapy training was to keep a calm demeanor no matter what the patient said, and I did my best.

Jimmy was calmer now, and, for the first time, he told me what had happened to him. While his father was away at war, a neighbor had molested him. Vastly relieved to have him back in a rational state, I didn't press for details.

Jimmy and I parted on friendly terms, but I was severely shaken for hours, and I had serious misgivings about the profession I was embarking on. This wasn't the therapy results I expected from my work with patients. My use of Freud's theory to make the interpretation that saved me from severe injury or death was uncharacteristic of my previous therapy and nothing I learned in supervision. I was amazed to hear the words come out of my mouth. It was a canny intuition, informed by past learning, but bursting out with sheer survival force.

When I was later able to talk to Dr. Baer, he absolved me of all responsibility, which I greatly appreciated, but I remained unsettled. Was the practice of clinical psychology as unscientific as the Iowa academic faculty said? Was my profession anything better than quackery?

Chapter 5

Clinical Psychologist

My new job as staff psychologist at the Minneapolis VA Hospital was great. Every week there was a teaching conference featuring eminent psychologists from the University of Minnesota. This is how I met Starke Hathaway and Paul Meehl, two preeminent psychologists of the twentieth century. Starke was a co-author of the Minnesota Multiphasic Personality Inventory (MMPI), perhaps the first scientific test to measure personality and psychopathology. I had already studied the MMPI, but now I interacted with experts on the test and with psychologists who were both scientists and practicing clinicians. These role models helped me resolve my doubts about clinical practice.

At the University of Iowa, science had been on one side of the Iowa River, clinical practice on the other, and I was torn between. The Minnesota psychologists, on the other hand, melded science and clinical practice and demonstrated the traditional academic value of an open mind: Meehl was intrigued by psychoanalysis, but Hathaway rejected it entirely. Nonetheless, the two showed respect for each other's opinions.

Hathaway took a special interest in me, and I delighted in our conversations. (His opinion that all psychologists should leave posterity their autobiographies inspired me to write an earlier version of this memoir.) He was a slight man with Einsteinesque white hair flying off his head. His piercing blue eyes were somewhat unfocused yet conveyed the impression that he missed nothing. He was a shy man and seemed to regard women as an exotic species; apparently, I was a specimen worth studying. He soon told me that I was hysteroid, a conclusion illustrating the acumen of a master clinician. One day, in a friendly, avuncular fashion, he said, "If you ever need an abortion, I know where you can get one." My mind went blank. Intellectually, I knew what an abortion was, but I couldn't process the thought that I'd ever need one. It was unthinkable, and, therefore, I was having trouble thinking. Hathaway immediately picked up on my mental confusion. My reaction revealed a telling interference with cognition with repression as its cause. This is how repression affects thinking. It stops logical processes, a phenomenon called blocking. I'd already taken the MMPI as part of my training at Iowa. It clearly showed what in the 1950s was interpreted as hysteroid personality characteristics, so I wasn't surprised by Hathaway's observation, but I was impressed by his perceptiveness.

Although it may seem presumptuous that Hathaway made such a comment to me, I took it as a friendly, helpful gesture. At that time abortions were illegal, and he no doubt had encountered many a young woman in desperate need of such information. He seemed genuinely interested in me and my career. For example, he recommended me for a staff position in the department of psychiatry at the University of Minnesota. The idea was immediately quashed—no women allowed, but I was surprised and heartened by his high opinion of my abilities.

But what did Hathaway mean when he said I was hysteroid, that is, tending toward hysteria? He was referring to a person, nearly always female, who tries to present herself in a good light, with a tendency to deny unpleasant realities. Sound like anyone

I've already described? Like my mother? Like Mrs. Bucket of *Keeping Up Appearances* fame? Such an individual wasn't necessarily considered neurotic (a term still easily understood, but no longer used in medical diagnosis). No, it was a description of personality.

From my accounts of sexual traumas in the first chapters, it's clear how sexuality came to be a repressed, dangerous topic for me. How would a person acquire a clear-eyed view of sexuality when fervent male sexuality and illegal coercion had been brushed aside and elemental facts of anatomy and sex were withheld?

Hysteria is a time-tested male explanation for women's behavior. Men have been trying to figure women out since time began, and their views have often been wrong-headed, self-serving, and not a little arrogant. As I've been writing, the words of a patient, a young woman philosophy student, keep coming back to me. Referring to her visit with her psychiatrist, she said with great indignation, "Do you know what he said to me? 'You don't know what it is to be a woman.' But he thought he did."

Hysteria goes back to the ancient Greeks; the word itself comes from the Greek word for womb. Then, and for many subsequent centuries, indispositions of women were attributed to a wandering womb. Such problems could include shortness of breath, insomnia, irritability, fainting, fearfulness, and inappropriate sexual behavior. From time to time, since Hippocrates, there has been a treatment used for hysteria consisting of a mix of clitoral and vaginal stimulation to orgasm. During the 19th century, for example, doctor-assisted genital stimulation that induced "paroxysm" was used as a treatment. Such stimulation generally consisted of internal vaginal stimulation with a straight vibrator, often in combination with manual massage of the external clitoris with the fingers or a water spray. The ensuing paroxysm was thought to center the wandering uterus back into its "normal" position. This was regarded as a medical treatment without recognition of its sexual implications (Pfaus et al., 2016).

The development of hysteria in women was a cultural by-product. Women were falsely believed to be less intelligent than men because their brains are smaller, even though women's brains aren't smaller in proportion to overall size. Educating women was often considered a waste of time. They were regarded as too psychologically delicate for books and education, and they were to be systematically shielded from unpleasant facts. This atmosphere was well portrayed by the adorable lily-of-the valley purity of Edith Wharton's 19th century heroine, May, in *Age of Innocence* (1920). Actually, as an aspiring young writer, Wharton had to fight to pursue her vocation. Such mental effort wasn't thought to be good for women. (These strictures were only for the upper-class white women; no thought was given to the delicacy of other women.)

Hysteria's association with women took another giant leap forward in the late 19th century when Freud and Breuer published *Studies in Hysteria* (1895/1955) which traced the symptoms of women patients to incestuous relationships with their fathers. However, late in his life, it was reported that Freud no longer believed that his patients told him the truth about their incestuous experiences. Had Freud begun to wonder, "How could those nice men do such an awful thing?"

Although Freud stated that hysteria is not limited to females, it became associated with women anyway. Soon it was used as a political tool. In 1908, an attempt was made to delegitimize the cause of the suffragettes by accusations that they suffered from hysteria (Gilman et al., 1993).

"Hysterical" has several different meanings. It can mean excessive emotionality or something extremely funny, but hysteria also had psychiatric meanings. In the 1950s, patients with hysteria might be diagnosed with conversion reaction, meaning that the repression of an emotional conflict had been converted to a bodily symptom (examples to be given later), but by 1980, the term "hysteria" had fallen into such disfavor among women that the American Psychiatric Association removed it from its diagnostic manual. Today, the diagnosis dissociative disorder is used instead. However, the diagnosis of histrionic personality disorder is still in the diagnostic manual. It refers to individuals who are dramatically seeking attention: Think Kardashian.

My hysteroid tendencies developed not only from sexual trauma, but the ways it was poorly handled, which reflected the culture of the times, and my mother's personality. However, I'm not interested in promoting the blame-the-mother routine. If we blame my mother for my problems, who do we blame for her problems?

The blame-the-mother routine got way out of hand in the last century. It's bad enough to have a mentally ill child, let alone be blamed for it. Harriet Shetler, one of the founders of the National Alliance for the Mentally Ill (NAMI), told me her heart-rending, hair-tearing experience. (NAMI provides education and advocacy for people with mental illness.) Harriet fell victim to psychoanalyst Frieda Fromm-Reichmann (1948) who propounded the idea that schizophrenia is the result of a mother who is both overprotective and rejecting at the same time, dubbed the schizophrenogenic mother. A prominent family therapist, Dr. Carl Whitaker, took this view and Harriet and her husband, with the hope that their child might recover, entered into family therapy with Whitaker, even living in a hospital ward for a time. It was an awful, dreadful experience, like being brain washed. The theory was totally unfounded; the child never recovered. However, Harriet sure ended up with a head of steam. A woman of action was born.

So blaming Mom isn't in my repertoire. I know little of my mother's individual history, but we do know that early 20th century culture handicapped women with a lack of information and opportunity on the excuse of protecting them. She was "hysteroid" herself, but my father's extreme idealism and foibles also didn't help my development into a realistic person. In late life, I reread *Main Street* (1920), by Sinclair Lewis, and I was embarrassed to recognize so much of myself and my family in the book. When I was younger, I found the book boring. I missed the satire entirely.

It is one of the ironies of life that we often end up at least somewhat like those we otherwise reject. This was the case for me and my mother. We shared an abnormal psychological tendency for denial: failure to recognize inconvenient information especially that connected with repressed information (historically for women—sexuality). From a small beginning, denial can grow into a habit. Contemporary American society no longer shields girls from sexual knowledge and conversation; consequently, the hysteroid personality style is less common than previously.

I first became aware of my mother's tendency to denial when I was eight years old. A tableau was to be staged at the Universalist church, and Mother was to be a Biblical character, the disciple known as Doubting Thomas. She was excited about her role. The morning of her performance, I awakened covered with the red rash of chicken pox, but I didn't feel particularly sick.

Mother looked at my red splotchy skin and declared, "Isn't that cute. She scrubbed herself with Dutch Cleanser to be clean for church."

"No, I didn't," I vehemently protested several times. Mother wouldn't listen to me, so off we went to church where I exposed all the people there to my illness, and Mother successfully acted out her pose. When it was definitively revealed to her that I had a contagious disease, she thought it was funny that she'd been mistaken. I told this story over dinner to some psychologist friends who startled me by observing how self-centered my mother was. I had never thought of her that way, yet the shoe fit. However, it wasn't so much selfishness, but more a matter of wishful thinking. She wanted to be in the tableau, and her wish that I not be sick allowed her to gloss over the obvious facts. Denial had become a habitual way of thinking, or not thinking. She didn't consciously take me to church with chicken pox. The result was selfish behavior, but its source was complex.

My mother's tendency toward denial showed in her reaction to animal sexual behavior. One spring we were all in the backyard when we observed one bird atop another thrusting vigorously and pecking it on the head. My mother asked my father, "What are they doing?" My father thought this was hilarious. Next spring, the same situation, and my mother asked again, "Roy, what are they doing?" Both my father and I laughed heartily. But what did pecking the female on the head have to do with mating? I didn't have a clue. (I intuited that they were engaged in a sexual act, but its mechanics were unknown to me.)

Mother couldn't bring herself to talk to me about sex. One day, when I was eight or nine years old, while looking for something in my parents' chest of drawers (at my mother's request), I ran across what looked like a balloon. It was about five inches long, made of rubber, but unlike most balloons, it was a dull tan in color. I tried to blow it up.

"Mom, this balloon won't blow up," I complained. I'd found my parents' condom supply.

She looked up from her bed horrified. "Put that back! Leave those alone!" She refused to explain what they were, and I didn't learn about condoms or contraception until I was in my twenties.

My brother was no help either. When I was about seven and walking home from school with John, I heard him say "fuck," and I asked him, "What does 'fuck' mean?"

He wouldn't tell me. That made me angry so I followed him down the street shouting, "Fuck, fuck, fuck." John tried to run away, but I chased him, yelling, "Fuck, fuck, fuck."

Finally, desperate, he stopped and I caught up to him. After extracting a promise from me to stop yelling fuck, he said, "'Fuck' is something a man does to a woman," and refused to say more. I didn't know the meaning of the word till years later. There was no one to ask.

My own sexual history was unremarkable according to the statistics of Kontula and Miettinen (2016). Like most girls, I found the delights of self-pleasure, perhaps a little early, by age ten. I went to bed each night with my nylon panties on, which puzzled my mother. I had found that a delightful experience could be mine by stroking the silky, panty crotch. Somehow, I knew I shouldn't mention this to my mother, and I didn't connect it with sex. It was something that was mine, and I was desperate that she not discover a way to take it away from me, like the pleasure of my Linus blanket and sucking my thumb. As for my Linus blanket, she got it away from me by telling me that she was going to make it into a nice new blanket. Instead, she put it in the middle of an ugly, scratchy quilt made from my father's old wool suits.

With the onset of puberty, I developed a lively interest in boys. A lesbian overture from Peggy, an eighth-grade schoolmate, went nowhere. Why would I want her to stroke my clitoris? I could do that myself. For me, it was boys, boys, and boys. I hadn't had a crush since Kenneth in first grade. That attraction ended when he asked me to pull up my skirt in the cloak room.

"I will not," I said.

"Why not? Gloria did."

Now, age eleven, I had a total crush on Jim Smith, who sat in front of me. His daring appealed to me. He'd walked across the dizzying heights of the railroad viaduct crossing Tallmadge Road. Besides that, he'd found a dead body in the woods in the valley of the Little Cuyahoga River. Jim became a jet pilot and died at an early age in a crash. Alas, I only managed to get to one grade school dance with him. The boy who sat behind me was another story; he dipped my pigtail in the ink well.

I had serial crushes on boys: Bud, Paul, the basketball player, Johnny, with the wavy brown hair, Hirsch, Dick, Ronnie, Chuck, Bruce, and many others, a pattern that continued until I married. In high school, I began to attract boyfriends; they were good to me, and I enjoyed the attention and physical affection they lavished upon me. However, repressive forces were at work, and I managed to remain unaware of the significance of penile erection until I was much older. Now, on my first job in Minneapolis, I was married, becoming more mature, and shedding my hysteroid tendencies.

I still wanted to learn more about psychotherapy. I didn't consider my personal therapy with Dr. Baer complete, and I was eager to continue with Dr. Meehl. He was Hathaway's prize student, but the two men were different in their personalities as well as their viewpoints. Hathaway's nickname among the students was Stark Raving Hathaway. He was regarded as "schizy," while Meehl was open about the fact that he suffered from manic depression (later called bipolar disorder), as well as epilepsy. Meehl was about five feet ten, a handsome man except for a weak chin, which he later disguised with an immaculate beard. He was brilliant, quick, and breathtaking in his breadth of knowledge and mastery of complex concepts. (When depressed, he was slowed and quiet.) Meehl had an open mind, strong ethical imperatives, and a winsome, charming personality. He was zany, unconventional, and highly original. I quickly decided that I wanted him for my new therapist, which proved a wise choice. He had an intuitive grasp of my problems, since, as it turned out, we shared the same illness.

At that point in my life (1958) I was unhappy about my marital choice, but otherwise I felt fine. Meehl and I decided that I was mildly neurotic, but when I later developed a major depression in 1984, it was apparent that these earlier depressive symptoms were those of an underlying bipolar vulnerability. By 1984, other members of my family had fallen ill with bipolar disorder.

It was lucky that I was aware of the hereditary component of the disorder, because many individuals with bipolar disorder spend years before they're correctly diagnosed, sometimes with terrible consequences. Misdiagnosis as schizophrenic is particularly tragic. A devoted daughter told me this horrifying story: When she was a girl, her mother was confined to an Illinois state hospital, diagnosed and medicated as schizophrenic. As an adult, the daughter began to suspect that her mother's diagnosis was actually bipolar disorder, and she mounted a determined campaign to have her correctly diagnosed and treated. She was ultimately successful, and her mother not only recovered and left the hospital but became a successful executive secretary in Chicago.

In another case, the son of a wealthy family spent a year in an expensive, private mental hospital, misdiagnosed and medicated for schizophrenia when bipolar disorder was his correct diagnosis. Because he wasn't properly diagnosed and treated, he later became manic and got involved in a financial fiasco, which is typical of the out-of-bounds behavior of the manic phase. However, no one understood that his aberrant behavior was a product of mental illness. As a result, he was disowned by his family and sent to prison without proper legal representation or treatment for the depression that inevitably ensued. Fortunately, his distressed girlfriend and I figured out the situation and got him help. Countless others suffer less dramatic, but nonetheless significant, negative consequences because of misdiagnosis.

Meehl and I began a classic psychoanalysis with me lying on a couch and Meehl sitting behind, listening to my free associations three times a week. Meehl was intensely interested in psychoanalysis and had begun an analysis himself.

While I was in therapy with Meehl, I noticed another patient, a short, nondescript man who attracted my attention because his furtive manner suggested that he didn't want to be recognized. Later, I saw his picture in the newspaper and identified him as the novelist, Saul Bellow. In an amusing turnabout, Bellow modeled aspects of the character, Herzog, after Meehl.

Although the process of free association intrigued me, my condition deteriorated, and I was not merely troubled and unhappy about my marriage, but depressed. Why did this happen? At the time, I thought that it was the result of the psychoanalysis, which is a stressful procedure. Hours spent introspecting interfere with reality testing and focuses attention on negative thoughts and experiences. For vulnerable individuals, the fourth step of the Alcoholics Anonymous program, which involves a review of a lifetime of misdeeds, carries a similar risk. However, in retrospect, I think my depression probably had to do with the onset of the Minnesota winter and seasonal affective disorder (SAD). However, SAD wasn't a recognized illness at the time.

Now, it wasn't a matter of my getting therapy so I would be a good therapist, I was sick. Meehl was patient and infinitely kind. He allowed me to call him at home, which was fortunate because I was suicidal for months. During this time, I was obsessed with thoughts of killing myself. Should I throw myself into the river? Should I jump from a ten-story building? I was acutely aware that most suicide attempts are unsuccessful. Such was my pessimism that I had no faith in a successful attempt but wasted my time and tortured myself with this suicidal preoccupation. In retrospect, it's interesting how different this episode was from the one in 1984. At that time, I was slowed and lost my appetite, symptoms of a major depression (often called a melancholic depression). During the 1958-59 episode, I was miserably preoccupied with suicidal thoughts, but carried on my life with this secret misery.

Meehl was always able to calm me down and never seemed to mind that I called him. How did he do it? Strange as it may seem, given the fact that Meehl was an important, brilliant professor, he listened and conveyed to me a compassionate, sustaining interest in my welfare. A psychotherapeutic relationship decreases the likelihood of suicide; never underestimate the power of a relationship.

Once, when I was suicidal, Meehl invited me to visit him at his home; I was overwhelmed by this kindness. He was a character, full of surprises: While I was there, I was startled to see a cat wandering about with a metal apparatus attached to its head. "Oh, Tom," he said, as though it was nothing out of the ordinary. "He was used in some experiments on brain stimulation and needed a new home."

Meehl and I correctly decided that couch analysis wasn't helpful for me, and we switched to face-to-face therapy. Meehl's therapy was unorthodox in the sense that he talked a lot about himself and gave advice; he was flexible and practical. As I agonized over what to do about my marriage, he finally said, "I don't think you'll ever be happy in your present marriage." What a relief. I soon filed for divorce.

Meehl also helped me professionally. He advanced my name as someone to teach an evening class at the university, an affirmation of my intellectual worth that was much needed. One day, Meehl asked me a surprising question: "Do you find thinking pleasurable?" At the time, I was puzzled by his question, and, after some thought, replied that I didn't. (I'd floundered in depression for months.)

"For me, thinking is entirely pleasurable," he said.

As a fellow psychologist, I was intrigued by this revelation. Here was a man who was a genius, or at least near-genius, who talked about thinking in a new way. I was mystified by his question for years until I later had the leisure to pursue my own curiosity and learn the exquisite joy of thinking. It's this pleasure that urged me to all my creative work. For at least some people, thinking is "addictive" in the sense that it's intrinsically rewarding.

Both addictions and creativity are more common among bipolar individuals, and evidence is mounting that they share a related genetic basis. To be clear about what I mean by "thinking," I'm not referring to obsessive thought. Obsessive thoughts may occur, but they don't go anywhere. By thinking, I mean problem solving that is goal oriented, that is, thought processes motivated by the intrigue of solving a puzzle or problem.

I suspect pleasure in problem solving is behind all creative work and is an essential feature that separates us humans from other primates. The achievements of modern humans don't require everyone to be creative—just enough so that the rest can use the ideas produced by those able to think of them. It's the partnership which is often crucial. For example, Ron Chernow (2004), biographer of our brilliant and bipolar founding father, Alexander Hamilton, makes the point that it was by working in tandem with George Washington that Hamilton made his greatest contributions. Washington was a man of consummate good judgment and provided an anchor for the more tempestuous Hamilton.

The neuroendocrine dopamine is responsible for the rewarding, pleasurable addictive experience of thinking. High levels of dopamine characterize hypomanic and manic states (and several other abnormal mental states). As Fred Previc (2009) spells out in his book, *The Dopaminergic Mind in Evolution and History*, dopamine played a crucial role in human evolution, and individuals with high dopamine states are associated with creative surges throughout human history.

Meehl was going through a religious conversion experience when I was in therapy with him, and I was influenced by his views. Although it's often regarded as irrational for a scientist to be a Christian, science doesn't explain everything. Even if you accept the idea that the universe was formed by the Big Bang, where did the Big Bang come from? If you ask enough questions, you eventually find some that are unanswerable using scientific methods.

Meehl, like many other intellectuals, took the "leap of faith" and became a believer. My father had told me that I should believe in God, and I seized this opportunity to straighten out my religious views. Through Meehl, I was introduced to a retired minister, Woody Ching, and Pastor William Buege who instructed me in the Christian religion. Eventually I was baptized. Religion isn't taught in the schools, and I was surprised at the gaps in my understanding of American culture because of lack of knowledge about the Christian religion. The conversion was a positive experience for me. It gave me time-tested rules to live by, a feeling of belonging, and I was often comforted by a sense of God's presence. Dramatic religious experiences frequently occur among bipolar individuals, though not in my case. Because of my teenage experience hearing voices, I avoided excessive preoccupation with religion.

While I was working at the VA hospital and still in therapy with Meehl, antidepressants came into use, and he suggested that I try the new antidepressant Parnate (a monoamine oxidase inhibitor no longer often used). It worked amazingly well, and I was impressed. However, in retrospect I wonder if I got better because of the antidepressant or because the long winter was over. With regret at the loss of Meehl's company, now that I was well, I discontinued therapy.

During my work at the Minneapolis VA hospital, I happily found new women friends: a social worker, Lucile Spriggs, a psychiatrist, Margaret Bailey, and a librarian, Margaret Alverson. I got along well with the staff, and they were a fun, sociable group. However, I had a horrible experience with the head of psychiatry, Dr. Simon. When I left my husband, Lucy told me that I could get temporary housing at a VA facility, which I did. Unfortunately, the bill for this housing didn't reach me, and it came to Dr. Simon's attention that the bill was unpaid. I learned from Lucy that, during coffee break in the conference room, Dr. Simon had opined to the gathered staff that I was a dishonest and unethical person, a psychopath. Here I was again, run afoul a male authority figure. Luckily, my friends stuck up for me; the bill was paid, and Dr. Simon apologized.

Apparently, I was different from other women. Sometimes people thought especially well of me, sometimes not. I stood out for good or ill, even in high school. As a student, we were all being rowdy on a school bus, but the bus driver singled me out as the leader. He called the police, and I was astonished to be taken off the bus to a squad car. Fortunately, the policeman was satisfied with my explanations and simply drove me home.

On another occasion, as an adult married woman, a conservative Lutheran church elder branded me a Communist. Again, there was no basis whatsoever for this opinion, and at the behest of the minister who knew me, the man apologized. I've often reflected that I'm fortunate to be living at this time in the United States of America because I might have been burned at the stake at other times and places. I actually was once pronounced a witch. While crossing from the United States to England on the Queen Elizabeth, I met the Spanish novelist Ramon Sender, who immediately pronounced me a *bruja* (witch) and shunned me thereafter. He came to this opinion because of my long, slender feet, which he considered a sign that I was a witch.

Although I suffered from depression and anxiety while working at the VA, I had plenty of energy and worked well. With the expert mentoring that I received from Meehl, Hathaway, and my immediate supervisor Harold Gilberstadt, I became convinced that psychotherapy works and developed my own philosophy of treatment.

I approached clinical work with an attitude of discovery. That's what made it so interesting. I was always thinking, "What's wrong here? How can this be fixed?" I'd form hypotheses and look to see if the data fit. My method of working was to make a careful diagnosis and then choose the treatment, depending on the patient. While this sounds like a common-sense approach, some practitioners give the same treatment to all their patients, be it medication, psychoanalysis, or behavior therapy. Most commonly, I used interpersonal psychotherapy, which relies heavily on the healing power of the therapeutic relationship. But I also used supportive therapy, the psychoanalytic techniques of free association and dream analysis, and behavior therapy. I became expert in psychodiagnosis and evaluated hundreds of patients for internists, neurologists, psychiatrists, and others.

One of my first patients had the forbidding diagnosis of pseudoneurotic schizophrenia. This diagnosis, no longer in use, referred to persons with many neurotic symptoms and evidence of a thought disorder, but no obvious psychosis. Norman (pseudonym) was seriously depressed, withdrawn, and preoccupied with obsessive thoughts, but he was exceptionally intelligent. When I saw him for a diagnostic interview and psychological test evaluation, we got along well, and I thought I could help him with psychotherapy. The rest of Norman's treatment team, a psychiatrist and social worker, thought that he wouldn't respond to psychotherapy and would have to be hospitalized for the rest of his life, but they agreed to let me try.

Norman was single, twenty-six years old, and trained as an accountant; I thought he might benefit from Starke Hathaway's practical approach to psychotherapy. Since I didn't thoroughly understand his ideas, I asked Starke to explain. He began by saying, "Psychotherapy is like a bug in a cup."

"What do you mean?" I asked. "I don't get it."

"The bug is the patient running around in the cup, unable to get out. The therapist's job is to put a twig in the cup so the patient can climb out."

I couldn't think how to apply this idea to Norman, but I knew he needed an approach that didn't stir him up—no discussion of early life experiences, no dream analysis, no probing questions. Instead, we talked about his concerns, especially his future employment, a treatment called supportive psychotherapy.

After a few months, Norman recovered. He left the hospital and was soon engaged in full-time employment as an accountant. I was pleased, relieved, and elated. Psychotherapy does work, I thought. Norman's recovery was especially sweet since the senior staff had thought it unlikely. His recovery boosted my morale as a psychotherapist and encouraged me to use my own judgment in accepting clients, even those others thought hopeless.

These next experiences as a therapist illustrate various aspects of repression, the unconscious, the problems they can cause, and their treatment. Some are from later years of practice including other settings. However, John (pseudonym) was a VA patient, one of my first, and another experience that convinced me that clinical psychology was a valid profession. John was also a prime example that hysteria isn't limited to women. He entered the hospital with a strange symptom; he was unable to close his mouth, but the physicians couldn't find a physical reason for his problem. His diagnosis was conversion reaction, which means that an emotional conflict has been converted into a physical symptom. John's jaw started working again before psychotherapy began. But to my surprise, the disappearance of his symptom wasn't considered the end of his problem. The psychoanalytically oriented senior staff wanted to know what was behind the symptom. Why had his mouth been stuck open?

What was the underlying conflict? I was to answer these questions and help John resolve the conflict.

John was thirty years old, married, the father of one child, with another on the way. He worked as a repairman for the telephone company and was an active member of a Methodist church, where he taught Sunday school. These were important facts involved in the central psychological conflict. John's work, going into homes to service telephones, exposed him to many lonely women in various forms of dress and undress. He was sorely tempted, obsessed with adulterous thoughts, but tortured by the hypocrisy of a Sunday school teacher contemplating adultery. His wife's pregnancy heightened the conflict, precipitating his illness.

Though the central conflict was clear, what did it have to do with his original symptom—inability to close his mouth? John regularly reported his dreams, but the "royal road to the unconscious" led me nowhere. Then he went home from the hospital on pass, got drunk, and ended up in bed with another woman (the mother of a former girlfriend).

This experience jolted John into finally reporting the essential information that made sense of his symptom. When he was seventeen, his family received a telephone call reporting that his father was lying dead—burned to death in a house of prostitution. In order to hide the circumstances of the death, John and his uncle went to get the body and were directed to an upstairs room. Upon opening the door, John saw the charred body of his father in the prostitute's bed, dead—with his mouth fixed open. This traumatic sight was the basis for John's symptom since, in John's religious language, the wages of sin are death (with an open mouth). John's psychotherapy and knowledge of the source of his symptom set off a series of healing discussions between him and his wife which led to a deeper level of intimacy and trust. They were extremely appreciative of my help and planned to name their baby, Julie, but, alas, the baby was a boy.

Patients of this type aren't common, and I was lucky to have the chance to work with John. Our treatment team also saw a man who for years had the symptom of walking on his heels. His diagnosis was also conversion reaction. When the psychiatrist on our team interviewed him under the influence of sodium amytal (commonly known as truth serum), the source of the symptom became obvious. Jeff (pseudonym) had been on a ship in the Pacific during World War II, and everyone was under strict orders: no lights. However, Jeff lit a cigarette. Enemy aircraft overhead saw the light in the vast dark of the night, and the ship was bombed. As the ship was sinking, in order to reach a life boat, Jeff had walked on his heels to lessen the pain from the burning hot deck. He had done a terrible thing, and now, these many years later, treatment relieved him of the symptom that had resulted.

Traumatic events may elicit strange symptoms, and people *do* sometimes repress memories that nonetheless affect behavior, as Freud observed. In this case, it was Jeff's guilt that prompted the symptom. What he failed to remember without psychiatric help was the connection between his wrongful behavior and the symptom. It was truly amazing that the symptom, which had persisted for years, disappeared with insight gained from the sodium amytal interview. Had authorities known that Jeff was responsible for the ship's bombing, he would have been court-martialed and severely punished. In effect, Jeff punished himself with his symptom, but needless to say, his symptom was a minor inconvenience compared to what the Navy would have done to him.

In another instance, a patient was hospitalized with a complete loss of memory for who he was. In his case, the guilty trauma, which was also recovered with the aid of a sodium amytal interview, involved his embezzlement of a large sum of money.

The return of the repressed, Freud's term for manifestation of a repressed memory, can also come in the form of a dream. Kerry (pseudonym) reported a nightmare in which a large, red object approached his face, awakening him in fright. The patient was a gay male and it wasn't hard to guess that the large red object was an erect adult penis. Because he was frightened and perceived the penis as so overwhelmingly large, I inferred that he'd been molested as a child, but I didn't explain the dream to him. I let him find the meaning himself by free association. "What comes to mind when you think of the large red object?" I asked. There was a pause.

"Oh, my God," he said. The repressed returned. He'd completely forgotten (repressed) repeated instances of childhood sexual abuse. His subsequent dreams contained details of the surroundings where the abuse occurred. Later, he returned to the place of his abuse and validated the details in his dreams. I was Kerry's fourth psychotherapist. Now in his twenties, he'd first begun therapy at age seven. All three previous therapists missed the sexual abuse.

The return of repressed memories is often triggered by something that reminds the person of the experience they have repressed; smells can be especially evocative. Jena (pseudonym) had clear, never-repressed memories of incest so I didn't think of her as harboring a repressed memory. To me, her conscious memories were so awful that I couldn't imagine what was left to repress, but sometimes there is a special, painful hurt. Jena often vehemently complained about her severe allergy to the smell of apple blossoms, yet she was never sniffing or sneezing when she complained. I found this peculiar, as though she were unconsciously trying to catch my attention. I began to suspect a repressed traumatic experience associated with the smell of apple blossoms and decided to test the possibility.

Without telling her my hypothesis, the next time she complained about her allergy, I asked her, "What comes to mind when you think about the smell of apple blossoms?" It was like opening Pandora's Box; she snapped into a flashback of dreadful emotional intensity. She was reliving the time after her father first raped her. She was walking up a dirt country road in the springtime to find her mother at the neighbor's house; the air was filled with the scent of apple trees in bloom. Although Jena remembered being raped, she'd repressed the memory of her terrible journey in search of her mother, perhaps because disappointment in a mother's protection is one of the cruelest wounds of incest trauma; Jena's first rape was not to be the last.

Traumatic memories are sometimes expressed as hallucinations. Although psychotherapy with schizophrenic patients was unusual at the time, I had two patients with schizophrenia in long-term psychotherapy (in collaboration with psychiatrists). I was eager to learn as much as I could about every form of mental disorder.

Mary (pseudonym), one of my most memorable patients, told me, "Every night before I go to sleep, a group of people gather around my bed, talking."

"No, Mary," I said. "That's not possible."

"Oh, yes it is. It happens every night."

"No. No. You're imagining this."

"No, I'm not. This really happens, and I'm going to prove it to you. I'm going to buy a tape recorder, and we'll see who's right."

Oops, I'd made a mistake. I'd jeopardized my relationship with Mary, although my ability to help her depended on our having a strong relationship. When she returned for the next session, I asked if she'd bought a tape recorder.

"No, I don't need to," she triumphantly proclaimed. "You can't prove I *didn't* see them." Notice that she was making the sophisticated point that it's impossible to prove a negative. I was amused; I admired the agility of her argument, and quickly agreed with her. Much later, I realized that Mary's hallucination was a post-traumatic stress reaction.

She had already told me about many instances of childhood abuse, but it was months before I heard about the experience that conjured her nightly vision. One day as she was leaving, she turned back and poked her head around the door, saying, "I was raped," and quickly she was gone.

At our next meeting, having broken the ice, she was able to tell the story. The first incident occurred when her family was visiting relatives. Her alcoholic father took her, then but a girl, to a back bedroom and raped her. When she screamed, the relatives gathered around the bed, talking. This was the experience repeated in her nightly vision. The incident wasn't reported; her mother ignored the problem, and Mary was forced to submit to this incestuous relationship for years.

I learned a lot from Mary, including how easy it is to discount mentally ill individuals. For example, during a meeting between me, Mary, and a third party, I talked about Mary as though she wasn't there. At our next therapy session, Mary gently let me know that she didn't appreciate my talking about her like she was invisible. I was dismayed by my insensitivity and apologized. Mary handled the lapse with good judgment and grace.

Mary actually hadn't been referred to me in the first place. She'd been so confused on the occasion of our first interview that she came into my office by mistake. Because of a clerical mix-up, I didn't find out about this until much later. Although she was on anti-psychotic medications, her thought processes were so mixed up that I couldn't make sense of what she was saying for the first several sessions. However, she did make it clear that she wanted to pursue therapy in the hope that she could recover for the sake of her child. She was strongly motivated. I saw Mary for supportive psychotherapy twice a week for five years at a severely reduced fee paid from public sources. However, for several months because of a glitch in public funding, I received no payment at all. I saw her anyway since it was my policy to see patients even if they couldn't afford the usual fee.

Despite poverty and a highly traumatic history, Mary had the courage and wit to overcome daunting obstacles, take good care of her daughter, and live independently for many years. I lost track of her, and then after about ten years, she contacted me. She questioned her diagnosis of schizophrenia and thought it should be PTSD. She did have PTSD, but by all our criteria for schizophrenia, she also warranted that diagnosis. For example, at one point during my work with her, she wasn't doing well and her medication was changed. I asked her how she was doing with the new medication.

"Much better," she said. "Now I have much more privacy."

I was puzzled. "What do you mean?" I asked.

"Well, before, my mother could see everything I was thinking."

"What?" I said. I couldn't understand what she was telling me. Later, her psychiatrist, Dr. Max Smith, explained to me that she was talking about thought broadcasting. Mary saw everything she was thinking written in the air, and, therefore, she believed her mother could see what she was thinking. This is a symptom pathognomonic (specific) to schizophrenia. Mary's case was an unusual example of the effects of a traumatic experience.

Since my personal and professional experiences were replete with examples of how the unconscious and repression affect behavior, I, along with many other therapists treating victims of abuse, was startled when the ideas of repression and the unconscious were rejected as unscientific as a result of the "false memories" controversy (Loftus, 2003). Unconscious processes are difficult to demonstrate scientifically, but that doesn't mean they don't exist. Given the large number of women (and men) who have been traumatized, it's important to recognize the power of the unconscious and the therapeutic tools useful to unravel the effects of traumatic events. The proper retrieval of repressed memories requires care to avoid contamination of the evidence, but the valid recovery of "forgotten" (i.e., repressed) memories is possible.

Skepticism also still exists about the meaningfulness of dreams. Some say that dreams are random neurological events, but here are some simple examples to the contrary. After I remarried, there was a dinner that I planned to attend with my new husband; I had forgotten that my first husband would be there. The night before the dinner, I had a dream in which I was at the dinner and encountered my first husband. The dream warned me of a circumstance that I'd forgotten, and it prepared me for what might be an awkward situation.

Here is a second example of a dream that prompted me to remember something I had forgotten. In the 1950s, girls were warned to be careful about the appearance of their underwear. After all, we were told, you could end up in the hospital, and people would see your panties. I'd decided that I should throw out a pair of panties I'd resolved to wear for the last time that day. However, when I went to bed, I forgot and threw the panties in the wash rather than the waste basket. During the night, I dreamed that someone saw me in my raggedy panties because I hadn't thrown them out, and I was embarrassed and ashamed. Was this dream an instance of a part of my brain so conscientious that it felt compelled to "speak"?

At another level was the dream told to me by my colleague, Bill Jackson, who was dying of cancer. "I dreamed I was floating in an inky, black nothingness merged with the universe." I felt the chill of death; Bill was calm, but I wasn't surprised when he died the next day.

Dream analysis has a long history reaching back to the Bible and the ancient Egyptians. It's even part of Americana. Founding fathers Dr. Benjamin Rush and President John Adams engaged in a long correspondence involving the analysis of dreams (McCullough, 2001). Dreams can't be dismissed as simply the product of random neurological events; however, individuals may vary in their capacity for meaningful dreams.

Arguments about Freudian theory have been part of my life for over half a century. In the late 1960s when I reviewed the scientific literature regarding Freud's ideas about the psychology of women, I found no support for them, but, on the other hand, I've observed phenomena (hypnosis, dreams, and symptoms consistent with repression) that support other of Freud's ideas. A nuanced evaluation is necessary.

So far, I've illustrated support therapy and the use of psychoanalytic techniques. The next case features behavior therapy, and a drug-free treatment of agoraphobia (fear of going outside). As already suggested, the sexes differ in the prevalence of mental disorders. Men have a higher rate of early-onset schizophrenia, autism, and attention deficit disorder while anxiety, panic attack, and depression are more prevalent among women (McCarthy et al., 2012). Panic attacks can occur as a single symptom or in addition to another disorder, such as depression, bipolar disorder, or agoraphobia. The latter was Nancy's (pseudonym) problem. She'd been a stay-at-home mom, but now she found herself unable to leave home although she wanted to rejoin the work force. She also experienced panic attacks, which are an integral part of agoraphobia. They are dreadful experiences, and often patients become so fearful of having a panic attack that they won't leave home. I've had two panic attacks myself, and because of my professional training, I knew what they were; otherwise I would have believed that my life was in danger. The attacks are so frightening that fear of another attack can become a major problem in itself.

Nancy's insurance covered only three months of therapy, and she preferred treatment without medications, so we developed a plan within these constraints. Using the knowledge I had gained from reading the literature on the behavioral treatment of agoraphobia, we made a list of her fears and began with the mildest one. The idea is to gradually develop the person's tolerance for feared behaviors. I had her begin by walking away from her home to the point where she felt a bit anxious, and then she was to return, repeating the venture until she could go farther and farther away without anxiety. She took her young daughter with her; the presence of another person, or even a pet, can be an anxiety reducer. She went to church with her family, sitting in the back to reduce her fear of no escape. Sitting up front, or in the middle of a row would have been more difficult. Once she realized what a panic attack is and that she wasn't going to die, she was able to "calmly" endure a panic attack that occurred when she attempted dinner out with her husband. Gradually, we upped her goals until she surprised me by reporting that she'd made a long bus trip in the company of her daughter. By the end of three months, Nancy was well and soon had a job. I could never have gotten such an effective, quick result with other therapies.

I can't leave the topic of my clinical experiences without giving you an example of the mistreatment of a psychiatric patient illustrating the problem of *Bias in Psychiatric Diagnosis* (2004), title of a book edited by Paula Caplan and Lisa Cosgrove, and a problem underscored by Phyllis Chesler in her 1972 book, *Women and Madness: When is a Woman Mad and Who is it Who Decides?*

Debbie (pseudonym) was a young woman student with few financial or family resources. Because she'd been adopted, her family history of lupus was unknown to her. (Lupus is a systemic autoimmune disease that can affect any part of the body causing pain, fatigue, and multiple symptoms, including depression. It can be hard to diagnose.) Debbie was depressed and she attempted suicide more than once. As a condition of further treatment, her HMO required her to sign a statement that she would never again attempt suicide. However, she took a lethal dose of medication and crawled under bushes in an out-of-the-way place. A passing runner spotted the tips of her shoes, called police, and her appointment with death was canceled. Her HMO considered that she had violated her contract and refused to provide her with any further psychiatric care, which is how I came to be involved in her case.

I talked to her former psychiatrist at the HMO who described the suicide attempt as manipulative and attention-getting, but I didn't agree. For example, contrast Debbie's suicide attempt with this one: While on a locked psychiatric ward, the patient hanged herself in her room while dialing 911 on her cell phone. Not surprisingly, she was immediately rescued. Debbie had nothing to gain by her suicide attempt, but because she violated the no-suicide contract, she was told to find new mental health care on her own, which isn't easy when you're sick, a stranger in the city, and have no money or family resources.

Debbie had been given the stigmatizing diagnosis of borderline personality disorder. Individuals with this diagnosis, mostly women, were regarded as difficult to treat, manipulative, attention seeking, untruthful, and a general pain in the ass. When I received Debbie's psychiatric records, I found that her former psychiatrist had misconstrued her behavior to fit this diagnosis.

Debbie was described as a lesbian. "Not that there's anything wrong with that," as Jerry Seinfeld would say. But beneath a surface-tolerant attitude, lesbianism had serious, negative implications in psychiatric circles at that time. Being a lesbian was described as an identity disturbance and considered part of the borderline personality syndrome. Debbie denied being a lesbian, and I could find no evidence of lesbianism. However, in a tour de force of circular reasoning, since lying was regarded as characteristic of borderline personality, Debbie's denial that she was lesbian was regarded as a lie, and further evidence that justified the stigmatizing diagnosis of borderline personality and the HMO's dumping her.

The no-suicide contract never made sense to me. Active intent to commit suicide is almost automatic grounds for a judicial finding of mental incompetence, which can justify involuntary commitment. If a patient is mentally incompetent, how can she be held responsible when she breaks a contract? Is the HMO on sound legal ground to deny treatment? Years later I got an explanation for the no-suicide contract; the psychiatry department didn't make money, and the no-suicide contract helped the bottom line by ridding the HMO of patients requiring expensive care.

Debbie was not a difficult patient. She was always on time for appointments and worked responsibly in therapy. The more I got to know her, the more evidence emerged that the diagnosis of borderline personality disorder was incorrect.

Here's how she stacked up according to the *Diagnostic and Statistical Manual of Mental Disorders-IV* (APA, 1994). A diagnosis of borderline personality disorder required that the patient meet at least five of nine criteria: (1) frantic efforts to avoid abandonment (no); (2) a pattern of unstable and intense interpersonal relationships (no); (3) identity disturbance (no); (4) impulsivity (yes); (5) recurrent suicidal behavior (yes); (6) affective instability (no); (7) chronic feelings of emptiness (no); (8) inappropriate or intense anger (no); (9) transient paranoid ideation or severe dissociative symptoms (no). Debbie satisfied only two of the nine criteria.

As I thought about Debbie, I became convinced that her behavior and symptoms didn't hang together as any psychiatric disorder, and I began to suspect that she had a physical disease. She and I talked it over and she tracked down her biological parents. When we learned that her biological mother had lupus, her physician was able to make the correct diagnosis. Although joint and muscle pains and rashes are common symptoms, Debbie hadn't complained to me of these more tell-tale symptoms. I hadn't guessed that she had lupus; I had only figured out that the depression, which is a common symptom, didn't make psychological sense. She got treatment for lupus, recovered from her depression, finished a Master's degree, overcame enormous obstacles, and landed a good job. This was a fine woman that the HMO and her psychiatrist were willing to discredit and throw on the scrap heap of life. While this kind of treatment could happen to a man, it's more common among women. More women have lupus; more women are depressed; more women attempt suicide. Sad to say, her former psychiatrist was a young woman who had passed her boards in psychiatry.

Chapter 6

Fast Forward

In 1961, I remarried; we moved to Los Angeles, and I gave birth to a child in 1964. It was this pregnancy, childbirth, and care for my son that focused my attention on women's issues. During the pregnancy, my life and his had been threatened by preeclampsia, a disorder I'd never heard of. Preeclampsia occurs in 5-8% of pregnancies and is characterized by high blood pressure, swelling, and protein in the urine. It can end in convulsions and death. Women, along with the topics peculiar and central to us, were (and remain) neglected topics. We still don't have good scientific information about the causes of preeclampsia.

I had decisions to make about natural childbirth and breastfeeding. After all those years of education, I hadn't been given a sliver of information on these topics. Information wasn't readily available, and it wasn't scientifically based. Women weren't even included in the samples scientists studied, a problem that still exists. This is especially crucial when the research involves our health. Here are two examples: In 2013, the Food and Drug Administration ordered the makers of the sleep aid Ambien (zolpidem) to cut their recommended dose in half for women. The dosage had been based on research with men, with the result that women had been overdosed for twenty years. Not only is Ambien addicting, it is known for giving people bizarre sleep-walking experiences that can be dangerous or embarrassing. Second example: Women were advised to take a daily baby aspirin to prevent heart attack, a strategy later shown to be valid only for men.

After I gave birth to my son, I had a breast cancer scare and surgery; fortunately, the tumor was benign. Finally, after months at home, my curiosity set me on a mission to look for scientific information. This was during the time that the Women's Movement was unfolding; Betty Friedan's *Feminine Mystique* was published in 1963. Her book was a sensation, but it didn't ring bells for me. She wrote of "the problem that has no name." She was addressing the women who wanted something more than a husband, children, and home. The women Friedan appealed to were like one I saw later in my clinical practice. Here is how this woman's dismayed and mournful husband described his wife, "She got her boots, her IUD, her job, and she was out the door." This woman was fed up with the constraints of her role. On the other hand, I was a product of the first round of the Women's Movement with different problems that had names, like job discrimination and sexual harassment.

The phrase "the personal is political" hadn't been coined yet, but that was what happened to me. My experiences moved me to political action in the form I knew best: the science of psychology. Each day when the baby sitter arrived, I went to the UCLA library to get books and Xerox articles on relevant topics.

I started by reviewing the evidence regarding preeclampsia and the desirability of breast feeding, which I had decided to do, but I still wanted to know what facts were available. Then Eleanor Maccoby (1966a) published *The Development of Sex Differences*, a treasure trove of scientific information. I was informed, challenged, and intrigued by what I read. However, I was galvanized by statements that women are less analytical than men (Witkin et al., 1962). Skeptical, I was curious to know the evidence for this idea and set out to investigate. Careful research showed that the conclusion that men are more analytical than women boiled down to data on sex-related differences in spatial perception, particularly differences on a supposedly new dimension of personality and cognition called field dependence-independence (to be considered in more detail later). Bottom line: Researchers had conflated a sex-related difference in spatial perception into an unwarranted conclusion that men are more analytical than women, an idea that fit with a willingness to downplay the abilities of women. The results of my research challenging these ideas were published in the prestigious journal, *Psychological Review*, and were well received (Sherman, 1967). (For a readable update on sexist, slanted interpretations of the research literature, see Cordelia Fine's 2010 book, *Delusions of Gender: How our Minds, Society, and Neurosexism Create Differences.*)

Restive at home, I then started working part-time in the War on Poverty in Venice, California, but that job didn't last long. The director wanted to hold my hand walking around the work place. How could he imagine that this open harassment was okay? I put a quick stop to the hand holding, but then he wanted me to go on a trip with him. I refused, and the next day when I came to work, my desk was gone. I brought this up to a senior woman on the staff and got a "so what" response. Were we all expected to be his little harem? I quit. But what if I hadn't had a husband who supported the family? The hypocrisy of this man also got to me. Here we were working on an idealistic effort to help the poor, and this was the way he behaved. He went on to become a professor at a prestigious university. I wonder how many women he harassed during his career.

As the #MeToo movement has revealed, the problem is still with us. Nineteen percent of a recent sample of women reported workplace sexual harassment (Thurston et al., 2018). However, this underestimates the size of the problem. The Equal Employment Opportunity Commission (EEOC) reports lifetime estimates of on-the-job sexual harassment as high as eight in ten women. (In 2013, 17.6 % of the complaints filed to the EEOC were from men.)

The positive side of my being jobless was that it left me more time, along with the incentive, to work on what now became a book-length project reviewing the scientific literature on the psychology of women (Sherman, 1971). More and more topics of interest came to my attention. Every time I turned over a rock, a question popped out. I began the book with a chapter on biological sex differences. Some of the lesser known facts: Males not only have a shorter life span, but more males than females die in every decade of life. Beginning before birth, females physically mature more rapidly than males and are even born slightly earlier. Neither "male" hormones nor "female" hormones are limited to their respective sexes. Women produce androgens (and testosterone) and men produce estrogen. (Ironically, it turns out that the female sex drive depends on "male" hormones.)

The second chapter dealt with psychological sex differences involving some controversies unresolved to this day. Maccoby (1966b) not only reported that men were more analytical than women, but she also concluded that males have advantages in spatial ability and mathematical reasoning, topics discussed in more detail later. The averred difference in mathematical ability has been a serious obstacle for women. The belief itself has deterred women from pursuing the course work or sometimes, as in my case, they were actively discouraged.

One area where males do better is a specific form of space perception: spatial visualization, the ability to grasp space relations as they change in space. This isn't a clean-cut difference; many females are as good as or better than males, and the ability is important to a limited number of tasks (architecture, aspects of geometry, or the female sex-typed task: following a dress pattern).

However, the largest psychological difference between the sexes is not in cognition, but the fact that males are more "physically aggressive," a characteristic based in genes and hormones.

This is certainly not to say that females can't be aggressive or mean, but a look at the sex ratios in jails and prisons world-wide provides a practical fact not to be overlooked. It is sometimes said that women are more emotional than men, but isn't anger an emotion? This fact is conveniently overlooked in comparisons of the sexes that denigrate women.

There is an aspect of male physical aggressiveness that isn't the subject of much research: joy in physical combat. Will Mackin, author of *Bring Out the Dog* (2018), revealed that, although he missed the camaraderie he experienced during the Iraq war, he also missed the adrenaline, excitement, challenge, and ferocity of the combat experience. For some men, war is fun, terrible as it is. Mackin is an admirable man, a warrior, but it's notable that this mentality is rarely found among women (or most men). Historically, our government was set up under civilian control partly to prevent motivations like this from gaining the upper hand in decision making when it might be ill-suited to our overall welfare as a nation.

The next chapters in the 1971 book dealt with Freud's theory of feminine development. Although now passé, it was a topic of considerable interest in mid-twentieth century America. I've already discussed aspects of the theory and more will be considered in a later discussion of the female orgasm. Other chapters dealt with topics such as sex roles, menstruation, pregnancy, childbirth, and menopause. The book was finished in Madison, Wisconsin, where we moved so my husband could take a job at the University of Wisconsin. It was the first scientific book on the psychology of women; it sold well and was used in pioneer Women's Studies courses. I was invited to write articles and give speeches all over the country. NOVA, the Public Broadcasting System's television series, came to Madison and filmed me for a presentation, but the footage was cut at the last minute and never aired. In 1971, I began teaching perhaps the first course on the psychology of women; it was at night under the auspices of the UW extension psychology department. (The regular psychology department was hostile to the idea.)

However, I had no regular job. Hannah Gavron's book, *Captive Wife* (1966), described my dilemma. Many professional women whose husbands got jobs in a new city were captive to the situation, unable to find a suitable job in the new location. Sadly, these circumstances sometimes had devastating effects: The author of the dissertation on which that book was based committed suicide.

I finally went to talk to Dr. Norm Greenfield, head of the psychology section of the Department of Psychiatry at the UW Medical School. He didn't have a job for me, but he offered me the use of some of the facilities for research. Imbued as I was with the Iowa emphasis on empirical research, I hoped to begin a research career.

I did a study on field dependence, following up on my theoretical article in *Psychological Review*. One of the measures of field dependence is the Rod-and-Frame Test. The task posed by this test is to determine how vertical the rod is while perception of it is being influenced by a frame around the rod that is adjusted to different degrees of tilt. Women were found to be more influenced by the frame (field) in making judgments of the tilt of the rod. Hence, they were deemed more field dependent, that is, dependent on the context. The implication was that women were less able to make objective judgments. This went along with the idea that women were more psychologically dependent and less analytical than men. I remained curious about this. Also, if women *were* more field dependent, could they learn to be more independent? That is, could they become more accurate in their spatial judgment with practice?

The research was a shoestring operation, financed by a $500 grant from the American Psychological Association's Society for the Psychological Study of Social Issues. Since the room was borrowed, I couldn't alter it to paint it black. The room had to be pitch-black in order to conduct the study properly, so I dyed old sheets black and covered the walls and ceiling with black material. Now I needed the apparatus for the Rod-and-Frame Test. What to do? Sister Austin Doherty, PhD, head of the psychology department at Alverno College in Milwaukee, generously offered to buy the apparatus and lend it to me, and Dr. Greenfield provided access to a subject pool. The results of the study supported my theoretical ideas and showed that practice can improve performance on a spatial task, a new idea. I published the results in *Perceptual and Motor Skills* (1974). It was a pilot study to be followed with additional research, but I wasn't allowed to keep the room in order to continue. Now what?

It's often said that women don't do as much significant scientific research as men, but the obstacles are daunting. The opportunity to pursue an original research idea requires status, power, money, and colleagues—assets available to many fewer women than men. However, the discrimination doesn't end there. Significant achievements by women are often ignored or attributed to men.

Events took a turn for the better when I was contacted by Corinne Koufacos, who had recently received her PhD from the UW psychology department. In 1973, Corinne, Leticia Smith (PhD in sociology), Jackie Macaulay (PhD in social psychology), and I, with the crucial help of UW psychology professor, Dr. K. U. Smith, set up the Women's Research Institute. K. U. was an exceptional man, a brilliant maverick who was deeply interested in civil rights for women and African-Americans.

We directors of the institute were a diverse group. Corinne was a tiny Greek immigrant with jet-black hair and flashing dark eyes who came here after World War II, taught herself English, and made her way through to a PhD. She was smart, shrewd, practical, hard-working, idealistic, and socially astute. I got to know Leticia through Corinne. She was a small woman, like Corinne, and also an immigrant, from the Philippines. Unlike the rest of us, Jackie came from a wealthy family. She later became a lawyer and devoted herself to representing individuals who otherwise couldn't afford legal representation. With Corinne in the lead, we developed and put on an excellent series of seminars and conferences about women's issues.

Since we had little funding at first, we worked as volunteers, but I decided I needed to get some kind of outside, regular, paid employment. While continuing to work with the Women's Research Institute, I took a consulting job at Central State Hospital in Waupun, Wisconsin. This meant a considerable drive in all kinds of weather—an adventure in itself. Central State Hospital was a maximum security facility for those then called the criminally insane, which mostly consisted of the worst of the convicted sex offenders.

Rape is a consummate women's issue. In a recent sample of women, 22% reported sexual assault (Thurston et al., 2018). Why do men rape? I hoped to find out. I arrived there convinced that with my expert knowledge of psychotherapy, these sex offenders would recover and offend no more. I had a surprise. These men were highly resistant to treatment. They were essentially addicted to their aberrant sexual behavior, and like all addictions, this behavior was hard to change. However, in the case of addiction to aberrant sexuality, a slip in behavior—a rape or sexual abuse of a child—had much more serious consequences than the typical slip of someone addicted to drugs, alcohol, or gambling.

These sex offenders had trouble taking responsibility for their behavior, and they were persistent and ingenious about justifying themselves. I had previously dealt with psychopathic personalities, but never before was I immersed in an experience that exposed me to so many psychopaths (also called sociopaths and antisocial personalities). How well they could lie and deceive. How well they could place the blame elsewhere. How well they automatically took a self-serving position. It was an eye opener. Some examples: Sam (pseudonym), convicted four times of rape, demanded of me, "I've thought of rape a hundred times and didn't do it. How come I don't get credit for that?"

Another example: An educated man who had studied for the ministry said this about the victim of his rape, "She wanted it as much as I did." This he said during a group therapy session; the rest of the group hooted. They might not recognize their own flaws, but they could see his. He had threatened his victim, a young teen, with a linoleum knife. She was so upset by the experience that she required psychiatric hospitalization—not exactly eager, consensual sex.

Indifference to traditional morality was demonstrated in a different way by Harry (pseudonym), who was imprisoned for the second time because of an incestuous relationship with his daughter. He and his family seemed without guilt or shame. When I walked into the room for a therapy session with his family, he was cheerfully seated with this teenage daughter contentedly sitting on his lap. His wife, unperturbed, was in the room along with her attractive oldest son, home on a visit from military service. He was the product of an incestuous relationship between the wife and her own father. The message from them was clear: We're just one big, happy, incestuous family. We don't need therapy. Observing their utter lack of shame, I had no illusions that I was getting anywhere with this patient or his family.

Robert (pseudonym), also incarcerated a second time because of an incestuous relationship with his daughter, was different from the happy-go-lucky Harry. He was a rigidly moralistic member of the Seventh-day Adventist Church who, though he hadn't been able to resist incest, scrupulously observed a difficult diet in order to conform to his religious beliefs.

It comes as a shock to many people that individuals with apparently strong religious beliefs engage in behavior far outside the norm, but outward righteousness often serves as an effective cover for immoral behavior. Unscrupulous individuals manipulate their public image to form a screen so that in private they can do as they please without eliciting suspicion. The perpetrators of many types of sexual abuse (and other crimes) escape punishment because of their status and skillful manipulation of public opinion. This was illustrated in the scandal of Catholic priests' sexual abuse of children. It has also been a dynamic in the #MeToo exposés, as well as the epidemic of sexual abuse of psychiatric patients that occurred in Madison (discussed later).

My experiences at Central State Hospital fundamentally altered my world view. I was stunned to recognize and understand that some people's minds and personalities are much different from mine or that of most other people. Psychopaths can lie with more credibility than many people can tell the truth. For this reason, to evaluate people like this, a factual history is absolutely essential. Psychopathic personalities are regularly portrayed in the movies or on television, but it's hard to grasp that such people really exist, let alone recognize them in real life. They can be unusually likeable and charming. However, they are liars and unreliable, and the worst of them can hurt and kill without regret.

While I was consulting at Central State Hospital, I continued to be deeply involved at the Women's Research Institute. Professor K.U. Smith advocated a systems approach to social problems. He thought that all viewpoints needed to be heard in order to work out social problems successfully: Feedback was crucial to make a social system work. Accordingly, in 1974, when we decided to hold a conference on the topic of rape funded by the Wisconsin Humanities Institute, Corinne insisted that the rapists be represented. I was horrified. We were going to invite a convicted rapist to speak on our panel? It took some argument, but Corinne convinced me, and it worked out well.

Next, Corinne proposed that we sponsor an interchange of audiotaped conversations between rapists from my therapy group at Central State Hospital and rape victims, though not between the victim and her particular rapist. This was a bold and exciting idea, and we arranged it in cooperation with the Madison Rape Crisis Center. It was a fascinating experience. The men were far more engaged than in a typical group therapy session. One young man made this revealing comment about the rape he committed: "I didn't do it for sex. I could get sex from plenty of women. I wanted to humiliate her. I wanted her to feel like a snake was crawling all over her body." The last part he said slowly, drawing it out, hate oozing from his voice. Later, he was paroled, and he viciously attacked again.

His statement emphasizes what I and others learned: Rape is primarily about the need to dominate and humiliate, not sexual gratification. Those who blame the victim for inviting the attack are missing the point. However, attitudes toward rape remain retrograde. In 2012, prominent Republican Rick Santorum, who opposes abortion, wouldn't even make an exception in the case of rape. Later the same year, Missouri Republican, Todd Akin, made this profoundly ignorant statement, "If it's a legitimate rape, the female body has ways to shut that whole thing down."

Central State Hospital was a depressing place, and the head of the hospital, Dr. Sherbert (pseudonym), must have been bored because he began to amuse himself at my expense. Among the patients was the infamous Ed Gein, inspiration for the movie *Psycho*. One day when I was in my office, a workman appeared and began to erect a partition to the office, working behind me. I was accustomed to myriad distractions and paid no attention. Later, I got up and went out into the hall to get a drink of water. There I encountered Dr. Sherbert. "Did you meet Mr. Gein?" he asked.

With horror, I turned around; there was Mr. Gein; I'd never seen him before. He was a slight old man, standing there with his tools—saw and hammer. I nearly fainted. The good doctor cackled, "Hah, hah, hah. I guess he was taking your measure," referring to the fact that Gein made a lamp shade from the skin of one of his victims. Gein had murdered two women. He got away with the first murder, but not the second. When Gein was arrested, the body of his latest victim was found beheaded, strung up and gutted like a deer. Around the property were numerous items that Gein had made from the tanned skins of the bodies of women robbed from their graves.

I was appalled by Dr. Sherbert's behavior, but the other hospital staff, who were great to work with, assured me that I'd been in no danger—that Gein had been harmless for years. I resolved to take it as a macabre joke, but a second incident made me decide to discontinue my employment at Central State Hospital.

One day Sam was in a violent rage when he entered my office for a therapy session. He said Dr. Sherbert told him that I was responsible for the rejection of his petition for parole. This wasn't true; I hadn't even been consulted. Sam glowered at me. This was a maximum-security facility, and there were security guards, but not outside the door. Before any guards could arrive, I could be dead or seriously injured. I was on my own and curiously calm.

"I had nothing to do with your rejection for parole," I said.

"Yes, you did. Dr. Sherbert told me you did."

"No, really. I had nothing to do with it."

"Well, either you're lying, or Dr. Sherbert is lying."

I knew this patient well and gambled on his good sense. "You know Dr. Sherbert and you know me. Which do you believe?"

He looked at me awhile and finally said, "I believe you," and his rage subsided.

Although the job at Central State Hospital was interesting and paid well, after the incident with Sam, I got out as soon as I could wrap things up. This time I didn't discuss the incident with anyone else on the staff. I knew in my bones that Dr. Sherbert and the others would say either that Sam was lying or that Dr. Sherbert had been misunderstood. The latter is possible, but I knew Sam well enough to be dead certain that he wasn't lying. My life had twice been on the line, and I couldn't afford to take a chance on Dr. Sherbert's "fine" character.

What had I learned about why men rape? Some experts on sexual assault think that perpetrators have been sexually abused as children. I don't know if this is usually the case, but it was true of Sam. Finally, after years of incarceration and months of therapy, Sam told me a crucial fact: After his parents separated when he was eleven, his mother had him sleep in the same bed with her. The memory still made him furious. In a rage, he announced emphatically, "I told her I wasn't going to sleep with her anymore!" The combination of sexual arousal, guilt, and sexual frustration must have been excruciating. But did therapy successfully cure him of rape? Sam eventually was paroled, but

I don't know what happened to him or whether he committed further offenses.

I still wonder where all the hostility toward women comes from. These men at Central State Hospital represented the extreme of violent rape, but what about the much more common gratuitous hostile, even sadistic, mean behavior that women encounter? One interesting dynamic is feelings of entitlement to a woman's sexual favors and self-righteous anger when denied.

Cervantes uncloaked this sexism four centuries ago in *Don Quixote* (1615/2003). He told the story of Marcella, a young, beautiful woman who, in order to avoid suitors, had hidden away tending sheep in the remote mountains of Spain. How dare she? Her persistent suitors found her; she turned them all down, and one of them, Grisóstoma, died, it is said, of a broken heart. His death was blamed on Marcella who was decried as cruel and heartless. She confronted these clueless, rejected suitors pointing out that had the situation been reversed, no one would have criticized a man for not responding to a love-smitten woman. She said that Grisótoma's death was caused not by her cruelty, but his obstinacy. She ended her defense saying, "I am free and do not care to submit to another."

I was gratified to find comments about Marcella's story on the Internet in the context of the "nice" male friend who therefore feels entitled to sex. Guys: Friendship doesn't mean you're entitled to sex. Male sense of entitlement to sexual gratification is common. Hence, a woman who arouses sexual desire in a man may be subject to his anger if she refuses him, or even if he, himself, is not in a position to gratify his wishes. Nonetheless, he may see her at fault for his thwarted desires. This certainly complicates life for women negotiating potential #MeToo situations.

Sometimes men with power think they can get away with sexually exploiting women so why not? They may even brag about their ability to gratify their sexual desires at will, and amuse each other with accounts of their exploits, like telling stories about the big fish they caught. There is a "boy's club" culture that condones and even celebrates the sexual exploitation of women.

Does this relate to Dr. Sherbert's behavior? Was he part of a lascivious male group? His manipulation of psychiatric patients to place me in danger was later repeated in the actions of Dr. Mauston when I was a witness for the state in their prosecution of him for sexual misconduct with a patient. In Madison, Wisconsin, in the 1980s there was a hot bed of sexual misconduct with patients, and, according to investigators, it involved cooperation in defense, discussion of possible victims, and camaraderie among the perpetrators. One of these perpetrators was a good friend of Dr. Sherbert. Dr. Yallow (pseudonym) was the chief forensic psychiatrist for the state of Wisconsin and frequently consulted at Central State Hospital for many years. This man was later convicted of multiple instances of sexual misconduct with psychiatric patients. He tried to blackmail a witness and cooperated with other perpetrators by harassing the witnesses against them, including myself, with robo-phone calls in the middle of the night.

My experience at Central State Hospital prompted me to write an article "The Coatlicue Complex: A Source of Irrational Reactions against Women," which analyzes this problem at a deeper level (Sherman, 1975). The ideas were also presented at a symposium entitled "Power and the Sexes," chaired by Agnes N. O'Connell, PhD, at an American Psychological Association Convention in 1976. The use of the term "complex" was something of a tongue-in-cheek poke at Freud's theory of the Oedipus complex. Although the article is speculative, we need some new ideas if men are going to gain a better understanding of themselves.

Coatlicue refers to the Aztec Goddess of earth and death, the mother of the Gods. She is depicted wearing a necklace of human skulls and a skirt of writhing serpents. She symbolizes the power of life and death that every mother holds over her infant and represents a profound fear of women, a source of irrational motivation to suppress and control women. Unfortunately, this may not simply be a problem for individual men, but rather an attitude that has become institutionalized among men in general. If men are to relate to women in more mature ways, they will need to confront a host of irrational attitudes.

Meanwhile, my work with the Women's Research Institute continued, but we were isolated from the main action in the Women's Movement on the East coast, and I wanted to reach out. I'd done pioneering work in my own field, but I wondered what other disciplines would look like when viewed through what I called the prism of sex. This became the title for a conference funded by the Rockefeller Foundation. The question was: How had male intellectual dominance affected various fields of study? Corinne suggested that we bring in Dr. Evelyn Torton Beck from comparative literature to work with us. (Evelyn later became a professor at the University of Maryland and an outstanding advocate for Jewish and lesbian women.) Together Evelyn and I wrote the grant proposal, invited the guests, and ran the conference.

The papers were excellent. The contribution of fellow psychologist, Dr. Carolyn Wood Sherif, won a prize from the Association for Women in Psychology. Also notable was the paper on abortion by Kathryn Pyne Parsons (later Addelson). These were the days before abortion was legal, and her pioneering paper dealt with moral questions of abortion. We decided to publish the papers as a book, *Prism of Sex: Essays in the Sociology of Knowledge* (1980). Evelyn and I wrote the Introduction, but Evelyn's apartment building burned down, and she wasn't able to help with the final editing and development of the manuscript, which fell completely on my shoulders. The book was well received, even translated into Japanese. Looking at the book now—how things have changed. Ironically, the increase of women in mental health services has been such that men now complain that it's hard to find a male therapist. Today, women are well represented in nearly all areas of academia, except in the STEM disciplines (science, technology, engineering, and mathematics).

In 1975, the Women's Research Institute held a conference on "New Directions for Research on Women" sponsored by the American Psychological Association and funded by the National Institute of Mental Health and the Ford Foundation. Together with Dr. Florence Denmark, later President of the American Psychological Association, we developed a great lineup of contributors and excellent papers that were later published as a book (Sherman & Denmark, 1978).

Starting in 1976, I also devoted considerable time working with Editor Georgia Babladelis as Associate Editor for the new APA journal, *Psychology of Women Quarterly*. (Later, I served as its Book Review Editor for many years.) As an editor, I encouraged young psychologists to submit papers on important topics, for example, the effects of child care, which finally bore fruit (Etaugh & Bridges, 2013). Another important question was whether abortions have a negative effect on mental health. The answer is "No," but this controversial question took a long time to resolve (Biggs et al., 2017; Steinberg et al., 2018).

During the 1970s, I also began research on women and mathematics. From a conversation with Dr. Eleanor Maccoby, I learned that Dr. Elizabeth Fennema, an Assistant Professor in the University of Wisconsin mathematics education department, was interested in sex-related differences in mathematics performance. We teamed up, and it was a good partnership. Liz was a strong, practical person who had a position that made the research possible. On the other hand, I had expertise in statistics and research design, and the intellectual energy to devise and write a research plan that was successfully funded. Amazingly, Liz never had a single course in statistics.

At the time, it was widely believed that women are constitutionally impaired in their ability to master mathematics. Like physical strength, weakness in mathematics was commonly considered a female handicap. As a consequence, women were discriminated against in science and engineering, and even in medicine and law, where the role of mathematical expertise is problematic. What was the truth? I was curious to see what could be learned, relishing the challenge and opportunity.

As I started to investigate the question of women and mathematics, I sought to identify all the variables that might affect women's performance, as compared to men. An obvious variable is the extent of prior education in mathematics. Shockingly, the research literature was such a mess that many of the published studies that purported to show male mathematics superiority hadn't even controlled for previous mathematics education.

A second obvious factor is general intelligence. There is no evidence that males are generally more intelligent than females, but there are many varied aspects of intelligence, and a person with so-so verbal skills may be an excellent mechanic, and that person is more likely to be male than female. On the other hand, women often perform better than men on a variety of verbal tasks.

If there were an intellectual attribute that interfered with women's mathematics performance, I was able to narrow the candidates to one factor: spatial visualization, the ability to imagine spatial relationships changing in three-dimensional space. The most common way this sex-related difference manifests itself is in direction finding. Getting lost is a stereotypic female attribute, and women often use a different direction-finding strategy than men. They tend to memorize turns at notable landmarks rather than navigating by north, south, east, and west on the basis of a mental map. However, the sex-related difference in spatial visualization is a relative matter; some women are better than many men.

When I talked about this with my colleague, Corinne, I brought up a Wechsler intelligence test question about how to find your direction if you're lost. Corinne's answer gave me a good laugh: "Look for a man—that's how a Greek woman would answer."

In addition to intellectual factors, I also wanted to measure the effect of attitudes. I knew a lot about test construction from my training at Iowa, and I also benefited from conversations I'd had with Starke Hathaway about the construction of the Minnesota Multiphasic Personality Inventory (MMPI). Starke explained to me that, despite the vaunted empiricism of the MMPI, the initial generation of the items was intuitive. The items were subsequently winnowed by empirical test. This was the procedure I followed, easily generating the initial items for the Fennema-Sherman Mathematics Attitude Scales. The items were then tested for reliability and validity before being included in the final form.

I thought about what variables should be included and felt certain that level of anxiety was important. While I was a student in Iowa City, I became familiar with the Taylor Manifest Anxiety Scale, devised by Dr. Janet Taylor Spence, later president of the American Psychological Association. There was evidence that women are more anxious than men, and that anxiety has a negative effect on complex kinds of intellectual performance (Taylor, 1953). Could it be that women's performance in mathematics was adversely affected by their level of anxiety?

Math anxiety was not a major personal problem for me. As a college student, I had a friend, Nancy Langsdale Shera, who was majoring in chemistry and was terrific in mathematics. I expressed concern to her about whether I could master college-level courses in mathematics. "Math is like any other subject," she said. "Study it, and you can do it." She was absolutely right. However, the course work is sequential; you have to do your homework, and you can't bullshit your way.

The math anxiety scale turned out to be the one that generated the most interest. As expected, the study showed that high school girls experienced more math anxiety than boys, and that high anxiety adversely affected mathematics performance. An attack on the problem of math anxiety was popularized in the Women's Movement by the razor-sharp Sheila Tobias in her book, *Overcoming Math Anxiety* (1978).

Other scales measured the attitudes of significant others (mother, father, teacher) toward the individual as a learner of mathematics. We thought that if you received positive attitudes and encouragement from significant others, you were more likely to do well in mathematics, and our results confirmed these expectations.

In my case, my father was a key positive influence. One day when I was in the eighth grade, I came home from school upset because I couldn't understand the word problems that Miss Lemler introduced that day. My father patiently showed me how to approach these problems and figure them out. Too bad my high school math teacher wasn't equally enlightened. When women are given the idea that they can't learn math, it's hard to try. Women can find encouragement in Lynne Osen's book, *Women in Mathematics* (1974). Her historical account describes the lives and contributions of women geniuses in mathematics from the Greek Hypatia of Alexandria into the early 20th century. The belief in the possibility of mastery is the beginning of success.

Liz and I also measured boys' and girls' perceptions of mathematics as appropriate only to the male sex-role. We wondered whether girls shied away from mathematics or underperformed because they thought it was a masculine subject, unsuitable for females. In our samples, students increasingly perceived mathematics as a male subject the farther they advanced in their education. For girls, perceiving mathematics as sexually neutral correlated modestly with good mathematics performance.

The first article with Fennema (1977), "Sex-Related Differences in Mathematics Achievement, Spatial Visualization, and Affective Factors," was well received. Many years later University of Wisconsin professor, Dr. Tom Carpenter, surprised me with a phone call: The National Council of Teachers of Mathematics had chosen the article as one of the most important published during the last century; it was to appear in a volume entitled *Classics in Mathematics Education Research* (Carpenter, Dossey & Koehler, 2004). I was hugely pleased.

The supposed female mathematics incapacity has largely been put to rest thanks in part to a research effort I helped put in motion (Fennema & Sherman, 1977; Hyde & Mertz, 2009), but questions persist as to why more "geniuses" in mathematics are male (Breda et al., 2018). However, great progress has been made. Entrance exams to medical and law schools had contained questions involving advanced mathematics that weren't even relevant to the practice of medicine or law, but the questions had effectively screened out women. Armed with scientific data and the efforts of people like Sandra Tangri, PhD, a social psychologist with the Commission on Civil Rights, entry tests for medical and law schools were made fairer. (Sandra and I served together on the American Psychological Association Committee on Women.)

Today there is a healthy representation of women in both law and medicine, but participation in STEM disciplines still severely lags. There are many women competent to succeed in these fields, but a major problem is that they don't feel they belong. This is not surprising. Human relationships are the bedrock of well-being. Researchers have found that a lack of belongingness is a factor in whether or not women persist in the course work leading to STEM careers (Lewis et al., 2017). It is uncomfortable to be in a situation in which you are the only woman, especially if the males seem to be a buddy-buddy group. It's awkward, and even well-intentioned men may fall prey to their unexamined sexism.

In *Why Aren't More Women in Science?* (Ceci & Williams, 2007), the authors' discussion of "subtle beliefs about who should participate in science," in other words, bias, reminded me of a funny incident that occurred when I was asked to give a talk for Psi Chi at the Eastern Psychological Association convention (Sherman,1976). (Psi Chi is the honorary psychology society I was elected to at Case Western Reserve University.) Dr. Jerome Kagan, prominent male psychologist, was chosen to introduce me. During the introduction, he allowed as how I had "luckily" come across the important topic of the talk. Groans were heard from the largely female audience, but the poor man hadn't a clue about what he'd said. I talked to him privately afterward, but he still didn't get it. I finally laughingly told him, "Ask your wife. She'll explain it to you."

During this time, one of my most memorable experiences as an activist psychologist occurred when I served on the APA Task Force on Sex Bias and Sex-Role Stereotyping in Psychotherapeutic Practice (Brodsky et al., 1975). I had been asked to write the literature review, and Dr. Carolyn Payton, a member of the task force, went over it with me. She was a pioneer in the civil rights movement, a psychology professor at Howard University, and a smart, tough, Black woman. She offered the sweetest, most insightful, gentle criticism of a draft of my literature review. She carefully pointed out the flaws in my writing style: timid, tentative, and full of qualifiers. "Oh! Oh!" I thought. I learned more about myself in that five minutes than in a year of psychotherapy. It forever changed my writing style. (Tentative, hesitant writing and speaking is still a common problem for women.)

I continued to work on the question of sex-related cognitive differences and published an entire book on the topic (Sherman, 1978). Dr. Paula Caplan used it in her course on the psychology of women and wrote me a glowing fan letter, which was gratifying.

Meanwhile, other psychologists struck out in new directions. In 1979, Lenore Walker published *The Battered Woman Syndrome*. This ground-breaking, eye-opening book was read worldwide and has saved many lives. Walker pointed out how easily women can be led to accept the excuses of male perpetrators. "Oh, I didn't mean to do that." "I'm so sorry; I'll never do that again." Unfortunately, data showed that, however well-intentioned the man, he often failed to control himself so that a cycle of violence developed, even increasing in severity, leading to a fully beaten-down woman, the battered woman syndrome.

Unfortunately, I was unable to continue my work on the psychology of women. The way the Women's Studies program at the University of Wisconsin was set up, you had to first be a member of a regular department in order to be part of the program, and I couldn't get a position. However, in 1986, the UW Psychology Department did hire Dr. Janet Hyde, who had provided a successor for *On the Psychology of Women* by coauthoring a popular text (Hyde & Rosenberg, 1976). She also made a name for herself in the area of women and mathematics. I never found my way to a suitable position.

We were able to keep the Women's Research Institute going for only a few years. I had hoped that we could establish a link to the Women Studies program, but that was not to be. The institute was largely dependent on my ability to write fundable grant proposals, and I was reluctant to assume this responsibility in what became a highly negative political environment during the Reagan presidency.

In 1981, shortly after Ronald Reagan's election, I was in Washington, D.C., as a member of the National Institute of Mental Health Small Grants Review Committee. We were to decide which research projects were to be funded. The session had barely started when it was interrupted by an individual who came in and conferred briefly with the director. It was then announced that a decision had been made not to fund any proposals that had to do with sex or race. We were told to sort through the proposals before us and put aside any such proposals, which weren't to be considered regardless of merit. Thus began the insidious influence of the political right on the impartial conduct of scientific affairs in the United States. I was shocked by this blatant ideological move. How quick, how bold, how shameless it came.

The Women's Research Institute became increasingly isolated as the local Women's Studies program gained ascendancy. Our descent into obscurity was ensured when my final research proposal to the National Science Foundation was rejected in a particularly demoralizing way. A woman researcher that I greatly respected launched an *ad hominem* attack against me, to the effect that I was a wild-eyed feminist whose research couldn't be trusted. NSF had a policy of sending to the applicants the reviewer's comments, so I saw what she said. Her behavior made me sick. I was keenly disappointed, but I could see the handwriting on the wall: I had to abandon research on the psychology of women.

These were wonderful years of creative work and achievement. Although I wasn't successful in pursuing a full-time research career, I met a lot of wonderful women and had the opportunity to contribute to society in important ways.

Chapter 7

Female Orgasm: Fifty Years Later

Critical readers asked, "What is a scientific review of the literature on female orgasm doing in the middle of a memoir?" Sexual ignorance was a wrenching problem for me, and it's still common.

Knowledge is power. In order to make informed choices, women need to know what to expect from intercourse. Women's sexuality and women's bodies are personal, yet they are subject to political control. Is information about women's sexuality also subject to cultural suppression? Is information freely shared and openly discussed? I think not. As a young woman, I wasn't sure what an orgasm was, and it was difficult to get clear information. To the question, "What is an orgasm?" the response was, "You'll know it when you have one." What do young women today know about orgasmic response? For example, do they realize that brief sexual hook-ups are unlikely to result in intense sexual pleasure? When these experiences don't, do they understand why?

In any case, the female orgasm deserves a place in my memoir. The discovery of intense sexual pleasure was a major event in my life. I'd started out with great expectations only to be repeatedly disappointed. Then, when I was in my early thirties, and well into my second marriage, intercourse began to result in an entirely new, different experience: an intense whole body feeling of sexual ecstasy. Was this the experience men were having? Was this the vaginal orgasm? It had come solely from vaginal intercourse.

The female orgasm became a "fixation" during the 1950s as Freudian theory took hold. Men would anxiously ask, "Did you come?" Women began to fake orgasms, hilariously demonstrated by Meg Ryan in the 1989 movie, *When Harry Met Sally*. This concern emanated from Freud's *Three Essays on the Theory of Sexuality* (1905/1975) in which he distinguished various stages of development, the phallic-oedipal stage from ages three to six and the mature genital stage from puberty onward. As part of the theory, Freud declared that clitoral stimulation, and the orgasms derived from it, represent an infantile stage while mature orgasms, resulting from vaginal stimulation, are deeper and felt throughout the body. Thus, a woman requiring clitoral stimulation to reach orgasm was thought to be stuck in an infantile stage. A goal of psychoanalysis was to help her overcome her neurosis and learn to transfer clitoral pleasure to full vaginal enjoyment. "Frigid" became a term of derision.

People were preoccupied with the female orgasm. Why weren't more women having orgasms from vaginal intercourse? What was the problem? Was it where the clitoris was located? In some women, was it too far away from penile action so that it missed out? The question was researched. Measurements were taken with maybe yes, maybe no results. Meanwhile, Marie Bonaparte, a Freudian psychoanalyst, was so sorely vexed to be anorgasmic that she had surgery five different times to move her clitoris closer to her vagina. It didn't work (Wallen & Lloyd, 2011). However, Bonaparte had a point. Recent research has shown that the clitoris-vagina distance ranges from 1.6 cm to 4.5 cm (Lloyd et al., 2005), and a closer location does facilitate orgasm during intercourse (Vaccaro, 2015).

For more than fifty years, the vaginal/clitoral orgasm controversy bubbled. Kinsey et al. (1953) claimed (incorrectly) that the vagina lacked the necessary nerve endings to create an orgasm. Feminist Anne Koedt (1970) maintained that the vaginal orgasm was a sexist myth. However, it is now clear, that "vaginal" orgasms do occur, that is orgasms resulting from penile intercourse alone. Since 1971, book-length treatments of the scientific literature on the female orgasm have appeared (Fisher, 1973; Komisaruk et al., 2006; Mah & Binik, 2001), but assessment of the research literature has been hampered by the absence of agreed upon definitions of female orgasm, though progress has been made (Kontula & Miettinen, 2016; Mah & Binik, 2010).

Dr. Osmo Kontula and female co-author Anneli Miettinen (2016) defined the female orgasm as "sexual pleasure ending in relaxation and a very good feeling" (VGF). However, the VGF orgasm doesn't cover more intense experiences.

Here is a montage of some more dramatic descriptions of orgasm from a *Cosmopolitan* magazine posting entitled *21 Women Describe What Orgasm Feels Like to Them* (Ruderman, 2018): "It feels like I have an electrical current running directly through my vagina. It's just this crazy moment where every single cell is screaming 'yes.'" "I would describe it as like a giant explosion that starts deep inside me, almost like ... radiating from my belly button through my clitoris." "I have so much pleasure going on inside of me, the only thing I can do is feel my body react, whether I start shaking, or feel a wave of hot and then calm wash over me. It's almost confusing—something feels so good it almost hurts, so you want more, and you want it to stop at the same time and then you cross a line into an orgasm, and then when it's a big one, it just totally consumes you." "It's like melting and exploding at the same time. You don't have any control, and it's maybe the only time in your life when you're not worried about anything but that very moment." These experiences are more than a very good feeling and can be called a full body ecstasy (FBE) orgasm.

A still deeper dimension of this FBE experience is provided by Safron (2016). He discussed the role of continued, uninterrupted rhythmic stimulation of the vagina in producing synergistic, synchronized widespread brain activity, which he likened to a trance state. He pointed out that this can result in a peak experience of pair oneness that transcends self and promotes strong pair bonding. This would increase investment in the union, therefore, enhancing the likely survival of the pair's progeny and genes.

This maximal FBE experience is conveyed in a poem entitled "You and I" written by a Chinese woman poet named Guan Daosheng in the 13th century quoted in *When Red is Black* (Qui, 2004).

> You and I are so crazy
> about each other,
> as hot as a potter's fire.
> Out of the same chunk
> of clay, the shape of you,
> the shape of me. Crush us
> both into clay again, mix
> it with water, reshape
> you, reshape me.
> So I have you in my body,
> and you'll have me forever in yours too.

Oneness, equality, and mutuality are strongly expressed in this poem. Given such dramatic descriptions, it's not surprising that women can distinguish between orgasms. Sexually active undergraduate women described a clitoral orgasm as localized, intense and satisfying, but a vaginal orgasm was stronger, longer lasting, deeper, a whole-body experience with throbbing feelings, and more psychologically satisfying (Butler, 1976; Clifford, 1978; Pfaus et al., 2016).

Researchers King, Belsky, Mah, and Binik (2010) asked, "Are there different types of female orgasm?" The answer was essentially, "Yes." Using the Orgasm Rating Scale, they reported on 276 women rating orgasm experience with a partner and 227 women rating orgasm by solitary masturbation. The Orgasm Rating Scale (Mah & Binik, 2010) covers ten dimensions of female orgasm including both VGF and FBE experiences: pleasurable, relaxing, loving, building/swelling, flooding, flushing, spurting, pulsating, quivering, ecstasy. The results indicated that orgasms with a partner were generally better than solitary masturbation, but about ten percent of the women rated their partner-orgasmic experience as less satisfying than masturbating alone. Nearly ninety percent of the women were pleasurably satisfied with their partner sex experience, but only a minority appeared to have experienced FBE orgasms. This was also the case for orgasms from solitary masturbation.

The experiential differences between orgasms of clitoral versus vaginal stimulation can be explained by the fact that researchers Barry Komisaruk, Carlos Beyer-Flores, and Beverly Whipple (2006) have shown that the clitoris and vagina have different pathways to the brain.

Masters and Johnson (1966) and Shere Hite (1976/2003) found that about twenty-six percent of women experienced orgasms from vaginal stimulation, while about seventy percent experienced orgasms exclusively from clitoral stimulation. A look at recent research shows similar results. Debby Herbenick (2018) surveyed a thousand women ages 18-94. Only 18 % had orgasms with penile penetration alone; for 37%, clitoral stimulation was helpful; 36 % required clitoral stimulation for an orgasm, while 9 % didn't have an orgasm no matter what.

Kontula and Miettinen (2016) conducted systematic research on the female orgasm in Finland where equality of sexual enjoyment has been seen as a women's rights issue. Five national sex surveys using random samples of over 8,000 women ages 18-80 have been conducted. Based on their VGF definition of orgasm ("sexual pleasure ending in relaxation and a very good feeling"), more than ninety percent of men usually experienced orgasm during intercourse compared to 46-56% of women. They reported several results that surprised them: It had been thought that women could improve their orgasmic response during intercourse by masturbation practice, but this didn't increase the frequency of orgasms. Also, experimentation with different partners did not increase the frequency of orgasms. Furthermore, advancement in the equality of women wasn't accompanied by an increase in sexual enjoyment. Over the sixteen years from 1999 to 2015, women's orgasmic capacity declined from 56 % of women experiencing orgasm in intercourse always or nearly always to 46% in 2015. Only 6% reported always having an orgasm, and, remember, this is defined as a "very good feeling."

Three points seem clear from this research: First, Freud was wrong; lack of orgasm from penile stimulation alone is far too common to be abnormal; it does not indicate neurosis or immaturity. However, the medicalization of women's sexual responsiveness continues to be a concern (Kaschak & Tiefer, 2001). Second, there *are* two kinds of female orgasm: the very good feeling orgasm (VGF) and the full body ecstasy orgasm (FBE). VGF and FBE seem better descriptors than clitoral versus vaginal orgasm since orgasms can also occur from stimulation of the nipples, the cervix, the ear lobe, the anus, or merely by thinking (Komisaruk et al., 2006; Pfaus et al., 2016). However, it's not clear whether these reported orgasms are VGF or FBE orgasms, or both. Third, many women aren't having pleasurable experiences during heterosexual intercourse. Numbers ranged from 90% satisfied among Canadian women (King et al., 2010) to only 50% usually satisfied among Finnish women (Kontula & Miettinen, 2016). According to Herbenick (2018), most American women reported pleasurable sex, but 9% reported none, a small percentage but a sizable number of women. Most studies of female orgasmic response have been among heterosexuals, but *Our Bodies Ourselves* (2011) provides a broader lesbian, bisexual, gay, transgender, queer (LBGTQ) perspective.

Another controversy during the last fifty years has to do with the so-called G-Spot. The G-Spot got its name from a German gynecologist, Ernst Gräfenberg, who first identified it as a particularly sensitive part of the vagina located on the anterior (front) wall of the vagina (Gräfenberg, 1950). Research has confirmed that there is such an area, but it's not a spot that can be pushed like a button. The G region is a better name. It's an area that not only has vaginal erotogenic tissues but also anatomical and neurologic clitoral excitatory characteristics (e.g. the clitoral bulbs). Actually, Gräfenberg's interest was in the fact that when this area is stimulated, some women ejaculate a liquid, which consists of secretions of periurethral glands (Skene's glands) and urine (Salama et al., 2015). This squirting, which may occur during orgasm, can wet the bed sheets. This has embarrassed some women, but it's not an incontinence problem.

What about the woman who wants to have FBE orgasms, but isn't having them? There is a genetic component to the female orgasm, so she may get some idea of her orgasmic potential by consulting her mother and sisters (Dawood et al., 2005; Dunn et al., 2005). As a practical matter, if she's not having orgasms, she may prefer to have intercourse only at night. In this way, if she doesn't have an orgasm, the aroused and engorged sexual areas can subside overnight. Otherwise, the engorgement may be a source of discomfort.

But what do we know about how to facilitate FBE orgasms? We know two gambits that are unlikely to work: masturbation practice and experimentation with different partners (Kontula & Miettinen, 2016). Regarding experimentation, Kuperberg and Padgett (2016) reported that 75% of college students engaged in a casual sexual encounter with a stranger or acquaintance at least once. However, it doesn't seem to be making them happy. Wade (2017) reported that half of freshmen were concerned about their mental health and 10% were depressed. The hook-up culture stresses the ideal of an emotionless sexual union, the exact opposite of the type of relationship that promotes orgasm (Kontula & Miettinen, 2016).

What will work? The intense pleasure of the FBE orgasm is most likely to occur in the context of a stable trusting relationship with a male capable of providing an adequate amount of rhythmic, uninterrupted penile thrusting. Moreover, the woman must give herself to the experience, not thinking about other things, but giving the sensations her mindful attention (Adam et al., 2015). Even then, it may take women some time for trust to develop. According to Kontula and Miettinen (2016), the key to more frequent orgasms is "being in the mind and in the relationship." However, let us not ignore the obvious; the most common factors preventing orgasm are fatigue and stress (Kontula & Miettinen, 2016). Moreover, medications can inhibit sexual response, notably antidepressant medications, for example, selective serotonin reuptake inhibitors (SSRIs), including Prozac, Luvox, Zoloft, Celexa, Lexapro, and Paxil (Pfaus et al., 2016).

Women are still faking orgasms, 67% in one sample (Muehlengard & Shippee, 2010). Ironically, when a woman doesn't have an orgasm, it's often the man who's upset. He sees this as a negative reflection on his abilities as a lover. The reasons women fake orgasms range widely. Some fake orgasms in order to preserve their partner's feelings and the relationship. However, others fake orgasm for the practical reason that they want intercourse to stop (Salisbury & Fisher, 2014).

An FBE orgasm is a partnership experience, and the male is obviously a vital factor. For example, in terms of duration of intercourse, less than a minute wasn't enough for an orgasm, but what is the usual duration for intercourse? Among 500 couples, the median (mid-point) of intercourse duration time was 5.4 minutes (Waldinger et al., 2005).

We don't have much scientific data on women's sexual experience in longitudinal perspective, but we can review my experience. I had discovered the pleasure of clitoral stimulation at least by the age of ten. Accurate information about sexuality hadn't been easy to get. In high school biology class, we'd been taught that babies result from the union of a sperm and egg, but the teacher left out all the enthusiasm and details of how they got together. The big thing I didn't know was that a penis grows and gets hard with sexual excitement, and then its size goes down as excitement dies or with orgasm. As a little girl, I'd seen a whole circle of erect penises with my own eyes, but the significance was dissociated and repressed. I also had no clue how motivated boys and men were to have sex. Although I had gotten the impression that intercourse would be an ecstatic experience, it wasn't. I couldn't figure it out. After several VGF experiences with different partners, I decided that this was simply the way things are, and I didn't worry about it. I wanted to get married; I didn't want to go through life alone; I wanted children so eventually I married. The first marriage was a mistake, but well into my second marriage, I began having FBE orgasms. Why? The proper conditions finally arrived. I had a stable continuing relationship with a competent partner, and for some reason I adopted a "relax and enjoy it" attitude. My first sexual experience was at seventeen and now in my thirties, I began experiencing regular FBE orgasms.

Why did it take so long? Earlier we explored the concept of repression. Was my delayed responsiveness related to early sexual abuse? Probably. But in the end I think it was mainly a matter of finally having the right conditions.

Kontula and Miettinen (2016) asked why women are so altruistic as to provide sex when they receive no intense pleasure from the experience. However, some women do not altruistically provide sex; they charge. Other women are essentially coerced into sex. Still others are willing to provide sex in order to obtain marriage, children, status, financial support, or a significant-other relationship. Relationships are of central importance to human well-being, and beginning in early adolescence, women often risk venereal disease and pregnancy in hopes of developing a sustaining relationship with a male. Many women deeply love their male partners and enjoy giving them pleasure. So long as the sexual experience isn't disagreeable or painful, many women *are* altruistic and simply accept the level of sexual pleasure they receive as a fact of life.

Like Kontula and Miettinen (2016), I was surprised by the difference between the sexes in sexual pleasure. Is this a fact of nature? Or, has sexual trauma contributed to this result? Nearly

26% of college women reported that they were victims of attempted sexual assault or rape (Koss et al., 1987), and about a third of all women reported being victims of domestic violence at some time during their lives (Huss, 2009). These traumatic events would hardly be conducive to the relaxed, trusting frame of mind linked to FBE orgasms.

Women today are better informed about male sex drive, the mechanics of intercourse, contraception, abortion, and LBGTQ issues; however, making wise decisions about sexual participation remains a challenge. The facts suggest that the sexes have a long way to go in the development of harmonious relationships of equity.

Chapter 8

On the Front Line

The next years of my life were a mess. I finally got a good job as a clinical psychologist with Madison Associates (pseudonym) only to discover that it harbored two psychiatrists (Jenkins and Mauston, pseudonyms) who were having sex with their patients. I escaped to another private practice group, and eventually became a witness for the state of Wisconsin in their case against Mauston. When he was exonerated, I was run out of the practice. This chapter is a condensed version of events, centering on the issue of sexual misconduct with psychiatric patients. A recent study found that in California nearly thirteen percent of psychiatrists were formally disciplined for sexual misconduct (Morrison & Morrison, 2001). Although the problem is serious, the Citizens Commission on Human Rights International reports that only twenty-seven states currently define therapist sexual misconduct with a patient as a criminal offense.

In the 1980s, the women's movement proceeded apace, and I was well known in Madison because of newspaper articles, radio, and TV appearances about my work on the psychology of women. The publicity helped me get the job at Madison Associates. Dr. Bill Jackson, head of psychology, was a Cracker Jack clinician, and psychiatrists Harold Lubing, Max Smith, Ben Tybring, and Bob Linden were dedicated, compassionate clinicians. I was happy with my new job. I liked my colleagues and I enjoyed the work—back to the challenges of diagnostic consulting with physicians and psychiatrists in hospitals all over Madison—back to fascinating encounters with people's individual problems and the challenge of helping them gain mastery.

Unfortunately, after a few years Bill Jackson died, and other key partners were looking toward retirement. The changed composition and dynamics of the group were to have fearsome consequences for me. As fate would have it, my service on a task force of the American Psychological Association landed me on the front line of the battle for women's civil rights. The task force, which I mentioned before, had the formidable name of Sex Bias and Sex-role Stereotyping in Psychotherapeutic Practice, but during the first meeting of the task force in Washington, I was told its real focus: therapist sexual misconduct with women patients, a problem Phyllis Chesler had written about in *Women and Madness: When is a Woman Mad and Who is it Who Decides?* (1972). Members of the task force began to fill me in.

At that time, it was estimated that as many as twenty percent of therapists engaged in sexual misconduct—almost entirely male therapists with female patients—far more transgressions than I would have guessed. With my characteristic naïve, romantic view, I pictured the patient and therapist hopelessly in love—this despite the fact that I knew Dr. Miller at Iowa Psychopathic Hospital had sex with his patient while she was hypnotized.

My romantic ideas about sexual misconduct proved to be completely false. Most transgressors simply take advantage of the situation—the all-knowing, all-giving therapist with a sick, confused woman needing help: "Here my dear, let me offer you true consolation, love, and care." But some professionals take blatant advantage of the power discrepancy between doctor and psychiatric patient. Dr. Yallow (top forensic psychiatrist for the state of Wisconsin) intimidated a bipolar patient so effectively that he had sex with her on the desk in his office for thirty years before he was caught. According to the public record, he commanded, "Drop your skirt," threatening that he'd see to it that she would be committed to a state mental institution for the rest of her life if she didn't comply. Having had sexual intercourse with her once, he blackmailed her to continue by threatening to tell her husband. What a nightmare life she led. This was an important, powerful, intimidating man, and it's understandable that she was frightened into submission.

As is usually the case, this patient wasn't his only victim; three other women publicly charged him with sexual misconduct. About eighty percent of perpetrators abuse more than one patient. Experts on therapist sexual misconduct stress that sexual exploitation of patients often worsens their emotional condition and undermines their current and future trust relationships with doctors, the basis of all doctor-patient relations.

The APA task force asked me to serve as a liaison with a Wisconsin task force dealing with therapist sexual abuse, and that's how I became enmeshed in the problem at the local level. During the 1980s, three percent of the psychiatrists in Wisconsin were convicted of sexual misconduct by the Wisconsin Medical Examining Board (Goodwin et al., 1994). In addition, a highly regarded Lutheran minister who taught medical ethics, Bishop Lowell Mays, was found guilty of sexually abusing women who came to him for abortion counseling.

The successful predator's tactic of hiding behind a high-minded, respectable façade was on conspicuous display in Wisconsin. Two of the psychiatrists convicted of sexual misconduct were so well regarded by their local churches that the accusations against them were met with massive disbelief. Three had been president of a local psychiatric association, and some held influential teaching positions. The book, *Doc: The Rape of the Town of Lovell* (Olsen, 1989), gives an illuminating account of a perpetrator and how he manipulated his patients and public opinion. Although the book is about a physician rather than a psychiatrist, Jack Olsen's true crime story features many aspects of the Wisconsin situation: cunning predator conduct, manipulation of community opinion, and callous amorality.

As the rash of accusations against Madison psychiatrists began, I was shocked and surprised by each new case. Of those that directly affected me, the first accused was Dr. Jenkins, the young, good-looking psychiatrist in the office next to mine. He sought my favor—took me for a ride in his new Mercedes, offered to write prescriptions for any drugs I might want. I didn't want any prescriptions, but he pressed the point. Was he trying to set me up for blackmail in case I discovered that he was having intercourse with his patient in the office next to mine? Probably; these were not nice guys. He was finally charged with sexual misconduct when the patient, his second victim, sought police protection after he physically threatened her. He is still in practice in another state.

Unbeknownst to me, Dr. Wanda Bincer, whose office I now occupied and the person I was hired to replace, had been discredited and forced out of her job by Dr. Jenkins in order to protect himself against an accusation of sexual misconduct. The way Wanda was treated was but a dress rehearsal for what I was to experience. Since this man was eventually disciplined by the Medical Examining Board and lost his job, I thought all would be well, but his case was only the start.

My next encounter was with a psychiatrist known for his religious counseling. I was interested in the intersection of religion and psychotherapy and how religious concepts might be introduced into counseling for believers who shied away from secular therapy, an idea that Paul Meehl and I had discussed. At the time he was accused, I was doing marital counseling co-therapy with this seemingly pious, mild-mannered psychiatrist; I was trying to learn about Christian counseling. When the accusation against him became public, his private practice group quickly dismissed him, but he conned local evangelicals into hiring him at their counseling center. Such a smoothie was he that among his victims were two well-respected female mental health care providers. Eventually, he, too, was disciplined by the Medical Examining Board.

I'd seen justice done in Iowa and twice in Madison. As a result, I had no idea what a horror I was getting into when I became a witness for the state of Wisconsin in the case of Dr. Mauston who was accused of sexual misconduct. Lawsuits involving sexual misconduct were driving up the cost of malpractice insurance with the result that doctors had a strong financial incentive to aid and protect perpetrators. Having had one judgment of sexual misconduct against a member of their group, Madison Associates couldn't afford another.

It was an ordinary day in 1983 when I saw Dr. Mauston ostentatiously standing in the hall with a thick case folder open in his hands, like he was holding a big Webster's dictionary, an odd behavior. I came down the hall and asked what he was doing. He mumbled a concern that this patient might bring a false charge of sexual misconduct against him. Just then my next patient arrived, and we couldn't continue the conversation. He never brought up the subject again, nor did I. In retrospect, I realize that he was testing me, watching for signs that I'd heard something about the case from Wanda or from a social worker friendly with Wanda. This social worker told me that Wanda suspected Dr. Mauston of sexual involvement with a patient, but I didn't know the patient's name, so I didn't react when he flaunted the file at me. Doubtless, he was reassured. Subsequently, he was friendly and helpful, and often referred work to me that he couldn't handle. The report of Dr. Mauston's suspected sexual misconduct seemed to be malicious gossip, but it roiled around in my head. One of my peculiarities is that my mind registers incongruities, stores them, and at some point, without conscious effort, it adds them up to make a conclusion.

Later, another incongruous event occurred. I was present at the usual weekly luncheon meeting of our group when the question came up: Who should the group support for a special honorific position? To my surprise other candidates were passed over in favor of Dr. Mauston, but the selection process seemed phony. An ostensibly open discussion was held, though it seemed that a decision had already been made to choose Dr. Mauston. Why was he chosen? Why the subterfuge? Dr. Mauston seemed a nice enough man, but not the sort of person deserving a high honor. However, the group had a special reason for pushing his candidacy.

Dr. Mauston hadn't yet been publicly charged with sexual misconduct, but he and his partners knew the charge was coming since they had been informed a year in advance. His selection for a position of honor was part of a sophisticated public relations strategy to make a positive impression on members of the Medical Examining Board who were to adjudicate his case. Mauston's case wasn't decided until 1990, which gave time for a corrupt government to come into office and six years to manipulate the situation.

During a subsequent luncheon meeting, it was announced that Dr. Mauston had received the honor. At this time, it seemed to me that he should be smiling at everyone. Instead, he gave me an unusual furtive look which I read as checking me out for sign of an adverse reaction to his election. By this time, the charge against Dr. Mauston was public knowledge, and he commented to the group that he hoped he wouldn't be an embarrassment to his colleagues. To me this sounded like a hollow piety. My mind automatically added up his earlier odd behavior in the hallway, the social worker's report of suspected sexual misconduct, the phony selection process, and this strange look. I instantly realized that he was guilty. I was appalled and angered. Though I had no plan or conscious intent, I stayed after lunch, and Dr. Mauston and I were alone in the room, talking. He was flush with pleasure about winning the honor. Distracted, he bent over slightly to scratch the back of his leg. Was a mosquito bite bothering him? All the roiling thoughts of months coalesced in what I sensed as a chance to trap him into a confession. I thought myself exceedingly clever to perceive this moment of weakness. Without forethought, I uttered the fateful words which were to change my life forever, "I bet you're sorry you did it."

Taken by surprise, he answered, "It's not so bad is it, if I only did it once?"

I was immediately aghast at what I'd done. In impulsively satisfying my curiosity, I elicited a confession of guilt, which made me a marked woman. I had a secret, a big secret, which I resolved to keep to myself. A moment's reflection told me that if I tried to report his confession, it would be my word against his, and I didn't think my word would stand against that of a prominent psychiatrist. I was frozen with fear. Did this event tap into a previous trauma? In retrospect, I should have sought wise counsel. Instead, I decided that I should never, ever repeat this information to anyone. However, against my better judgment, I was later convinced to become a witness for the State of Wisconsin in their case against him.

My confrontation of Dr. Mauston was a canny, shrewd intuition impelled by idealism, but unwise in the extreme. He and his supporters quickly mobilized to discredit me, sow obstacles in my path, frighten, and destroy me. During the next several years I was often terrified and lived in a state of extreme stress. Dr. Mauston and his supporters tried to break me, and they did.

Mauston and I never spoke of his confession again, and I considered it water under the bridge. However, a few weeks later, I received a death threat. The male caller's voice slowly, deliberately, furiously voiced his venom, "I want—to smash—you—with a big boulder against the wall." Then he hung up. (No caller ID in those days.) The guy must have been completely bombed. The threat didn't make sense. How do you arrange to kill a person with a boulder? Nonetheless, I was concerned. Whoever it was, he desperately and intently wished for my complete obliteration. The next day at the office, I asked the secretarial staff if they had any idea who might have called me. No one did. I systematically ruled out all my male patients past and present. After a couple of days of my worried chatter about this at work, the newly hired administrative assistant, posing as my friend, definitively assured me I needn't worry. (This woman was an ex-addict, easily manipulated, and hired to achieve the group's purposes.) She could convincingly reassure me because she knew the caller was Dr. Mauston and had been instructed to cool me out. I had made a fool of Mauston, and he harbored a violent vengeance against me that persisted for years, even after he'd been exonerated.

The next sign that something was amiss came when board meetings of the group were closed, which meant I could no longer attend. (A specious excuse was given.) Following that, a fellow psychologist was abruptly ousted from the governing board of the group to be replaced by the social worker who had heard about Mauston's misconduct. Next, I was told that I would no longer be getting any referrals for psychological testing. They would all go to the other psychologist on the excuse that he was the sole support for his family. I objected, but it did no good. My final confrontation with the group came when a senior partner, claiming group financial hardship, confronted me in the hall with an "in your face" announcement of an extremely unfavorable, unfair change in my financial arrangement.

I resigned and joined Downtown Psychiatry (pseudonym), but Mauston and his allies made trouble for me there. I had no idea how nasty, mean, and relentless these guys could be. It was a continuation of Dr. Sherbert's M.O.: the incitement of psychiatric patients. I was clueless until one of my severely ill, bipolar patients told me that the psychiatrist handling her medications, one of Dr. Mauston's partners, had urged her to file a malpractice suit against me. Like Sam, she was in a high state of indignant outrage when she entered my office and threatened me with a law suit. After we discussed the situation, she calmed down and realized that the idea of a lawsuit was completely phony. This patient's report was a wake-up call. I had little factual information about these men and how they operated, but I was beginning to get the idea.

Dr. Mauston even referred a case to me *after* he knew I was a witness against him. I was surprised and leery, but I feared that a refusal to see the patient would be used against me since he and I were part of the same HMO. I gave him the benefit of a doubt.

This young woman's mother was consulting Dr. Mauston, and he doubtless told her that it would be good for her daughter to have some counseling. Maybe she'd like to visit with that nice Dr. Sherman. He could make suggestions for therapy sound like going for a pedicure. Here's the hook: The referral contained confidential juicy information about the father that the daughter didn't yet know. It was a ripe #MeToo feminist issue; her father had impregnated an employee who wasn't being quiet about it. Here's what I think was going on: The hope was that I'd take the bait, violate confidential information and tell the daughter. Then charges could be brought against me for disclosing confidential information.

The daughter was a likable young woman who wasn't at all upset because she didn't yet know about the family problem that would soon publicly engulf them. I couldn't help her with a problem she didn't know she had, and I was charged not to tell her about it. What to do? I finally decided on the following strategy: I said, "Ask your mother if she knows that I'm a witness for the Medical Examining Board in their case against Dr. Mauston." I never heard from her again.

On another occasion, a man purporting to be a humble workman dressed in white painter's overalls consulted me as a patient. Because of my expertise in the psychology of women, my clientele was almost entirely female. A male patient was unusual, but this was the scariest man I ever talked to. The things he told me made my hair stand on end. By a stroke of luck, I learned that he was actually involved in organized crime. My situation was like Billy Crystal's movie, *Analyze This*, in which he plays a psychiatrist and Robert de Niro plays a gangster. I felt like Billy Crystal. "Hmm, you know, I'm not quite sure I'm the right doctor for your case." Unlike the woman psychiatrist in the TV mafia series, *The Sopranos*, I wasn't one bit intrigued. I was scared. Was this man a plant? He owned a fortune in Madison property. Why was he trying to pass himself off as a simple workman? Some of this man's problems were outside my area of expertise, and I refused his case on that basis. But he didn't want to take no for an answer. He came and sat, expressionless, in his painter's overalls, outside my office. He never said a word; he just sat there. At first, I assumed he was waiting to see another doctor. He wasn't; he was trying to intimidate me. Did someone put him up to it? Did he or someone over him owe a favor? Although I was completely within my rights to refuse to take this patient's case, I got grief about it from an administrator of the HMO, a colleague of Dr. Mauston.

Many other unsettling incidents occurred, but on the day that Dr. Mauston was found innocent of the charge of sexual misconduct, he detonated his finest booby trap. Among my former patients was a woman he had referred to me. She had been a prostitute, but now she held an excellent secretarial position at a facility that was frequented by Dr. Mauston. At the time she came to me, I was puzzled because she didn't seem to need therapy, and I only saw her for a few interviews. Had the good Dr. Mauston suggested that a little counseling with the nice Dr. Sherman would be helpful for her? During our first interview, she surprised me by stressing that I should never tell anyone that she'd been a prostitute because she'd lose her job. She was extremely anxious about this. Most patients know that therapist/patient communications are confidential, but she needed my special and repeated reassurances.

Now, on the same day Dr. Mauston was found innocent of sexual misconduct, I received a phone call from her saying that she'd lost her job and believed I was responsible. She was wildly enraged. She didn't believe my denial and demanded to see me immediately, but I didn't think that wise since I perceived she might be homicidal. I hoped she would calm down. However, after work she was waiting for me in the underground garage and menaced me with her automobile as if to run me down. I don't know why she didn't. Perhaps my calmness made her realize that I was innocent. She wasn't a stupid woman. Perhaps she thought of the consequences to herself if she ran me down. It must have filtered through to her that this wasn't a good idea.

I doubt that she realized she was set up. Dr. Mauston was an excellent con.

I was further disconcerted the next day. On the front page of the local newspaper, an article appeared quoting a prominent local psychiatrist to the effect that it was such a shame that Dr. Mauston's case dragged on so long and that this worthy man had been needlessly abused. Dr. Mauston's case had gone on for years which gave him time to manipulate circumstances to his advantage. Eventually he was able to label as liars both me and the patient.

I was made out to be a liar by the testimony before the Medical Examining Board of the young social worker who had been elevated to a position on the board of Madison Associates. She was the one who told me that Dr. Mauston was suspected of being sexually involved with a patient. Now she perjured herself by denying she'd ever said that; this made me look like a liar.

As for Dr. Mauston's victim, I never met her, but here is what I learned later from the heavily redacted public record of the case. She began therapy with Dr. Mauston as a teenage incest victim and developed a crush on him. Many girls and women idolize their doctors and fall in love with them. If this happens, therapists are expected to abide by professional, ethical standards. They have an, "I'm not available," talk with their patients. If they're tempted to get inappropriately involved with a patient, they get supervision, and/or refer the patient to another therapist. They are not to have affairs with their patients. It is not only unethical; it is illegal in Wisconsin and many other states.

The patient got worse rather than better under Dr. Mauston's care, and, despite years of treatment from Dr. Mauston, she attempted suicide and was hospitalized. He saw her daily at the hospital, and the nurse's notes report observing inappropriate behavior between them. According to the public record, it was after her discharge from the hospital that Dr. Mauston engaged in fellatio with her in his office. She eventually terminated therapy with him, went to another therapist, and filed charges with the Medical Examining Board.

The patient was made out to be a liar when her diagnosis was changed from mild depression to borderline personality disorder, a diagnosis that included the implication of untruthfulness. This point was underscored by an expert witness hired by the defense who related an anecdote illustrating that lies are typical behavior for individuals diagnosed with borderline personality disorder. The change in her diagnosis was made by Dr. Mauston, himself, a self-serving alteration that aided his case.

Moreover, the patient was threatened that unless she recanted her accusation against Dr. Mauston, her father would be charged with incest, and the family would lose their source of income. Apparently, she made a deal. Her financial circumstances certainly changed. Previously she had been impoverished and received her psychotherapy from Dr. Mauston at taxpayer expense. Now I learned that she'd graduated from an out-of-state college and was in graduate school.

The trial was over; my reputation was in shreds, but the worst was yet to come. I was forced out of practice with the help of my own physician, Dr. Benedict (pseudonym), a man I had completely trusted. He had a fine reputation and practiced with an excellent medical group. Earlier in his life, he'd been a monk and had taken a vow of silence. During the time I knew him, his wife died, and we all felt sorry for him. He had a great façade of respectability. However, I once asked a doctor friend what he thought of him. His response: "Queer duck," so he wasn't able to completely hide his twisted nature. This #MeToo story features the tortured soul of a man driven by lascivious and sadistic sexual desires. As my physician, he knew I was vulnerable, and he groomed me to be his victim. There are bizarre elements to this story that aren't accidental. Instead, they're part of a predatory strategy to discredit the victim, especially a woman with a psychiatric diagnosis: In order to tell what happened, the victim has to talk about things so bizarre that she sounds crazy, and no one believes her.

Here is what happened: I came in for my annual physical, which normally included a gynecological examination. However, this year, Dr. Benedict announced that he wasn't going to do that part. I was annoyed. I wanted to get the whole thing done with. "Why can't you do the gynecological part?" I asked. He paused. He was thinking up his story.

"Look at my hand," he said.

He showed me his right hand which was all scrunched up and looked severely crippled and deformed. "Oh, my goodness, what happened?" I was distressed for him.

"I caught a golf ball. It was flying through the air, and I reached up and caught it."

I was skeptical. "And it did all that? How can you work?"

"Oh, I manage," he bravely replied. He kept it up. He really poured it on. I was hooked. I felt sorry for him. This fine, dedicated doctor with a severely damaged hand.

"Well, I suppose you really can't do the gynecological exam."

"I could," he said hesitantly. "I was just worried that it might not go as smoothly as usual, but we could go ahead."

I decided to proceed. How bad could it be? As he walked around the room gathering his instruments, I noticed that he was walking strangely, as though he wasn't sure where the floor was. Unfortunately, my avoidance of the drug scene left me without crucial information, and I didn't realize that he may have been on cocaine or some other drug. Instead, I decided the poor man was tired.

The pelvic exam was extremely uncomfortable; he poked around for a long time. Finally, he said, "I feel some kind of abnormal thickening here in the wall—maybe something wrong with the intestine. You're going to need a sigmoidoscopic examination."

Basically, this examination involves running a long, snaky thing through your intestines. The snaky thing has a light at the end of it, and the doctor can look for abnormalities. A few days later, Dr. J. H. Turgeson did the exam in an office down the hall from Dr. Benedict. It hurt like Hell. (In those days, no anesthesia was used.) Was Dr. Benedict listening out of sight in his office, enjoying my shrieks of pain?

"Ouch. Ouch. That hurts."

"I just have to go around this corner here."

I began screaming. "Stop. Stop it. God damn it, stop. Stop." More screaming.

"Just a little bit more."

After the examination was over, Dr. Turgeson apologized, "I'm really sorry about this. I don't see why your doctor ordered this test. I don't understand how he could have felt an abnormality in your intestine during a gynecological examination, and I don't understand why he insisted that I go so far. We don't normally try to go that far." I accepted Dr. Turgeson's apology; he was obviously sincere. It was a terrible experience, but no harm done. In retrospect, I'm lucky Dr. Turgeson didn't perforate my bowel.

Months later, I saw Dr. Benedict because of a bad cut on my leg that required stitches, and I noticed that there was nothing wrong with his right hand. His severely crippled right hand was miraculously healed. I put two and two together and was instantaneously furious.

I swore at him: "You son of a bitch. You son of a bitch. You told me you'd crippled your hand, and there's nothing wrong with it."

He responded by calmly calling for his nurse. In she came, her face beaming with adoration. This sweet, naïve woman would absolutely cover for him. I got the picture. In an intuitive insight, I realized what was going on. If I didn't control myself immediately, he would claim I was dangerous, that I threatened him, and I would be hauled off by the police to a psychiatric ward. His nurse would back him to the hilt. Who would believe me when I told them what happened? No one. A nice, good Catholic doctor was being maligned by a certifiable nut. I looked him square in the eye and said, "Can you stitch this up, pointing to my leg?" He nodded his assent; quietly sewed it up, and I left the office.

I later learned that I was not Dr. Benedict's only victim. Here is an account of another woman's experience with him: A highly intelligent friend of mine told me that he had prescribed such heavy doses of estrogen that her breasts ballooned. They were humongous, but think about it. How credible is it that a respected physician would deliberately give his patient excessive doses of estrogen in order to see her breasts grow? Even I found it hard to believe. "Gee," I thought, "I wish my breasts would grow," but there can be too much of a good thing. Her breasts were so large that they created back strain, and she was considering breast reduction surgery. There was even more to the story because she actually sold her house and moved away from Madison because of him. She said that he'd put something in her medical records that she didn't want other doctors to see, but I don't know what it was. At the time, I couldn't imagine what he could have said to make her sell her home and move to another city. Too bad I didn't consider this information more carefully.

Now almost forty years later, I recently told a friend that I was writing this book and mentioned Dr. Benedict's real name. Before I could continue, she said, "I remember him. I saw him just one time. I had a sore throat, and after looking at my throat, he said he could give me a breast exam. This is kind of embarrassing, but I let him do it."

As in the case of the #MeToo incidents, I think there are a lot more stories of inappropriate behavior out there—each of us keeping our own embarrassed silence.

Doc: The Rape of the Town of Lovell (1989), an expertly researched true-crime book, helped me understand the situation. It tells a remarkable story even more unbelievable than my own. Doc served a largely Mormon community in the small town of Lovell, Wyoming, where the women were trusting and naïve. When Doc did his gynecological examinations, his patients put their feet in stirrups and he draped the lower half of their bodies with a sheet. They couldn't see what he was doing. During the examination, what he inserted wasn't a specially warmed speculum as he told his gullible patients. It was his penis. Doc was a well-respected member of the community. His patients felt indebted to him and trusted him. He also had a devoted, loyal nurse. Many of his patients were extremely grateful to him for his legitimate medical services, and they were reluctant to say bad things about him or participate in his prosecution.

The same had been true for me. I had thought myself extremely lucky to have such a great doctor. When I called him, he'd make room in his schedule to see me the same day. More than once, I had bronchitis and serious complications were averted by prompt shots of antibiotics. When I suffered from overall muscle pain and severe pain in the right shoulder, he claimed that he stood up for me to his colleagues to support a referral for physical therapy. He said such referrals were limited under my insurance plan. On another occasion, he made a point of telling me that, against the objections of his colleagues, he'd supported my need for psychotherapy. What a good guy. Moreover, he went way out of his way to help when a member of my family became ill. I felt an enormous debt of gratitude toward him.

Smart, high status psychopathic male predators have a strong social advantage. For example, in the case of Doc in the town of Lovell, despite the fact that tests showed that the area nearby was dotted with the product of his unique gynecological examinations, some members of the community passionately and staunchly defended him. The lies of psychopaths can be amazingly convincing.

Although I didn't want to make a complaint to the Medical Examining Board, I had to get a new internist. I called Dr. Benedict's office to ask them to prepare a copy of my medical record. When I arrived to pick it up, the record was clearly incomplete. I argued with the clerk at the counter. "No, this is all there is," she said, and she even wanted me to sign a statement saying that I'd received the complete record. Then I glimpsed Dr. Benedict flitting in the background, between the stacks of files, and I realized he was hoping to get me hauled off to a psychiatric ward. He was waiting for me to lose control of myself and make some wild threat. The law in Wisconsin is that, if there is evidence of

danger to self or others, individuals can be involuntarily confined to a psychiatric ward for a few days. After that time, there
has to be a hearing to establish that they're a danger before they
can be kept longer. It sounds like a patient's rights are respected,
but what if people lie about you? It happens. I didn't want to risk
his calling the police. I picked up my incomplete record and left.

In view of what I learned later, my decision was wise. This
man's intentions toward me were highly malignant. Here's what
I found out years later when I read the part of the record that had
been withheld from me. I got the record as a consequence of my
hospitalization at Mayo's psychiatric hospital in Rochester. It
was included in materials Dr. Benedict had previously sent to
my neurologist, who sent it to Mayo at their request, who then
mailed it to me after my discharge. At the time I received the
records I wasn't in good shape; I stuffed the thick packet into a
file cabinet and didn't read its contents until years later. Gullible
as ever, I never guessed what this rat did. In his case notes on
12/15/88 he wrote that he talked to my colleague at work, Dr.
Mayberry (pseudonym), telling him that I was "psychotic and
threatening." The case note ended with the pious comment, "I'd
like to help this poor woman, but she's too hostile."

I was nowhere near psychotic and nowhere near any kind of
violent attack on him or anyone else. I've never been a violent
person. Perhaps, Dr. Benedict was trying to discredit me in case
I ever brought a charge against him. Perhaps, he was helping
Mauston as well, since it is known that Madison doctors involved
in sexual misconduct cooperated in victim-finding and later in
defense. In any case, he slandered me and violated a confidential
doctor-patient relationship. He damaged my standing with my
colleagues and prejudiced against me any physician who got
records from him. Unfortunately, by the time I realized what had
happened, the statute of limitations had run out which prevented
me from filing a law suit. These lies created difficulties for me at
Downtown Psychiatry and helped lead to my being forced out of
practice. Benedict was lucky that my colleagues at Downtown
Psychiatry, where I was working at the time, didn't tell me what

he had done. The docs stuck together. He is also fortunate that my lawyer didn't honor my request to get my medical records.

There is a moral here: If you become a potential threat to powerful people, protect yourself; make a record, and consider going to the proper authorities, even if you don't want to press charges. Otherwise, you may find yourself preemptively discredited.

Chapter 9

Depression is a Feminist Issue

This chapter partly concerns factual information about depression and bipolar disorder and partly my own experiences. Serious major depressions are up to three times more common among women than men (American Psychiatric Association, 2013; Weissman et al., 1996). Moreover, the problem is getting worse. According to Johns Hopkins University (2016), about thirteen percent of adolescent girls were depressed in 2005 increasing to slightly over seventeen percent in 2014, one in six girls. Depression is not only more common in women, but among those with bipolar disorder, depression is likely to be the first sign of illness, whereas for males, mania is the likely first sign. Manic periods also last longer in men than women. It's often said that there is no difference between the sexes in bipolar disorder, but a fine-grained analysis tells another story.

Bipolar II disorder, which is more common in women, is characterized by periods of depression with intervals of hypomania, the moods often swinging seasonally. Hypomania means an upswing in mood not as extreme as mania; it's a happy and productive state. It would be regarded as a supernormal good

150

mood, but for the fact that, in the context of bipolar disorder, it signals the potential for a move to an undesirably manic state. Antidepressants are particularly to be avoided with bipolar II disorder since they can set off a manic episode and a huge new bunch of complications: out of bounds behavior that can cause serious trouble, hospitalization, and more medications. Bright light therapy (BLT) is effective for bipolar II depressions, and it rarely elevates mood too much. If it does, treatment with BLT can be easily adjusted whereas you can't unswallow an antidepressant pill. Use of BLT, rather than antidepressants, also lessens the chance of being put on anti-manic drugs. Many psychiatrists don't see the need to treat hypomania with anti-manic drugs. They're reluctant to deprive patients of a happy, productive experience and prefer not to expose them to the risks and complications of additional drug treatment. Increasing numbers of health care providers understand that hypomania can be kept in check by regular periods of darkness at night. (Discussed in more detail later.)

Previous psychologists have focused on depression as a feminist issue, for example, Kaplan (1986) and more recently Hyde, Mezulis, and Abramson (2008); however, this chapter emphasizes a hitherto neglected source of the greater prevalence of depression in women: light deprivation (Chotai et al., 2004; Lyall et al., 2018). These depressions, occurring almost twice as often in women, can be severe and their remedy is too often the unnecessary and harmful use of psychiatric drugs. *Drugs are not effective treatments for depressions, especially not those based on light deprivation, which respond well to BLT.* Even non-seasonal depressions respond to BLT (American Psychiatric Association, 2010; Oldham & Ciraulo, 2014; Terman & Terman, 2005). Women need to know and understand this. Moreover, this is an issue highly relevant not only for women, but also for men, public health, and public policy since depression is the single greatest source of medical spending (Goetzel et al., 2012).

The problem of depression in women isn't new. In 1892, feminist activist Charlotte Perkins Gilman published *The Yellow*

Wallpaper, a semi-autobiographical, chilling account of a woman's descent into madness. To cure her "hysteria" and post-partum depression, the heroine's physician-husband provided her with a rest cure—rest and more rest—separated from friends and family, isolated in a room with striped yellow wallpaper.

The unwary woman today can fall prey to an even more destructive treatment: pills and more pills. Many more women than men take psychiatric drugs: drugs for sleep, drugs for anxiety, drugs for depression, drugs for serious mental illness, plus the drugs to treat the bad effects of the drugs they started with.

There are many problems with antidepressants. Although the American Psychiatric Association's (2010) guidelines for treatment of major depression recommend antidepressant drugs and report efficacy for them, Kirsch et al. (2008) found that the efficacy of the drugs over placebo is small. Moreover, the term "efficacy" is misleading because, although it sounds like the drugs are effective and curative, "efficacy" refers only to a short-term response (Whitaker & Cosgrove, 2015). Actual effectiveness is different. A careful research study showed that, after a year of treatment on antidepressants, only 11% of patients were well, a poor result indeed. The authors concluded that antidepressants are more harmful than helpful in the long run (Rush et al., 2004). Whitaker and Cosgrove (2015) came to an equally negative conclusion.

In those same American Psychiatric Association (2010) guidelines, seven pages of side effects for antidepressants are cataloged. The currently most popular antidepressants are the SSRIs (Prozac, Luvox, Zoloft, Celexa, Lexapro, and Paxil). Their side effects, as listed, include the already mentioned loss of sexual enjoyment, as well as diarrhea, agitation, insomnia, headache, serious movement disorders (akathisia, dystonia, Parkinsonism, and tardive dyskinesia), a two-fold increase in risk of falls including hip fracture, and weight gain, which can be considerable.

However, there are even more hazards attached to these antidepressant drugs. When you stop them, you're likely to have symptoms as bad as or worse than the depression they were meant to treat. Dr. Joseph Glenmullen (2006) has written an excellent book on the topic and how best to stop antidepressants. Discontinuation of them is like going through a drug withdrawal and can mean weeks of misery.

Antidepressants can also be a causative factor in stimulating violent behavior, even homicide and physical assault (Moore, Glenmullen, & Furberg, 2010). Tell that to the judge. (However, the prescription drug most associated with violent behavior is Chantix, the smoking cessation drug.)

Antidepressants also can backfire making you chronically depressed, even suicidal (Whitaker & Cosgrove, 2015). How can that happen? It's simple; your body makes its own neurochemicals, and it may stop making them when they're artificially supplied. For example, when you add a drug that increases the neurochemical serotonin (prescribed to relieve depression), your body may stop making it, leaving you with less serotonin than before. Worse yet, your body may never resume its normal occupation of making serotonin for you.

Pills not only adversely affect us directly; they harm us through our children. Antidepressants can even cause suicide in young people. The United States Food and Drug Administration (FDA) now requires a warning label about the risk of suicide. Moreover, there is clear evidence that antidepressants are harmful to the unborn and to nursing babies (Freeman & Gelenberg, 2005; Lugo-Candelas et al., 2018), including a significant increased risk of having an autistic child (Boukhris et al., 2016). Since 50 % of pregnancies are unplanned, women can unwittingly expose their babies to a harmful drug before they know they're pregnant.

Going the drug route, you may end up with a chronic depression like that experienced by fellow psychologist, Lauren Slater, author of *Blue Dreams: The Science and the Story of the Drugs that Changed Our Minds* (2018). Slater suffers from depression as part of bipolar I disorder, a serious mental illness that has caused her moods to swing from severe depression to manic psychosis. She was hospitalized five times between ages 13 and 24 for bipolar and eating disorders. Over the years, she was variously prescribed three different antidepressants (Prozac, Imipramine, and Effexor), and lithium, which is an anti-mania drug, and neuroleptics advertised as antipsychotics, including Geodon, Abilify, Risperdal, and Zyprexa, the latter meant to boost the nonexistent effect of her antidepressant. These antipsychotics aren't specific treatments for psychosis; instead they operate to shut down the brain. With the drugs, Slater has been more or less functional, but as a result of them, at age 54, she is grossly overweight, has high blood pressure, memory problems, diabetes, kidney and eye damage, and an early expiration date stamped on her forehead.

Both Lauren Slater and I are diagnosed with bipolar 1 disorder, which means that we've had episodes of both major depression and mania. Historically, people with this disorder experienced episodes of illness with normal periods in between, but this is no longer necessarily the case. Slater seems stuck in a chronic depression. (Or is it a chronic state of drug side effects?) Many people now suffer from "rapid cycling" in which they careen from one mood extreme to the other with little or no normal periods in between. This dire state is believed to be caused by the use of psychiatric drugs that have disrupted the usual course of the disorder.

When I read Lauren Slater's account of her illness, I felt bad. That could have been me, but it's not. Here, briefly, is what happened to me. Like Slater, I was on lithium and antidepressants (only briefly an SSRI) for sixteen years. However, I got so sick from the drugs that I feared for my life, and against medical advice, I went off the drugs completely. Now nearly twenty years later, using BLT and dark treatment schedules, I have had no mood swings, and at 85 I am in excellent mental and physical health.

Unfortunately, Lauren Slater's case isn't an isolated one. In casual conversation with people, I've been saddened and shocked to hear terrible stories of unnecessary suffering caused by drugs: the extremely overweight person on lithium for twenty some years whose kidneys are now so damaged that she must drink two gallons of water a day, the also now overweight person on her fourth antidepressant, who is nonetheless suicidal. Then there is the story of a friend's superstar cousin who developed bipolar disorder just after she graduated from college. She was beautiful, smart, and dynamic—the star of every school play. Then she started lithium and became so dull, she ended up working as a bagger at the grocery store. Then she hanged herself in her parents' living room.

These are anecdotes, but severe adverse effects of psychiatric drugs is a widespread problem documented in several books: *Mad in America: Bad Science, Bad Medicine, and the Enduring Mistreatment of the Mentally Ill* by investigative journalist Robert Whitaker (2002) and *Anatomy of an Epidemic: Magic Bullets, Psychiatric Drugs, and the Astonishing Rise of Mental Illness in America* (2010), also by Whitaker. In 2015, together with Lisa Cosgrove, a psychologist specializing in ethical and medicolegal issues who is affiliated with the Universities of Massachusetts and Harvard, Whitaker published *Psychiatry Under the Influence: Institutional Corruption, Social Injury, and Prescriptions for Reform*. These investigations reveal a shocking story of fraudulent science and collusion between medical professionals and the pharmaceutical industry. Not only have many mentally ill individuals not been helped by psychiatric drugs, their condition has been seriously worsened, often permanently. The seriously mentally ill are now dying fifteen to twenty-five years earlier than normal. They are dying from cardio-vascular ailments, respiratory problems, metabolic illness, diabetes, kidney failure, and other physical problems that accumulate as people stay on psychiatric drugs (Whitaker, 2010).

We Americans have been successfully conned by a well-orchestrated propaganda campaign promoting psychiatric drugs. Who hasn't heard that depression is caused by a chemical imbalance? The idea suggests that depression can be relieved by taking a chemical drug to correct the imbalance. However, even if this questionable description of the depression problem were correct, fixing it with a drug is easier said than done. Drugs do alter brain chemistry, but often not in a desirable way. Moreover, chemical imbalances don't need chemicals to correct them; BLT can correct brain chemistry naturally without taking a wrecking ball to the brain.

Drugs for mania are also hyped. Individuals are urged to take lithium with the claim that it's just like taking insulin for diabetes. However, diabetics aren't making enough insulin for their bodies to function properly, so it makes sense to take insulin, but nobody's body makes lithium. Unlike insulin, lithium isn't replacing anything the body naturally makes or needs. It does slow brain function, but get too much of it and it's a lethal poison.

In the 1990s, an idea called the kindling theory further promoted psychiatric drugs. The theory suggested that episodes of bipolar disorder are like epilepsy such that each episode increases the likelihood of another attack. The theory made it seem essential to keep taking drugs to prevent a worsened illness. However, the theory has turned out to be incorrect.

In its 152 pages, the American Psychiatric Association's guidelines (2010) for the treatment of major depression contain a couple interesting sentences. They recommend psychotherapy alone (that is without antidepressants) for mild to moderate depressions, describing psychotherapy as "equipotent with antidepressant medications," that is, equally effective (p. 47). Regarding BLT, they report that it "appears effective for seasonal affective disorder and nonseasonal major depressive disorder" (p. 51). Notice that BLT is acknowledged to be effective for seasonal, *as well as* nonseasonal depressions, an assessment also shared by others (Oldham & Ciraulo, 2014; Terman &Terman, 2005).

What? How does this make sense? Psychotherapy and BLT are acknowledged as effective treatments for depression, but for 152 pages they recommend antidepressants in spite of all their problems? The average person or doctor would probably not read far enough to find these recommendations or guess that non-drug therapies are effective. Given the difficulties associated with antidepressants, wouldn't it be logical for the American Psychiatric Association to recommend psychotherapy or BLT instead of problematic drugs?

How could this happen? Whitaker and Cosgrove's (2015) investigation revealed that the American Psychiatric Association (2010) guidelines for treatment of major depression were developed by a six-member committee all with commercial ties to one or more drug companies that manufacture antidepressants (120 ties altogether). These psychiatrists received huge financial benefits from these companies. Seventy-five percent of the studies they considered were funded by the pharmaceutical industry, and these studies were five times more likely to report positive results in favor of antidepressants. In 2008, 36 of 74 industry-funded studies of the popular SSRI antidepressants failed to find even a short-term benefit for the drug compared to a placebo. Shockingly, half of the negative studies were unpublished, or the results were misleadingly reported in a way favorable to the drug companies (Whitaker & Cosgrove, 2015). Many physicians, psychiatrists, and even scientifically trained behavioral scientists, like me, were taken in by what was appearing in the scientific journals. It took an investigative journalist to go behind the scenes to reveal how the science was cooked.

What does our government say? As of December 2017, the FDA's statement about antidepressants put the word in quotes, suggesting that antidepressants aren't what the word implies. They say that "the 'antidepressants' can help improve symptoms in some" people, not a ringing endorsement. However, the government that should protect us is not providing adequate leadership in this area.

What does the British National Health Service say? It doesn't suggest antidepressants for mild to moderate depressions; instead it recommends exercise, self-help groups, and/or psychotherapy.

I have gone into detail regarding antidepressants, but the story for other psychiatric drugs, especially the new antipsychotics is as bad or worse. Serious problems with the new antipsychotics, even brain shrinkage, have been detailed by Moncrieff (2009, 2013). These antipsychotics (e.g. Abilify, Clozaril, Zyprexa, Seroquel, Risperdal, Geodon) which were originally intended to treat schizophrenia, have now morphed into an all-purpose medication to calm the agitated. As such, they have become a hazard for the aged, particularly women.

In some cases, psychiatric drugs leave mentally ill individuals in a no-win situation: They suffer serious, adverse effects if they continue the drugs, and also if they stop them. This is particularly anguishing in the case of tardive dyskinesia. It is a side effect especially of the older antipsychotic medications, but also the newer ones, as well as antidepressants. Symptoms include tics and involuntary movements of the face and other parts of the body, and involuntary utterances like Tourette's syndrome. The movements may be almost continual, an exhausting, disfiguring social handicap, sometimes worse than the symptoms of the mental illness the drug was meant to treat. However, if the drug is stopped, the symptoms don't stop; they get worse. They may gradually wear off over the ensuing months or they may be permanent. Tardive dyskinesia afflicted two of my relatives.

Members of NAMI (National Alliance for the Mentally Ill), like my friend Harriet Shetler, had great hopes for the value of medications. I spoke to Harriet a few months before her death. She was blind and had been unable to read for some years. Harriet had received many deserved honors for her work on behalf of the mentally ill, but she confided that these honors were like hot coals on her head. Surprised, I asked, "Why?"

In a voice muffled by intense emotion, she replied, "My son never got well."

Her mother's anguish struck a chord deep within me. Would her son, who suffered from schizophrenia, have been better off without all the "anti-psychotic" medications?

Those of us in NAMI, concerned about serious, persistent mental illnesses, such as schizophrenia, major depression, and bipolar disorder, had an optimistic mind set. We had watched enormous scientific advances made in the treatment of heart disease, cancer, and HIV (human immunodeficiency virus). We expected that the same would be true for mental illnesses. What happened? Instead of cures, we got fraud, greed, and political collusion with the interests of the drug companies. I'm not saying there is no use for these drugs. I am saying they are overused, carelessly used, and fraudulently marketed. Light and dark treatments don't make money. Drugs do. The Clinical Psychobiology branch of the National Institute of Mental Health, headed by Dr. Tom Wehr, used to be devoted to issues related to chronobiology, the effects of light and circadian rhythms on human behavior. It was here that scientists discovered that BLT can relieve depression, and darkness can dampen mania. What happened to the Clinical Psychobiology unit? We need revived government support for this research.

Although this chapter concentrates on depressions occurring in reaction to light deprivation, there are multiple sources for depression. In our drug-happy (or not-so-happy) culture, depression is often a side effect of a medication, such as Chantix for smoking cessation, propranolol and other beta blockers for high blood pressure, statins to lower cholesterol, Singular for asthma, and—women take note—birth control pills. (An IUD is as effective and safer.) Depression can also be part of several physical disorders, such as low thyroid or lupus. If you're depressed, be sure your physician rules out physical causes.

Moreover, as already mentioned, perhaps the most common cause of depression is something bad happening to you, the problems-in-living depression. This kind of depression responds to treatments such as those recommended by the British National Health Service: self-help groups, talking therapies, and exercise. Yes, exercise is an effective prevention and treatment for depression (Rethorst et al., 2009).

However, depressions occurring in reaction to light deprivation are common among people in the north, especially women
(Chotai et al., 2004; Lyall, et al. 2018). SAD, which includes
major depressions, is effectively prevented and/or relieved by
BLT (Golden et al., 2005). SAD has a hereditary component; it
is characterized by lethargy, loss of interest, sleeping too much,
increased appetite, and weight gain (Levitan et al., 2006; Rosenthal et al., 1984; Rosenthal et al., 1987; Rosenthal, 1993/2013).
The weight gain associated with SAD is often a major problem,
and, again, women take note: BLT corrects the urge to overeat
and is an effective treatment for compulsive overeating such as
bulimia (Terman & Terman, 2005). SAD can start as early as
August 15, the day of the largest drop in ambient light, and can
last until spring or summer if untreated (Wehr et al., 2001).

The effects of the timing and intensity of light on human behavior are only now beginning to be understood. It's long been
known that people are cheered and activated by sunlight and
depressed and deactivated by its absence (think of the Greek
myth of Persephone), but it hasn't been understood that the behavior of some of us is much more affected than others: Mood
and activity levels can range from clinically depressed to manic.
Moreover, because the effects of light occur without an accom-
panying awareness, we may not understand how our behavior
has been affected.

With the invention of electricity, we no longer need to travel
to a sunnier clime to rid ourselves of the winter blues; we now
have lights strong enough to simulate the sun and relieve this
kind of depression. The sun's light is powerful. To give you some
idea, the daytime average home or office has a light intensity of
50-300 lux while at sunrise outdoor illumination is 10,000 lux;
at noon it is 100,000 lux. (Lux is a measure of light intensity.) In
order to effectively relieve depression, therapeutic bright lights
need to provide 10,000 lux of light. Please do not think that turning up the lights in your house or work place will do the job. You
will need a proper lamp yielding the necessary 10,000 lux of
light, which can be ordered from, for example, Northern Lights

Technology. The idea is to sit in front of the lamp for about a half hour through the seasons of low ambient light. The best time is usually early morning. The sun comes up early in the summer and later in the winter. Therefore, in order to fool your body that it's not winter, BLT is best in the early morning. You can read or eat your breakfast, not looking directly at the light. Within two weeks, the therapy is usually effective; it's not harmful to the eyes, and has negligible side effects.

In addition to simple BLT, triple chronotherapy is a new, quick effective non-drug treatment for severe, even suicidal, depressions, and it works in a few days to a couple weeks. It's called triple chronotherapy because it involves three therapeutic phases: wake therapy (preferred term for total sleep deprivation), sleep phase advance, and BLT. Moreover, it's effective (Gottlieb & Terman, 2012; Sahlem et al., 2014; Terman & McMahan, 2013; Wirz-Justice et al. 2005; Wirz-Justice et al., 2013).

What? Major depression and suicidal behavior can be quickly derailed by manipulating patterns of light exposure and sleep? Is this another flimflam cure? No, it actually works 60% of the time. Compare that to the 11% recovery rate after a year of antidepressant drugs (Rush et al., 2004). In order to understand why this treatment works, a fuller scientific explanation will be helpful, although this isn't a full review of the literature. Later discussion of the development of the Evolutionary Origin of Bipolar Disorder-Revised (EOBD-R) theory will also clarify some points.

First, why is this treatment called *chronotherapy? Chrono* refers to clock and the fact that we, like all living things, have clock genes inside us: Clock genes determine when flowers open and close, depending on ambient light; when animals hibernate; when we are hungry, and when we are sleepy. Our behavior is ordered by biological clocks that function on a daily and seasonal basis. When our clocks don't function right or function differently than other people, we're perceived as disordered. For a more detailed discussion of chronobiology and the role of melatonin, see Wirz-Justice (2006).

Scientists have long speculated that winter depression is a sort of hibernation under the control of clock genes. Dr. Tom Wehr and his colleagues at the National Institute of Mental Health (NMIH) (2001) provided stunning evidence to support this view. They showed that a genetic factor controlling vulnerability to seasonal major depression is connected to the human biological clock in a way similar to that found in hibernating animals. Moreover, they demonstrated that it is the change (the largest drop) in the amount of ambient light during mid-August that triggers the neurochemical cascade of events that result in the behavioral changes of SAD and winter major depression. These changes also include increased eating and weight gain, especially among women. Importantly, this research underscores again the tie between obesity and depression, both serious problems for women. The EOBD-R theory (Sherman, 2012), and an increasing number of facts, support the view that individuals with SAD, major depression, and bipolar disorder have inherited different genes affecting their chronobiology, how they respond to changes in the intensity and timing of light. These genes come from Neanderthal, a people who lived through the Ice Ages (Dannemann & Kelso, 2017; Simonti et al., 2016). It is theorized that the Neanderthal adapted to the long, cold winters by developing genes to shut down during winter and revive with fair weather. The winter shutdown, which we call depression, saved energy and helped preserve the Neanderthal. On the other hand, during good weather, they had the energy they needed to "make hay while the sun shines." This explains why both the early waking time and BLT work; they fool the body that it's not winter.

But how does keeping people awake contribute to triple chronotherapy? Tom Wehr and his colleagues at NIMH used to be linked to the old St. Elizabeth's psychiatric hospital in Washington DC. There they observed that when depressed patients lost sleep, they regularly came out of their depressions, an interesting and puzzling fact. They decided to see if *deliberately* keeping a depressed patient awake would relieve depression. It did. Thus was born the crucial wake component of triple chronotherapy. Why does this work?

Wehr and I independently arrived at the conclusion that mania, the opposite of depression, is an emergency response. During mania a person has super energy and no felt need for food or sleep. During emergencies, people often go without sleep, and deliberately depriving depressed patients of sleep fools the body that there is an emergency, hence triggering it to revive from its deactivation. This is part of the EOBD-R theory (Sherman, 2012), and it explains why wake therapy works. However, it raises a question: Does everyone have the capacity to switch from depression into activation with loss of sleep, or only those with bipolar heredity? Triple chronotherapy is being offered as a specialty at Chicago Psychiatry Associates, but it can be found elsewhere.

Chronobiology also underlies dark therapy, which calms mania. The patient is kept in the dark, signaling the body that it's winter, hence moving it to deactivation from its extreme state of super energy. The original research on the use of darkness to calm mania, also done at NIMH, required the patient to stay in total darkness for fourteen hours at night, gradually reduced to ten hours (Wehr et al., 1998). However, patients in a general psychiatric practice balked at this interference in their life style. As a result, Phelps (2008) introduced amber tinted sun glasses that filter out the most activating form of light, blue light. The glasses are worn part of the time instead of remaining in total darkness, which seems to work (Henriksen et al., 2016). Dark therapy is also part of my own self-prescribed program; I have successfully used a regular routine of seven to eight hours of continuous darkness in sleep or rest during the night to prevent mood swings. Long periods of lying in the dark can be boring or a time for distressing thoughts. This I've avoided by listening to recorded lectures, non-emotional material, which is, nonetheless, of interest.

More discussion and detail about therapies for depression (and bipolar disorder), BLT, and triple chronotherapy can be found in an online publication *Depression and Bipolar Disorder: Evidence-Based Natural Treatments and a New Theory* (Sherman, 2015). Also, consult the EOBD articles for a much better understanding of the theory underlying these treatments (Sherman, 2001; 2012).

In terms of my own bipolar illness, it started with a depression beginning in 1984 which was when I started the medications. During the period of Mauston's trial and their harassment of me, I was mostly okay. However, after only two years, I began having physical ailments caused by lithium: pervasive muscle pain and peripheral neuropathy, manifested by numbness in the right foot. These symptoms should have been recognized as side effects of lithium, but Dr. Benedict, and a neurologist he sent me to, incorrectly assured me that they weren't. Dr. Benedict and my psychiatrist strongly urged me to stay on lithium. It was emphasized to me that professionals were especially hard to treat because they second-guess their doctors, and I promised them that I would leave my treatment to them; unfortunately, I kept my promise. These side effects didn't go away until fourteen years later when I stopped the psychiatric medications. Meanwhile, I suffered, and I wasted time and money on ineffectual treatments for the side effects. These included massage, physical therapy, and the services of a chiropractor, who turned out to be a dangerous fraud.

The first sign of my major depression began in January the morning after I returned to Wisconsin from a Florida vacation. I wept uncontrollably for about four hours, even though I wasn't depressed or upset about anything. The crying was apparently a physiological response. The episode baffled me. It had never happened before and has never happened since. (However, it reminded me that I had once incongruously burst into tears after childbirth, a phenomenon known as Baby Blues. However, that was a brief minute, not four hours.)

I felt more or less normal for a while, and then I began to develop symptoms of major depression: early awakening, difficulty sleeping, loss of appetite, slowing, and impairments in concentration and sense of time. I realized something was wrong when I spent an entire morning reading two newspapers without remembering any of what I'd read. These symptoms used to be diagnosed as a melancholic depression to acknowledge that it is a different type of depression from the SAD typical for younger women. (I was 50.) An anomalous feature of major depression is that the diagnosis doesn't necessarily include the emotion of feeling sad, inadequate, or rejected. My depression originally was more of a shutdown such as William Styron (1990) described in his book, *Darkness Visible.*

The onset of the illness was marked by a nightmare in which I dreamed that I existed in a world totally devoid of light. The dream may have marked my neurophysiological switch into deep depression, which is known to occur during the night.

My brother and sister had already fallen ill with bipolar disorder, and the knowledge that a great-aunt had been put in a mental hospital in late life helped me understand what was happening, but I was surprised that I didn't feel "depressed." I certainly wasn't suicidal. On the contrary, I was dedicated to my self-preservation. I desperately wanted to be well. I feared losing my husband, my job, and my friends, and in the end, except for a few friends, I lost them all.

In retrospect, three factors brought on the depression: genetic vulnerability, a shift in neurophysiology related to menopause, and the winter season, especially the sharp contrast between the intensity of light in Florida and Wisconsin. Perhaps if I'd had hormone replacement therapy, or if I had known to use light therapy, I would have been okay, but that's not what happened. Although menopause isn't a mental health hazard for most women, it is for women with bipolar heritage, who are also more vulnerable to PMS and postpartum depression. I asked my gynecologist about hormone replacement therapy, but at that time the health risks were thought to be substantial, and he wouldn't prescribe it.

I learned about light therapy later when I led a depression support group for NAMI. A fellow member of the group was a patient of Dr. Wanda Bincer, whom I had replaced at Madison Associates, and who also had bipolar disorder. This was in the early days of light therapy, and Wanda had ferreted out the information from the psychiatric research literature and used light therapy herself. I added light therapy to my treatment repertoire, but, unfortunately, my psychiatrist also advised me to continue the medications, which unbeknownst to me were already having increasingly severe adverse effects: emotional dulling and cognitive impairment in addition to pervasive muscle pain and peripheral neuropathy.

There were times when my mood seemed normal, and I wanted to discontinue the drugs, but my doctors insisted that I stay on the medications. Like many another American, I devoutly believed in the pharmaceutical solution, and I did what my doctors told me to do. As a result, I stayed on the lithium and antidepressants. I rarely felt really well, but I was more or less functional and settled for this existence.

The private practice group where I had been working began to harass me in multiple ways, and when I resigned in 1990, I said that I was leaving in order to write, a kind of polite way to accept the inevitable. I did write; I wrote an entire women's self-help book that was too mediocre to publish, and I wrote a book about my experiences with patients but decided not to publish it. I took up hobbies: duplicate bridge and water color painting. To my surprise, I had more artistic ability than before my illness and produced some creditable paintings. Clifford Beers (1908/1981) and Winston Churchill, who both suffered from bipolar disorder, also took up painting. Perhaps at such times the right side of the brain works better than the left.

However, during the 1990s my health continued to deteriorate. Although I saw a psychiatrist weekly, no notice was taken of the mounting adverse effects of the psychiatric drugs. I was grossly overweight, diabetic, and unattractive. I had numbness in my right foot, and I continued to ache all over. I was often maddeningly slow. I couldn't think well, and my memory was failing. I had lost my husband's respect and my place in his heart, and though I was frightened, I struck out on my own. The divorce was final in 1995. After the divorce, I lost thirty pounds, got my diabetes in control, and functioned somewhat better.

During this time, I did volunteer work for NAMI and served on its Dane County board. Harriet Shetler asked me to review Goodwin and Jamison's book, *Manic Depressive Illness* (1990), for a NAMI publication. The book ignited my interest in figuring out the causes of bipolar disorder (the later name for manic depression); this was a fateful decision that saved my life. My routine became regular trips to the University of Wisconsin libraries where I looked up articles and books about bipolar disorder. Despite cognitive impairment, I systematically reviewed the literature, taking notes, and photocopying hundreds of articles that I took home and read.

I already knew a lot about bipolar disorder from my personal and professional experiences. My first encounter with major depression had made a deep impression. As a student, I had been told to interview a sixty-year-old woman who was sitting, slumped in a chair in the hospital's locked ward. She hardly looked alive, but she was neither dead nor asleep. I got her attention, and she raised her head. I introduced myself and asked, "How are you feeling today?" After what seemed an eternity, she replied with a single word, "Depressed." No further interview was possible, but I'd been given a dramatic demonstration of the power of major depression. This woman's thinking and activity level were severely slowed. Left on her own, she might die of starvation because she had neither appetite nor the desire to initiate activity. These are classic symptoms of extreme major depression, and they have been consistently reported as far back as the ancient Greeks and the Old Testament.

In the case of bipolar disorder, making the correct diagnosis is both difficult and important. Even a depressed patient such as I described may be misdiagnosed, for example, as Alzheimer's disease. It happens. Psychodiagnosis had been one of my specialties. When I examined a patient, I started with a thorough diagnostic interview as I'd been taught by my mentors in Minneapolis who correctly understood the importance of heredity in the etiology of mental illness. The diagnostic interview included an inquiry into mental illnesses in the family, extending to aunts, uncles, grandparents, and cousins.

The purpose of the diagnostic interview is not only to gather facts, but also to evaluate the manner and demeanor of the patient—speed of response, vocabulary, eye contact, memory, mental organization—details that give clues about the underlying disorder. For example, while the speech of a depressed person is typically soft, halting, and slow, often with negative mental content, the speech of a hypomanic person flows on and on in a spirited manner, usually reflecting positive emotions, though irritability can also occur.

Mania is yet another matter. I almost never was called upon to interview a manic patient. The wild, self-aggrandizing speech and out-of-bounds behavior of manic patients (e.g. overspending, sexual indiscretions, verbal and physical conflicts, speeding, substance abuse) usually lands them in a locked setting within a week of the onset of mania. In contrast, because of the quiet, retiring nature of their symptoms, depressed individuals may not come to medical attention for months. Individuals in a manic state are impulsive, self-confident to an extreme, overactive, and have no felt need for food or sleep. They're often amusing, but they may be delusional, paranoid, and violent.

Here is an example of manic behavior that I observed in a rural Wisconsin courtroom. The patient was to be involuntarily committed and had insisted on a jury trial, which was unusual but within his rights. During the proceedings, this sixty-year-old farmer gaily skipped around the court room singing. This ability to make people laugh is typical of the manic state, and we all tried not to laugh. It certainly wasn't funny to the beleaguered family. They desperately wanted to see him locked up before he gave away the farm, which was an actual problem. (During a previous manic episode, he'd ordered a Cadillac while on the locked ward of Mendota State Hospital.) His behavior and moods were quixotic. When I first met him for the pretrial examination, he shook my hand with an excruciatingly painful squeeze. Then, he quickly kissed me on the cheek. This kind of impulsive, exuberant, outgoing behavior is also typical of mania.

Despite the dysfunction of manic and depressive extremes, there are positive characteristics associated with bipolar disorder: They're better educated and disproportionately found at the upper socioeconomic level of society. Many great leaders have had bipolar disorder. Among them are Alexander Hamilton, Abraham Lincoln, William Tecumseh Sherman, Teddy Roosevelt, and Winston Churchill (Ghaemi, 2011; Shenk, 2005). None of these men was psychotic, delusional, or oblivious to the advice of others. Aside from their energy, creativity, and charisma, they were honest, broadly knowledgeable, personally brave, and dedicated to the welfare of their nations.

Studies have also shown a positive correlation between bipolar disorder and creativity. Many outstanding poets, writers, artists, and composers have had bipolar disorder. Among them are Ezra Pound, F. Scott Fitzgerald, Sylvia Plath, Ernest Hemingway, Rachmaninoff, and Tchaikovsky (Jamison, 1993). Until recently, perhaps the most famous living American with bipolar disorder is Ted Turner, founder of CNN.

Bipolar disorder is complex, and not easy for the public to understand. For example, a person can be diagnosed with bipolar I disorder who shows only manic behavior, with no apparent history of a depressive episode, and hypomanic individuals can be tricky to evaluate. An expert on bipolar disorder, Dr. Ronald Fieve (2006), wrote a book on this subject in which he described the many such people he knew in New York City, including Donald J. Trump, whom he described as hypomanic. Such individuals can be charming, entertaining, and fun, as well as high achieving. However, individuals who are hypomanic can slip into mania, psychosis, delusions, and paranoia. When individuals have high status, their aberrant behavior may be overlooked. Their sexual indiscretions may be minimized as boys will be boys. Their financial disasters may be excused. After all, they made a lot of money, or so they claim. They may be seen as narcissistic, but megalomania is more descriptive. Their discourse jumps around in a word salad, but instead of recognizing this as a manic thought disorder, people may wonder if they have dementia. They repeatedly make wild, grandiose, untrue statements and may be described as pathological liars. True, but it's more serious than that; some of these statements represent delusions and some are paranoid. Sleeping only three hours a night may be admired as showing a hard-working energetic person, but it's actually a symptom of mania, a serious mental illness. Manic behavior is judged psychotic not only when the individual is delusional or paranoid, but also when behaviors are self-defeating. A person in a manic psychosis can be his own worst enemy. It can truly be a case of the emperor has no clothes.

In dealing with manic individuals, one of the problems is that they are infectiously amusing, and while we laugh, we forget that we're dealing with a mad man. It's important to understand that it's impossible to reason with manic individuals. Moreover, when cornered, at a point when we're prepared to dismiss them as fools, individuals in a manic state may surprise us by taking shrewdly effective, drastic action in reckless disregard for the welfare of others.

Bipolar disorder is an intriguing puzzle. How can a person keep up a routine of outrageous, but often amusing, behavior, with an uncanny ability to dominate the spotlight? How can an individual at one time be deeply depressed and at another, wildly self-confident and manic? This switch is one of the most amazing aspects of bipolar disorder. An individual in a short period of time can change from a stone-like depression into a mania. I had observed this first-hand at the Minneapolis VA Hospital. I had known the phenomenon existed, but it was awesome in action. How could this happen?

At the time, it was a mystery. Now, we know that neurochemical changes are responsible for such switches. Since the 1950s, we've learned that disturbances of neurochemistry are fundamental to bipolar disorder. However, as mentioned before, the brain's neurochemistry is delicately balanced with poorly understood neurochemical interactions, feedback systems, and compensatory mechanisms. For example, when depressed the brain may be low in serotonin, and when manic the brain may be high in dopamine, but it's not a simple matter to correct these states by adding chemicals to the brain.

Dopamine, which is involved in hypomania and mania, has as one of its functions the reward of accomplishment and problem solving. That sense of satisfaction when something is accomplished? That's the effect of dopamine. The dopamine neurochemical reward system builds into the human brain incentives for figuring things out, which may account for the link between creativity, achievement, and bipolar disorder. Achievement and creative activity can become almost addictive in bipolar individuals, and this characteristic is among the diagnostic criteria for hypomania and mania, described as "preoccupation with goal-directed activities." Unfortunately, the same processes that are linked to positive preoccupations with useful thinking and activities may also be involved in addictions, such as gambling and substance abuse.

In a sense, major depression and bipolar disorder reflect chemical disturbances of the brain, just as drunkenness can be thought of as a chemical disturbance of the brain caused by alcohol. However, in the case of major depression and bipolar disorder, the chemical disturbance is caused by natural changes in the brain's neurochemistry. What causes these changes?

In my search to discover the causes of bipolar disorder, I developed the Evolutionary Origin of Bipolar Disorder (EOBD) theory (Sherman, 2001), and EOBD-R, a revised version (2012). As I researched, I remembered the work of an early twentieth-century psychiatrist, Ernst Kretschmer, whose theory was so completely forgotten that Goodwin and Jamison (1990) didn't mention it in their voluminous text on bipolar disorder. Kretschmer observed that individuals with bipolar disorder tend to have a body build characterized by a thick trunk and a big head on a short, thick neck, with a tendency for fat to collect on the trunk and belly. The face was often unusually red. Evidence of this type of compact build was demonstrated by the crual index, the length of the thigh bone being longer compared to the lower leg. Kretschmer's theory intrigued me because, among my patients and individuals I knew with bipolar disorder, I could see for myself that there was a correlation with body build.

Was Kretschmer's theory valid? If so, what did it mean? I was curious and sought out every English-language publication on the topic and carefully studied the material. The conclusion of my own review agreed with the opinions of two of the top statisticians of the 20th century: Ann Anastasi and Hans Eysenck. Although they were critical of some of the research, they concluded that Kretschmer was correct; the build of individuals with bipolar I disorder is more compact than other people. A recent Hungarian study confirmed once more the validity of this relationship (Tóth et al., 2003).

Like the symptoms of bipolar disorder, this correlation became part of the puzzle. How could it be explained? I continued to work and to think. In the summer of 1996, I went to a three-day seminar in northern Wisconsin conducted by Dr. Frederick Goodwin. In 1997, I attended the Second International Conference on Bipolar Disorder held in Pittsburgh. Researchers were redoubling their efforts to find the genes responsible for bipolar disorder, and many of us thought that once the genes were found, effective treatment would soon be forthcoming. However, finding the genes proved to be difficult, and the genetic mechanisms are more complex than had been imagined.

The decisive step in my odyssey of discovery was serendipitous. I happened on an announcement of an archaeological tour of Ireland and decided to go. Western Ireland is known as an area with an increased incidence of schizophrenia. Why is this? I thought I might learn something useful, and I did, in an unexpected way. We were touring the National Museum of Ireland in Dublin, and I took advantage of the visit to talk to one of the curators. I was still thinking about what type of people had a thick, compact build, and I asked the curator about it. Without hesitation, he replied, "Neanderthal."

Bingo. This set my thinking off in a new direction. It wasn't long before I figured out that the thick, compact build of Neanderthal represents a cold-adapted physique that conserves heat as opposed to a slender, linear build that dissipates heat. I combined this information with research showing that light elevates mood and its absence depresses it. Moreover, the depressions of the subjects in the research that originally demonstrated SAD were individuals with (bipolar) major depression, not minor depressive mood swings (Rosenthal et al., 1987).

I had collected an array of facts, and it became a matter of connecting the dots. It seemed to me that bipolar disorder may have evolved among the Neanderthal as an adaptation to the severe Ice Age winters. Major depression could be seen as a kind of hibernation-like state while the speeded behaviors of hypomania allowed Neanderthal to catch up with all that was left undone during the bad weather. My research on the Ice Age uncovered the fact that sometimes there were only two to three months of reliable, fair weather, so this ancient people had to work fast. They had a lot to get done—courting, visiting, travel, and preparing for the next winter. The symptoms of bipolar disorder fit this scenario, even some that had totally puzzled me. For example, the lack of initiative, social withdrawal, and poor concentration of depression now made sense. This state isn't sadness; it's a partial shutdown. The tendency to inertia during major depression would aid the survival of a people who had to hole up together through a long winter. People who stirred things up would cause social conflict. The social withdrawal, lack of sexual interest, and lack of initiative characteristic of depression would be adaptive during this period, facilitating survival.

How about this question: If everyone was depressed during the winter, how would they cope with an emergency? What if there was a rock fall, a flood from a sudden thaw, a problem birth, or an enemy attack? How could people manage? It was then that I realized the significance of that ability to change from depression to mania: It can be seen as a further adaptation evolved to cope with emergencies. For a small group during the

Ice Ages, the charged-up self-confidence and manic ability to go without felt need for food or sleep helped people respond to emergencies. Mania is often thought of as a psychosis, but this isn't necessarily the case, and nonpsychotic mania is still adaptive during modern emergency situations. (Mania is judged to be psychotic when there is evidence of delusions and paranoid thinking, or/and when behaviors are damaging to the person, rather than helpful.)

It was at this juncture that Wehr and I began an email correspondence about mania. I ventured the opinion that mania is an emergency response, and I was pleased to find that he agreed with me though he'd arrived at the same conclusion by a different line of reasoning. He had observed that manic reactions are associated with sleep loss, and, because sleep loss is correlated with emergencies, he concluded that manic reactions are hardwired to sleep loss and are an emergency response. Now, as already discussed, sleep deprivation is being used in triple chronotherapy to quickly bring patients out of deep depressions without the use of drugs.

An apparent contradiction to the idea that bipolar disorder evolved as an adaptation is its association with a high rate of suicide, which is hardly adaptive. However, it's important to remember that seasonal changes in light aren't the only source of depression. As mentioned earlier, losses, social defeat, and rejection are universal causes of depression. Suicide is a complication of bipolar disorder, not intrinsic to the disorder itself. Although bipolar disorder was adaptive for Neanderthal during the Ice Ages, it isn't so adaptive today. Now, ironically, the symptoms of bipolar disorder often *lead to* social dysfunction which results in the experiences of loss, social defeat, and rejection that are the breeding ground of the hopelessness and despair associated with suicide.

The idea that bipolar disorder evolved as a climatic adaptation among Neanderthal was radically new, and I didn't want to foist an incorrect, ill-considered theory on the public. I knew little about paleoanthropology so I began to educate myself. I enrolled in a course on human evolution at the University of Wisconsin and sought out experts in paleoanthropology for their opinions. My instructor in human evolution, graduate student Chris Haller, was an advocate of Professor Milford Wolpoff's multi-regionalist school of paleoanthropology. They correctly thought that Neanderthal had interbred with other humans and that some modern humans have Neanderthal traits.

A contrary opinion was expressed by paleoanthropologist Chris Stringer who was a vehement opponent of the multi-regionalist view. Stringer thought that Neanderthals were a different and inferior species and that their physical appearance was so different from that of anatomically modern humans that the latter wouldn't mate with them. As a keen student of human nature, this idea struck me as laughable. Indeed, paleogeneticist Svante Pääbo of the Max Planck Institute in Germany could hardly suppress a smile when discussing Stringer's views on this topic during a television interview. (Stringer has since changed his views.)

Since there is overwhelming evidence that bipolar disorder is inherited, the genes had to come from somewhere. As I studied the problem, the idea that the genes descended from Neanderthal made more and more sense. Except for its novelty, I could find no evidence or reason to contradict the idea. It seems to me like the long-delayed "discovery" that all the world's continents had once been joined. If you look at the globe and mentally move the continents together, they fit. They were once one. It was obvious. In a similar manner, it seemed to me that the evolutionary origin of bipolar disorder was also obvious. What else accounted for the inertia of major depression? Why was it linked to low light conditions? Why did it occur more in winter than in summer? Why is major depression at least twice as common in women? The frequent abuse of women takes a toll (Thurston et al., 2118), but there is more to the story.

Having served as a consultant to the American Psychological Association's National Task Force on Women and Depression in 1987, I was familiar with the literature on sex-related differences in depression. As I thought through the question, I realized that during the Ice Ages Neanderthals faced severe survival threats during the winters. The excess incidence of modern-day winter depression (and overeating) in women could be explained by the fact that women, more than men, needed to have enough fat for reproductive purposes. Unless the body has a certain level of fat, there will be no menstruation, no ovulation, no conceptions, no pregnancies, no lactation, and no children. The buildup of fat reserves in women and their winter depressive shutdown helped preserve fat resources needed for reproduction. A similar idea has recently been expressed (Levitan et al., 2006). Thus, the evolutionary theory of bipolar disorder explains why SAD, bipolar II disorder, and major depression occur much more often in adult women than men though there is no difference between boys and girls in frequency of depression.

A theory's ability to explain known facts enhances its credibility. I wondered whether a sex difference in hibernation behaviors occurs across species. It does. Female bears hibernate more than males. Hibernation occurs in every mammalian order, and females typically hibernate more than males. As the pieces of the puzzle fell into place, I began preparing a scientific article presenting this new theory of the evolutionary origin of bipolar disorder.

Unfortunately, during this time, the accumulated effects of the psychiatric drugs were catching up with me, and I learned what it's like to be an impaired mentally ill person on my own. I was often taken advantage of, and I shudder to think what happens to other mentally ill individuals with less knowledge and even fewer resources.

From the beginning, I tried to hide the severity of my symptoms from everyone, including my family. I never thought consciously about this decision. Instead, I instinctively behaved like the lame wildebeest that moves to the center of the herd to hide its handicap from predators. People with mental illnesses are stigmatized and rejected, a fact I quickly learned. I always had a friendly chat with my local pharmacist when I brought in prescriptions to be filled, but not after he saw that first prescription for lithium. Tom physically recoiled, like he'd fired off a shotgun; our relationship was never the same.

By the late 1990s, there were periods when I couldn't think straight. I knew I was out of it, but I wasn't psychotic. In retrospect, I realize that I was cognitively impaired by lithium, but I didn't know that the lithium was doing this to me. At the time, I thought I was suffering from the effects of depression. I guess my health care providers thought so too. The prevailing belief among professionals was (is?) that individuals with bipolar disorder should stay on their medications, and I did. I trusted my doctors and health care providers to protect me from adverse medication effects, and I did everything they asked me to do. Every month, I dutifully had my blood drawn so the lithium level could be checked. I took the pills as instructed, but my health care providers let me down in a big, big, way. I was scared. Was I going to end my life in an institution like my great-aunt? I was an easy mark for any predator that happened along. What is shocking is how many of these predators were professionals. In addition to Dr. Benedict, here are some other examples.

My first psychiatrist violated medical ethics in two ways which were damaging to me: She talked to my estranged husband without my permission, and she put me into a drug trial without my knowledge or informed consent. Psychiatrists who recruited a sufficient number of patients for the medication trial were entitled to a free cruise. She got the cruise. The drug had horrible effects on me. I broke out in hives; my mouth swelled, and I had trouble walking and speaking. Her general attitude toward me and her patients was exemplified in a comment she made about another chronically ill patient, referring to her as a "cash cow."

And then there was my chiropractor. She saw me once a week to treat muscle pains, which, unfortunately, weren't amenable to treatment since they are a common, adverse effect of lithium. She had a variety of quack procedures like a phony apparatus to diagnose food allergies, but it was her fraudulent vitamin business that nearly did me in. She talked me into getting a blood test that would "scientifically" show if I had any vitamin deficiencies. If I did, she'd give me the vitamin, and we'd retest my blood to see if my condition "normalized." The blood sample was taken at a legitimate laboratory and sent off to be analyzed. When the results came back, she solemnly studied them and falsely declared that I needed vitamin B6, which she sold me along with other vitamins. Unfortunately, the megadose of vitamin B6 she recommended severely worsened my undiagnosed Charcot-Marie-Tooth disease and contributed to the health crisis that landed me in the hospital. I later showed the lab results to my internist who told me I never had a vitamin B6 deficiency. The whole thing was a scam.

I also had trouble with financial advisers. One highly recommended adviser charged me $1,400 for about an hour of advice I couldn't use. When I complained about the excessive fee, she announced that if I didn't pay up, she wouldn't return my financial records, which were my only copies.

As my condition worsened, I realized that I might become incapable of making decisions for myself. I couldn't remember any phone number beyond my own; had trouble checking bills and figuring tips; couldn't keep track of my keys; couldn't remember where I parked the car. The many highly paid professionals that I regularly saw performed with indifference, neglect, or incompetence in failing to diagnose the fact that I was suffering from adverse effects of lithium. I expressed concern to one of my psychiatrists about my memory. Instead of considering whether this was an adverse effect of medications, she suggested psychological testing for Alzheimer's disease, which only added to my anxiety. I myself had examined the intellectual functioning of hundreds of people, and at that time Alzheimer's disease could only be definitively diagnosed upon autopsy. I was concerned about a false diagnosis of Alzheimer's disease, which could contribute to a judicial decision that I was mentally incompetent, leading to involuntary commitment to a mental institution, perhaps for life.

What if I became manic? I'd never been manic. I thought about that. During a manic episode, some individuals spend money like it's going out of style and end up with legal and financial problems. After breast surgery for cancer, the mother of a friend became manic. After Margaret left for work, her mother, an elderly, pious Catholic widow, ordered a zillion telephones and piled their belongings together in the middle of the living room floor, planning to sell them. When Margaret came home from work, her mother announced that she wanted to go dancing. After hospitalization, she fell into deep depression.

Another example is the patient who told me that during a manic episode she remembered leaving Madison, and when her sanity returned, she was living with a man in Denver and didn't know how she got there. This kind of flight during a manic episode isn't uncommon. I knew of another woman who suddenly took off and was later found wandering the streets of Los Angeles, half clothed.

Inappropriate or atypical sexual behavior is another danger. One patient, who'd previously had a major depression, told me that, although she was engaged to be married, she struck up a conversation with an attractive stranger and took him home to bed with her. The next day she was shocked and dismayed by what she'd done. She was frightened that she was losing control of herself and afraid that such behavior would jeopardize her forthcoming marriage. The psychiatrist who had treated her major depression had failed to explain that she was also at risk for mania.

The possibilities frightened me, and I thought I would try to anticipate the problem. I had a fine lawyer that I trusted, and I talked to him about it. He agreed to take power of attorney if I became seriously ill, but when the time came, he was no help.

Chapter 10

Into the Maelstrom

During the winter of 1998-99, I developed new symptoms including a severe loss of strength and energy. Both my lower arms and fingers became so emaciated that I couldn't keep my watch on my wrist or rings on my fingers. I developed weird pains and tingly feelings in my hands, and they lost strength. I tried to replace a battery in my radio, but I couldn't do it. I kept trying and trying; I didn't realize that the problem was that I didn't have the strength to push back the spring. It was frustrating; I couldn't figure out what was wrong. I couldn't open bottles. I couldn't even replace a roll of toilet paper. When I pushed the button on the elevator, nothing happened—I hadn't pushed hard enough. It was scary and mystifying.

In spite of these difficulties, I was dividing my time between playing duplicate bridge in the afternoons and working on my theory of the evolutionary origin of bipolar disorder in the mornings. Like a hound on a scent, I was on the track of figuring out bipolar disorder's origin and cause.

But then I was date raped. This was a big, incredibly strong man who easily overpowered me. I later heard that he bragged of "having" twenty women since his arrival in the city, so I wasn't his only victim. Unfortunately, he was a good-looking, intelligent man who was well liked in my social circle. I wasn't hurt and hoped to ignore the incident, but, during a stressful moment, I confided in a close friend who betrayed my confidence. Word got around, and the rapist loudly declared his innocence. Before long, people divided into those defending the rapist and those defending me. Sound familiar? Blaming and defaming the victim and crass denials of guilt have been common as the #MeToo movement has unfolded. I had no proof of a rape; it was a "he said-she said" situation, which is why I had wanted to keep it quiet. I was well aware of the social advantages given high-status males.

The stress of the rape, which included gossip, hostility, and the deterioration of friendships, made my symptoms worse, including my cognitive function. It was difficult to get my bills paid, balance my check book, and take care of my taxes. Remembering appointments and getting places on time were serious problems. To keep myself functioning and amused, I continued to play duplicate bridge, put together puzzles, and read lots of books that were easy to read, yet interesting and amusing. I especially liked books that featured heroic males. I found it reassuring to read about strong, kind men. I reached out to the Rape Crisis Center, and they were a great help.

I struggled. Nonetheless, I continued to make progress on the research article I was preparing. Not all my intellectual abilities deserted me. I could still read and write. I wrote everything out first in longhand, but I had to make a lot of corrections for typos when the work went on the computer, and I had to make many revisions of the text. At one point my memory became impossible; when playing bridge, I couldn't even remember what was trump. I stopped playing for a while because I felt I was imposing on the others.

In my experience as a researcher, I had pioneered the idea that training could improve performance in spatial perception. "Hmm," I thought. "I wonder if I can improve my memory with intensive practice?" I had a computer program called *Counting* from the bridge expert Mike Lawrence, and I began to devote several hours a day to working with the program. In less than a month, my memory improved enough that I could return to the game, not that I functioned well, but I functioned well enough to get along. (Now, after years of no medications for bipolar disorder, I have nearly achieved the ranking in the American Contract Bridge League of Ruby Life Master.)

By the spring of 1999, it was painful for me to hold a pen in order to write; my temperature control went haywire, and I was abnormally cold. I feared that whatever was wrong with me might make it impossible for me to finish the article on EOBD, and I intensified my efforts. New research published in the *British Journal of Medical Psychology* excited my interest. Dr. Daniel Wilson (1998) had published an article showing that bipolar disorder has the medical epidemiology of an adaptation. In other words, he showed that bipolar disorder is too common to be the result of an aberrant gene, which supported my view that bipolar disorder originated as an adaptation. I was ecstatic to find a colleague who agreed with me on this point and began an email correspondence with him.

By August of 1999, I was heading into a health crisis. In addition to my other symptoms, numbness developed in my other foot. Even so, I was heartened. My muscle pains had been dismissed, and my deteriorating memory went unnoticed. Perhaps here was an objective symptom that the doctors would pay attention to. I made an appointment with my internist, and she scheduled me for some neurological tests. Time went by. Finally, I had an electromyogram and a nerve conduction test. The technician doing the examination excused himself and returned with a neurologist who repeated part of the examination. Then the neurologist stood up and said, "You have Charcot-Marie-Tooth disease."

"What does that mean," I asked.

"Make an appointment to see me, and we'll discuss it then."
He turned and left the room. The first appointment turned out to
be three months later.

Strange symptoms continued to occur. Bright red eruptions
began appearing on my trunk. "Nothing to worry about," said
the doctor. "They're just a reaction to the sun."

This didn't make sense to me. I was hardly out in the sun.
"But how can the sun have this effect through my clothing?" I
asked.

"Oh, the sun can do that. It's nothing to worry about."

Hair was growing all over my face. I hated the hair, and my
eye lashes had grown in crooked—every which way. I asked
the doctor about it. Her reply: "It's not uncommon for women
to grow hair on the face as they grow older." (I actually had
parathyroid disease from the drugs.)

In vain, I talked to a pharmacist about whether these symptoms were from my medications. The man acted like I was crazy.
I crept away. Every day I tediously plucked hairs from my face
with a tweezers, but what could I do about my eye lashes? If I
pulled them out, they would never grow back. I agonized over
my increasingly deteriorating appearance. My face sagged with
a typical depressive demeanor. No lipstick could correct a down-
turned mouth neurologically programmed not to smile. I was
frustrated with my medical care. I had talked to physicians and
pharmacists to no avail.

I made another appointment with my internist, but meanwhile my symptoms drastically accelerated. The area around
my mouth began to feel numb and paralyzed. I started to stutter
and have trouble breathing. I was trying to stop smoking and
used Nicorette chewing gum. The more anxious I got, the more
Nicorette I chewed. It seemed obvious that the numbness around
my mouth might be caused by the Nicorette so I stopped the
gum, and it improved. However, I was profoundly unsettled and
began to fear for my life. What did all this mean? Perhaps it had
something to do with the Charcot-Marie-Tooth disease. I repeatedly called the neurologist's office to get an earlier appointment

to no avail. He wouldn't even talk to me. I was told to wait until my fixed appointment.

I finally rebelled. I had promised my doctors that I'd leave my treatment to them, but I no longer felt bound by that promise. I consulted a book published in 1992 entitled *Adverse Effects of Psychotropic Drugs,* edited by psychiatrists John M. Kane and Jeffrey A. Lieberman. It contained information easily available to my physicians if they'd only bothered to check. It was quickly obvious that I was suffering from a multitude of adverse medication effects. I stopped taking all my psychiatric medications.

I had lost confidence in the local medical system and decided that I should try to get an outside, independent opinion. I searched my mind for doctors that had especially impressed me, and I remembered a physician now practicing in Lancaster, Wisconsin, a town not far away. I'd been there a couple of times when I'd been an expert witness at a trial held in their beautiful courthouse.

I arrived at the clinic where this doctor was working and when I got into his office, I was relieved to see the same old distinguished, gray-haired doctor. I poured out my story and happened to mention the name of Dr. Benedict. "Oh, yes," he said, "I talked to him just last night. We're old friends."

I was shaken to the core. It was like a children's Halloween tale. He didn't examine me, but he said that he wanted to do a diagnostic test that involved injecting me with iodine to see how it went through my system. I told him that my mother had this test and nearly died from it. He was unaffected and uninterested in this information. "There's nothing to worry about," he said.

Numbly I went out to the desk and scheduled the test that was to occur in another nearby small town. I was severely rattled— so much so that I left my glasses and some other belongings behind. I was exhausted and went back to my motel. I decided that I was too weak and upset to drive back to Madison, but I needed a nightgown and more clothing if I was going to stay on for the test. I had noticed a women's clothing store up the street and decided to go there.

I fell into conversation with the sales clerk, explaining that I had come to Lancaster looking for medical help. The woman kept asking me questions that led me to describe my symptoms in detail, which included abnormal coldness. She told me that I needed to keep my core body warmer and recommended some sturdy cotton panties as well as other items, such as a bathrobe that I was to sleep in. Her practical advice and friendly concern were a balm to my fractured ego. I bought more and more clothing. Finally, we added up the bill, and she put the clothing in a shopping bag. I tried to pick it up to carry it back to the motel, but I could barely lift it. I was simply too weak.

"Well, I don't think I can carry this back to the motel. I'll have to go get my car and come back," I said.

"That's all right," she said. "I'll carry it for you."

"Oh, no," I said. "You can't leave work."

"It's okay," she said. She picked up the bag of clothing, and we walked back to the motel.

On the way she said, "You have Charcot-Marie-Tooth disease, don't you? My son has it."

Charcot-Marie-Tooth disease occurs in 1 in 2,500 people, and here in this small town I encountered a woman who knew about it. It was an amazing life-saving coincidence. She told me that she was going to visit her son the next day and that I should wait in the motel for her. She promised to bring me a magazine published by a Charcot-Marie-Tooth disease advocacy group that listed the medications that are contraindicated. She stressed that it was important that I wait for the material.

I waited alone in the motel room all the next day. Labor Day weekend was coming, and I had made plans with a friend who canceled at the last minute. Now I had no plans. I hated holidays alone. Mostly, however, I worried about the test I was supposed to have. How could I have forgotten that it was Dr. Benedict who referred me to this doctor in the first place? What sense did this diagnostic test make? Was this man trustworthy? Usually physicians perform some kind of examination, and when they recommend a test, they give a reason for it. He'd done none of these things. Why was he so cavalier about my mother's adverse reaction to iodine? Why was he no longer practicing in Madison? (I later learned that there had been a complaint against him to the Wisconsin Medical Examining Board, but they wouldn't release any details.)

I certainly wasn't thinking clearly. Rather than recognizing that I should look for another doctor, I began looking up lawyers in the telephone book. I was planning to make out my will in case the test killed me. Suddenly, a light went on. "What are you thinking, Julia? If you're this frightened the test will kill you, call up and cancel the test," and that's what I did.

Somehow, I managed to pass the time. Before I left Madison, I perceived that I might be on the brink of a health crisis, and I made several requests of my lawyer. Now I hoped that he would be a source of help. I had asked him to get my medical records and the names of internists I could consult. However, instead of doing what I asked, he sent me a formal, legal letter to the effect that he wasn't complying with my requests because he considered them irrational. He thought I needed a psychiatrist, not an internist. This was a severe $4,000 disappointment that helped precipitate my manic episode. I thought that the lawyer acted in good faith, and I later settled with him for half that amount. However, had he gotten my medical records as requested, my life would have been starkly different because they would have revealed that I had an excellent legal case against Dr. Benedict who had violated confidence, libeled me, and damaged my employment opportunities.

I called friends and family, but some of them were away and others were taken up with their own plans. I felt bereft, lonely, rejected, and angry. By mid-morning the next day, the material had been left for me at the front desk of the motel. I didn't even know this woman's name, and she didn't leave a note. I had the impression that she didn't want me to contact her. The woman at the desk had seemed frightened of me. I found myself suffused by a sense of power. This was strange, but gratifying. What was it? Did my eyes glitter? What makes eyes glitter? Eagerly I took the newsletter upstairs and looked through it. That's when I learned that both lithium and mega doses of vitamin B6 were contraindicated as well as nicotine, which I'd already figured out. Alcohol was on the list too, but that wasn't a problem for me. I had already stopped the nicotine and lithium; now I also stopped taking vitamin B6.

What to do next? There was nothing for me in Madison so I thought, "Why not take a trip?" I'd go on the road, pretend to be crazy, and write a book about my experience. So far, I hadn't done anything strange, but now I decided to leave some things behind to make room for my new purchases. I piled these items on top of the desk in what seemed to me an artistic, but bizarre order, so people at the motel would remember me. "What did she do that for?" they would ask.

People often told me, "Let your hair down—be carefree." I'd go on the road. I'd have fun. I'd look for medical help in Iowa City or at the Mayo clinic. With these contradictory ideas I set out on the road to Iowa and into the heart of mania. I got a late start and drove all day. I got to Iowa City and decided not to stop. I went on to Marengo, Iowa. By now I had developed the idea that I was being pursued by enemies who wanted to do a medical experiment on me. My motel room abutted a cornfield, and amidst the tall, healthy stalks of corn a cacophony of insects squeaked their happy sounds into the night. I found a cricket on the floor of my motel room and got down on my hands and knees to talk to it. I thought the whole experience was charming. "Didn't Buddha talk to a cricket?"

The next morning, I was up early and drove to a local café for breakfast. Huddled in the corner was a group of teenage boys whispering to each other, but I ignored them and had friendly conversations with the other early morning diners. We talked about how the country was going to the dogs and agreed that the world was a dangerous place. "You know there are satellites in the sky that can watch your every move," they said. It's ironic that their ideas struck me as a little paranoid, but the interchange was congenial and pleasant. I paid my bill and left the café. Having bypassed Iowa City, I decided to aim for the Mayo Clinic.

I don't remember my exact route. Probably, I drove west on Highway 6 and linked up with Interstate 80 just east of Des Moines, turning north on Interstate 35 toward Minnesota. When it was getting late, I started trying to find a motel. Friends had often laughed at me for my careful trip planning. "We just stop at the first motel we see when we're ready. If it's full, we go on to the next." Well, the motels were all full—so much for a carefree weekend of fun.

I knew I was treading on dangerous ground; loss of sleep can trigger a manic episode. But what could I do? As it grew dark and I still hadn't located a motel, I thought about pulling over to the side of the road, but that's illegal, and I also thought it was unsafe. Besides, surely I'd find a motel. On and on I drove. Finally, I pulled into a gigantic truck stop. The flashing lights burst upon me; noises from the huge trucks thundered in my ears. To me they seemed like dinosaurs tromping the earth. Boom! Boom! Boom! The lights and noises confused and frightened me. By now I was exhausted. I pulled up to a restaurant, went in, and ordered something to eat. I had seen a motel near the restaurant, and I thought I would stay there. I saw a couple policemen having coffee and stopped to talk to them. They warned me not to stay at the motel because it was full of prostitutes. Now what to do? They said there was another motel on the other side of the highway, but when I got into the car, I felt frightened and confused again, and I was uncertain how to get over there. In retrospect, a bunch of prostitutes were the least of my problems. However, I decided to drive on,

After a while I became aware that I was being followed. I drove faster; the car following me drove faster, and we chased down the highway at one hundred miles an hour. I wasn't overly frightened because I wasn't totally sure I was being followed. Anyway, it would be fun to pretend that it was like a movie car chase. Wasn't I supposed to be having fun? Quickly I engineered myself in front of some other cars where they couldn't follow.

I was so proud of myself, but then we were off again, and they were still on my tail. Finally, I reached the Minnesota border, and I heard a car honk. I looked behind. I had been followed; it was the boys from the café in Marengo. They waved me good-bye and did a U-turn to head back to Iowa. At the time I thought, "Oh, and here I'd been afraid. Wasn't it sweet of them to escort me to the border?" In retrospect, I wonder if they'd been looking for an opportunity to steal my sporty-looking car.

You may be wondering how I could so confidently drive at one hundred miles an hour, but that's what mania can do. I had never driven such speeds before, darting in and out of traffic. In my normal state of mind, I'd be petrified to drive like that, and I wouldn't grossly violate the speed limits. But then, it was just me, the night, and the mania. At some point I heard over the radio that a young woman was missing, and the authorities were looking for her. I decided that I had some valuable insights on this problem and called the emergency hotline number. They didn't seem to appreciate my help. Then I got the idea to test how authorities would handle a mentally ill person on the road, and I called again. They weren't interested and hung up. At intervals I called my lawyer's answering machine to record a running account of what was happening so that I'd have contemporaneous documentation for my book. He was supposed to save the tapes for me. He didn't.

I realized that I needed help; I searched my mind for people who could help me and remembered my colleague, Dr. Wilson. He was head of a psychiatric hospital in Kansas, and I thought he could give me some good advice. Somehow, I got through to the hospital, but he wasn't available. This was later a source of embarrassment to me, but he was wonderfully courteous about it.

In retrospect, I marvel that I made some of these phone calls on my cell phone while rocketing along the highway. This is hard to do, and something I would never normally do as a matter of principle, but on I drove through the night. However, it was all catching up with me. As it got light, I started looking for a motel. Again, they were full. It was the weekend of the Iowa-Nebraska football game. On the third try, I became desperate and begged the woman to let me rent a room, if for a couple hours. She was a hard-hearted one and finally gave me a room from 10 am to noon at an exorbitant price. Such a greedy woman was she that she awakened me at 11:30 to make sure that I'd be out by twelve. I hauled myself from bed, got back into the car, and drove on. Finally, I stopped at a motel that would give me a room—on the third floor. There was no elevator. I was worn out by the time I got me and my suitcase to the room. I went to sleep.

I awakened still in a manic state. The daughter of a friend of mine in NAMI had become mentally ill on the road and the incident had been badly handled. Now, in my feverish state of imagination, I thought that I could do a service by testing how authorities would handle a mental breakdown on the road. I called the police and asked them to rescue me because I was being pursued. I tried to make it look convincing. I set up the room as though I'd prepared for an escape through the open window. As a final bit of convincing drama, I opened my Swiss Army knife on the bed stand. That was a mistake. Pretense and reality swirled in happy confusion as I greeted the arrival of two uniformed policemen.

"Take me to Jesse Ventura," I said. I had formed the idea that the former wrestler, who was now governor of the state of Minnesota, was just the man to give shelter to a lady in distress.

The two policemen were great. They quickly sized up the situation and smoothly assured me that they'd take me to the governor's mansion. I was deliriously happy. They packed me up and I chattered away as we drove off in the squad car.

"Oh," they said as if it was some incidental police business, "We have to make a stop to talk to this doctor."

We stopped at a building and met with an Indian doctor in an easily accessible first floor room. I talked briefly to the doctor, who, in all likelihood, authorized them to take me to the hospital. When we left, I asked, "We're still going to the governor's mansion, aren't we?"

"Oh, yes," they said. "We're on our way."

I kept up a steady stream of happy chatter, apparently not noticing that we'd entered a hospital. Me and my belongings had been piled on a wheel chair and cart, and we were about to enter a ward.

Now I came to my senses. "This isn't the governor's mansion," I said. Then I noticed a note on top of the cart, which I grabbed. It said that I had threatened the officers with a knife.

"Wait a minute," I said, "I never threatened you with a knife." The two policemen looked at each other, shrugged, and one of them took the paper and crossed that off.

When I had worked with NAMI on the question of the advisability of involuntary medication, I had read that in the state of Minnesota the authorities sometimes lied in order to involuntarily hospitalize individuals they thought needed care. This was a crucial piece of information, more sobering than an "anti-psychotic." I went on alert. The legal situation was this: If the police hadn't scratched out the statement that I'd threatened them with a knife, I could legally have been involuntarily medicated and involuntarily committed to a state institution.

My return to reality saved me from the worst, but through the door I went and it locked behind me. I was now on a locked psychiatric ward in Owatonna, Minnesota. It was Labor Day weekend, but a psychiatrist appeared who took a thorough history and gave me a brief physical and neurological examination. He told me that I was mentally ill and that he wanted me to take medications—a sleeping pill and Depakote, a treatment for mania. I refused medications. My body was already in an uproar because of sixteen years of medications, and I wasn't going to take any more.

"A little muscle relaxant to help you sleep won't hurt you," the nurse coaxed. Her tone revived a long-buried childhood emotional memory: the coaxing tone the witch used when she tried to get Snow White to eat the poisoned apple. However, at a conscious level, I had an excellent reason to refuse the medication. I'd recently gone through withdrawal from a minor tranquilizer, muscle relaxant, Serax, that had been prescribed for sleep, and I didn't want to do it again. Withdrawal from the minimum 15 mg nightly dose of Serax had resulted in several nights of frequent awakenings all night long. No thanks.

I spent that night on the locked ward in Owatonna, but the next day when I refused medications, the doctor said that I had to leave. He was annoyed that I didn't accept medication and said he needed the bed for patients who would cooperate with the treatments he offered. This seemed reasonable to me, but what was I supposed to do? Where was my car? They'd taken it upon themselves to bring me here and lock me up, and now they washed their hands of me. However, I was far more focused on getting out of this situation than expressing my opinions.

I called the policemen who had brought me to the hospital and asked them to come to pick me up. They wouldn't or couldn't. They did tell me that I could take a bus from Owatonna to where my car was. The nurses gave me a black garbage bag for my belongings and told me to go outside. I was too weak to carry the bag and dragged it behind me. I soon found that there were several of us—derelicts. The others were friendly and clued me in on what was going to happen. The bus drove us to a motel where the owner, an Indian, booked me into a room. When I was leaving the hospital, no one asked me if I had money to pay for a room. What happens to people without money? The motel room was disconcerting because it had a long, uncovered window across the wall to the hallway. I had no privacy. Was this a special observation room for people discharged from the psychiatric unit? I can't think of any other explanation. Possibly a little industry had grown up around dealing with people ejected from the hospital.

I had the whole day before me. What to do? I was out of cash. The first order of business would be to see if I could get a cash advance on my credit card. Owatonna was a pretty little place with a traditional town square. Across from the square was a bank, and that's where I headed. As I walked into the bank, I was amazed. Was I hallucinating? It was like stepping into a glade in a primordial forest: Greenish light magically suffused the room in a symphony of soft, chiming colors, descending from the stained-glass windows. I was dumb-struck. How could this be? I soon learned that, improbable as it seemed, it was real. The National Farmer's Bank of Owatonna, Minnesota, is a National Historic Landmark. It is a masterpiece of the great American architect Louis Sullivan. He'd been a mentor of Frank Lloyd Wright. It was he who coined the phrase, "Form ever follows function, and this is the law," meaning that buildings should grow organically to fulfill their functions, like trees. I gathered my thoughts and negotiated a much-needed advance on my credit card.

I had half-way wanted to become manic and psychotic because the psychologist part of me was curious. "What was it like?" Well, I got a bit more than I bargained for, but I learned something important about mania: Crazy could quickly shift to reality in the interests of self-preservation. When confronted with the door to a locked psychiatric ward, my mania had been replaced by realistic, shrewd, self-controlled behavior, reflecting an amazing shift in brain neurophysiology. I'd heard policemen experienced in dealing with psychiatric emergencies comment on such behavior shifts, but it was awesome to experience it first-hand. Moreover, despite my poor reality contact, its end result was a shrewd, stumbling access to the Mayo facility, one of the world's finest. It brings to mind sayings like, "Crazy like a fox," and the remark in *Hamlet*, "Though this be madness, there is method in it."

The psychosis was precipitated by abrupt withdrawal from medications, sleep loss, and the sense of emergency engendered by my failure to find effective medical help. The paranoid form the psychosis took reflected years of harassment and abuse, and the recent trauma of the encounter with Dr. Benedict's buddy. The rape also played its role. Both Dr. Benedict and the rapist had stuck their hands in my vagina. "Does that feel good?" the rapist wanted to know. Shortly after his ballyhooed forcible entry into me, he deflated like a balloon. When he reached inside me, was he looking for his lost penis? In my psychotic state, I imagined he was in league with Dr. Benedict and his buddies and that he had implanted a bug inside me so I could be traced.

After my teenage experience with hearing voices when I was invited to take communion, I never had another auditory hallucination, and I never had visual hallucinations, with one exception. During the night of my flight out of Iowa, on a couple occasions, I saw small pyramids of rainbow colors arising from the pavement in front of me. Whee, wasn't I having fun. What else would I see?

Later I tried to learn more about hallucinations. Apparently, a vision can occur such as Banquo's ghost in *Macbeth*, but so far as I can tell, organized, continuing visual scenes do not occur. In that sense, perhaps the portrayals of John Nash's mental state in the movie, *A Beautiful Mind*, were a bit misleading since it seemed as though he hallucinated whole scenes. On the other hand, I've heard reports of people carrying on conversations with a hallucinated person, such as a loved one who has passed away. I'm curious about this, but I have no desire to become psychotic again to find out more.

I had a whole day in Owatonna before me. What to do? The court house was on another side of the square. My father had been fascinated by our family genealogy and had often talked about going through records in various court houses across the country. I thought this might be a good way to pass the time, and I made my way into the building and began searching for records of Charles and John Schultz, brothers of my maternal grand-father. I found some possibly relevant records, but the Schultz name is common in the upper mid-west, and I don't know if they were actually relatives. I spent several hours contentedly record-ing information. I was fine until closing time, and I tried to leave the building. I couldn't get out. At first I panicked, thinking that I was trapped inside, but it was only that I was too weak to push open the door.

I still didn't know how I was going to retrieve my car, which was miles away. I remembered an old boyfriend who told me that he had volunteered on a crisis line. Roger (pseudonym) was a piece of work. I called him a cowboy tom cat, which greatly amused him. Whatever his faults, he was a good-hearted, practical guy, and I felt confident he would know what to do. I called him and explained the situation. "Okay," he said, "you go to the Chinese restaurant across from the square, and I'll pick you up there."

I figured it'd be a while before he got there so I went to the square and sat down on a bench. There was no one else in the park. It was a pleasant evening, but I still had on my trusty full-length L. L. Bean travel coat that could double as a raincoat. I sat there quietly, waiting. Carefully, I watched as each car came around the square. I didn't want to miss him. Overhead, I could hear the geese honking. They stirred something deep within me that made me want to get on the move.

It was getting dark and a small group of teenagers materialized on another park bench. "Cuckoo," they sang out.

I thought that was really funny, and I called back, "Cuckoo."

Soon cuckoo calls were rollicking back and forth, and we were all laughing. Suddenly, however, I got worried. What if we attracted the attention of the authorities? What if they found an excuse to put me back in the hospital?

I got up and went over to the teenagers. "Hey," I said, "I just got out of the hospital. I'm afraid if they hear us yelling 'Cuckoo,' they'll come and get me and lock me up again." Their faces were sober; they understood me exactly and were sympathetic. They promised to be quiet.

I went back to my bench, but I felt unsafe and exposed, sitting there in the dark. Where was my friend? I decided that perhaps I'd missed him, and that he was waiting for me at the Chinese restaurant, so I walked over there. I didn't see him anywhere. I asked the owner if he'd seen him, told him that I was exhausted, and sank into a booth. The owner went off, and I heard some excited chatter in Chinese. He came back and told me that he would take me to my motel. He seemed to know right where to take me. I understood that my friend wasn't coming, but I wasn't upset. I was confident that, somehow, he would help me out, and he did. He contacted my family and friends in Madison who began mobilizing a rescue.

Meanwhile I wasn't getting any saner. I felt unsafe in the hotel room because of the uncovered window exposed to the hall. The bed was in the line of sight of the window, and I thought that I'd feel less exposed sleeping on the floor. There wasn't room for the mattress on the floor, so defying all logic, I decided I'd be safer in the hallway, and dragged my mattress out there. Exhausted by my efforts, I fell into a sound sleep. When I woke up, I worried, "Was this going to get me in trouble?" I decided I'd better get out of the motel fast. I don't know if the desk clerk was aware of my little room rearrangement, but he checked me out without incident.

I took a taxi back to the other hotel, settled my bill, retrieved my car, and set out for Rochester. I hadn't had much sleep, and I was exhausted. I stopped and got a two-liter bottle of diet Pepsi, the smallest they had. However, instead of giving me energy, I began to feel totally awful. I arrived in Rochester and checked into a motel. The woman behind the desk took one look at me and asked, "Are you all right?"

"No," I replied.

I must have looked dreadful because she next asked, "Do you want me to call an ambulance?"

I thought, "Great, this way I can get into Mayo." I replied in the affirmative, and I was soon speeding toward the hospital in an ambulance. Upon arrival, I was put into a wheel chair, wheeled into a waiting area, and soon questioned by medical personnel. Ever honest, I told them that I had bipolar disorder, but that I wanted to see a neurologist to confirm that I really had Charcot-Marie-Tooth disease. I fully expected to be placed on the neurology ward. I waited a long time, but I was happy to wait. At last, I'd get some answers. Surprise! Surprise! I was wheeled into a locked ward.

"Hey, wait a minute," I shouted.

The door closed behind me. Apparently, Mayo had picked up a report that I had signed out against medical advice (AMA) from the hospital in Owatonna, and it was decided that I should be held involuntarily. I knew that in a few days there would be a legal proceeding that would free me. I wasn't too worried. The Mayo facility has a fine reputation, and I was confident that they would deal with me in a fair and competent manner. I decided that I should try to make myself comfortable and await my chance to find out what was wrong with me.

I was put in a private room. Again, there was a large, uncovered window. I assumed this was so that I could be kept under observation, but I decided not to worry about it. There was an adjoining, large bathroom that was windowless and provided some privacy. It had a toilet and a shower head, but it was bare, with a tile floor and a drain in the center. It wasn't a homey setup. It conjured scary visions—a woman cowering on the floor being hosed down by an attendant. I bade these ideas be gone and resolved to accommodate myself to the situation.

The nursing staff was pleasant and friendly. The nurse offered, almost insisted, on washing my clothes for me. She did the laundry in machines inside the nursing station, but when she returned the clothes, items were missing. How could she lose them in her own nursing station? Surely, she could see that clothing was missing. During my research for NAMI on the issue of involuntary medication and hospitalization, I had learned that in Minnesota, the tactic of deliberately provoking patients to "lose it" had been used. I was wary, and my rational self came to the fore. I knew that I was under continual observation and that any sign of untoward behavior would be used against me. I didn't say anything about the missing clothing as I thought it might have been an effort to provoke me. The incident, however, dimmed my enthusiasm for the nursing staff, and I decided that it was prudent to stick to myself. I was polite, but I was through with the happy chatter. Faced with a serious challenge to my freedom, the psychosis went into almost total retreat.

I was extremely angry about the fact that, despite all the highly qualified physicians and psychiatrists I'd seen over the past sixteen years, none of them had recognized that I was suffering from severe adverse medication effects. However, I thought it best to keep these opinions to myself and not share them with other patients. I was leery of ticking off the medical staff. Also I didn't want to foist onto other patients my own dreadful experiences. Perhaps they would fare better.

I was again offered medications, and again I refused them. I was exhausted and fell asleep without any need for medications. During the next few days, I put into effect my knowledge of how to calm a manic episode: Avoid stimulation and stay in the dark. Except for meals, I stayed in my room in the dark, lying quietly on the bed, sleeping or meditating. I put myself into a meditation state using the deep breathing technique pioneered by Dr. Herbert Benson (1975) in his book, *The Relaxation Response.* (Paul Meehl had recommended it to me.) This worked well, and though it wasn't intended to induce sleep, I found that I could use it for that purpose. I generally woke up one or two times during the night, and I would get up. One of the nurses would greet me and help me get a snack. Then I'd get myself back to sleep with the meditation technique.

The ward was clean, orderly, quiet, and well run. The food was excellent. I had found that a high protein, low carbohydrate diet worked best for me, and I was allowed to order two meals and eat the protein, fruits, and veggies, leaving the carbohydrates. I correctly thought that I needed nutrition to rebuild my emaciated arms, hands, legs, and feet that had been adversely affected by the lithium, B6, nicotine, and other medications.

Near the end of my stay at Mayo, I was served a dinner with a piece of roast beef clearly displaying teeth marks where someone had taken a bite. The sight grossed me out, but again I schooled myself not to overreact and calmly turned it back, requesting another dinner. I thought it might be a setup. If they were trying to provoke me, I wasn't going to oblige them.

There was one therapy event during my stay: I was invited to a group therapy session. I saw no reason to refuse, but I still wanted to be careful not to annoy the staff by talking against medications. One of the women in the group had recently been raped. Naturally, I felt sorry for her and talked to her at some length about my own experience. Afterward she thanked me. She said that it helped her a good deal. I was surprised.

Every day the head psychiatrist came around to ask me if I would take medications. Each day when I refused, he told me that if I didn't take the medication, I would spend the rest of my life in a state institution. It irritated me that he confronted me each day with the same question; I finally asked him why he did that. He looked at me sympathetically and said, "I have to document that you continue to refuse medication." He was only doing his job.

My main doctor, a resident, was a Peruvian Indian. He may have been newly arrived in this country, at the start of his residency. His English was uncertain; he was expressionless and spoke little. My case might have gone better if I'd had a more experienced resident.

The doctors, nurses, and staff didn't approve of me because I was refusing medications, and they weren't helpful. I don't think any of them seriously considered that I had an excellent reason for refusing medications. Their unwillingness to take me seriously was frightening in itself. I subsequently learned that a patient with Charcot-Marie-Tooth disease had died of the antidepressant, Zoloft. He wanted to stop taking the drug, but his doctors insisted that he continue to take it. They were afraid that he would become depressed. He didn't become depressed; he died.

Because I was a "bad" patient, the staff on the ward wouldn't help me make phone calls. The only way to make a phone call was to use a pay phone inside a single phone booth on the ward. In order to make a phone call, I had to wait in line for the phone to be free, and then I had to use the phone card that I luckily had with me. I had to punch in—it seemed like twenty numbers all in the right order and in proper tempo. It was extremely challenging. I certainly was glad I had refused all medications. I needed to have every bit of brain power I could muster to mobilize help on my behalf.

My reality contact was still wobbly for the first day or two. One of the psychiatrists was extremely handicapped, and when I saw him come on the ward, with the grandiosity suitable of mania, I thought, "Ah, Stephen Hawking has come to visit me." My mind cranked over; I looked at him again, and reality flowed through. "No, I don't know who that guy is, but he's not Stephen Hawking come to visit me." Governor Ventura didn't stop by either.

Finally, the neurologist came. I thought of him as "Tap-dance Mouth" because of his rapid-fire, staccato way of talking. I really liked him. He was competent and straightforward, which I appreciated. After some inquiry and examination, he confirmed that I had Charcot-Marie-Tooth disease. He also told me that it is an inherited, progressive disease and untreatable. The disease attacks the long nerves in the body, which explained the symptoms in my hands and feet, and also my breathing and speech problems. The phrenic nerve, which controls breathing and speaking, goes up to the brain and back; this makes it one of the longest nerves in the body.

Then he informed me that the psychiatry department thought that I suffered from a fixed paranoid delusional system, a rare, virtually untreatable disorder, and they had been planning to commit me to a state mental hospital. They thought that I didn't have a PhD in psychology and that this idea was part of a delusional system. Fortunately, the neurologist had done some checking on the Internet and found that I did have a PhD; the psychiatry department hadn't bothered. I was dumbfounded. This was gross incompetence.

Needless to say, this information severely shook my confidence in Mayo's psychiatry department, and I thought I'd better get out of there as soon as possible. The neurologist had scheduled some further tests, but I decided that I knew all I needed to know.

I called Harriet Shetler and she put me in touch with a NAMI contact in Rochester, a social worker for Freeborn County (what an ironic name). Through her, I hired a lawyer. Unfortunately, what he told me wasn't reassuring. He said that there were many patients institutionalized that he couldn't help because they were so impaired from medications that they couldn't cooperate with him. What if I hadn't spotted the policemen's lie in the note on the cart as they were pushing me into the locked ward at Owatonna? I would have been involuntarily medicated and possibly committed.

Toward the end of my stay at Mayo, I was staffed, which means that all the personnel gathered, and I was interviewed as a teaching demonstration. I guess I must have talked about Dr. Benedict at some point because the head psychiatrist began questioning me about him. He asked, "What do you think Dr. Benedict's motive was for the way he treated you?"

I had thought about this, but at the time of this staffing, I didn't know that Dr. Benedict had broken our confidential doctor-patient relationship, and that he had gone to my employer libeling me and irreparably damaging my reputation. I really hadn't wanted to think badly of this man. "Well," I said, "I read that sometimes Catholic doctors deliberately hurt..."

The psychiatrist cut me off. He wanted to demonstrate that I was thoroughly paranoid and involved in a fixed delusional system. Such a patient was rare and worth showing off. He was hoping to elicit some bizarre story that would justify the diagnosis. However, at that moment a young woman resident came to my rescue. "No, let her talk," she exclaimed.

"Hurrah, hurrah," I thought. I was allowed to talk again. I finished explaining that I'd read that sometimes Catholic doctors were encouraged to hurt their women patients in order to discourage sexual fantasies. My willingness to consider a benign explanation for Dr. Benedict's behavior shot down the fixed paranoid delusional system idea, but my explanation couldn't account for Benedict's instructions to Dr. Turgeson to conduct such a searching examination of my intestines, but I didn't bring that up.

The next day, out of the blue, my son showed up at the hospital. I'd been traced through Roger. Before my son talked to me or I even knew he was there, the hospital tried to get him to sign a statement that he would take responsibility for me so they could get me off their hands, but he refused. Perhaps it was just as well since it gave me more time to rest and for my mind to clear.

The afternoon before I left, I consented to try a dose of Depakote (an anti-manic drug) since I was uneasy about how I was going to manage bipolar disorder without medications. I was scared; some of the best psychiatrists in the nation had repeatedly told me that I'd spend the rest of my life in a mental institution if I didn't stay on drugs. I figured that it would be wise to find out the effects of the medication while I was in the hospital. However, shortly after I took the medication, the area around my mouth became numb, and I began to stutter and have trouble breathing. I am aware that my reaction was fast and extreme, but I certainly wasn't putting on. I think my body was simply in an uproar from the drugs, the withdrawal, and the stress. It simply said, "No."

The medical staff didn't believe me. If it had been legally permitted to medicate me, I'm sure I would have been given medications regardless of what I said. They had no in-depth knowledge of Charcot-Marie-Tooth disease or my sixteen years of medications and adverse reactions. They were only familiar with the common refusal of mentally ill patients to take medications. I had started my trip with the idea that I would see how a mentally ill person would be treated on the road. I found out, and the answer was not well. I now understand why many of the mentally ill prefer to live under a bridge.

I called my sister, and she gave me good advice that I carefully followed. I would be signing out of the hospital AMA and would be required to write out a statement. She told me to cause no trouble and to say in the statement that I realized that I had been mentally ill, but that now I had recovered. That's what I did, and things went smoothly. I worried that they'd find some excuse at the last minute to keep me. However, the legal proceedings were held. They could no longer legally hold me; my son returned, and I was released. It was a comfort to have my son with me, and he was a big help in getting me through the next months. Now I had to figure out how I was going to keep myself well.

Chapter 11

Discovery

Like many women (and men), I needlessly lost over fifteen years of my life because of mental illness; I wouldn't want that to happen to anyone else.

The mania and psychosis were gone by the time I left Mayo's psychiatric hospital. This may surprise you, but I've never had a delusion, hallucination, or mood swing again. However, there was a time shortly after I left the hospital when I was in such a state of despair that I considered suicide. What was my future? Life in an institution? How could I manage? Fortunately, over time, I found that I could rely on the answers I'd discovered through my own research. I owe my sanity and survival to discovery.

As previously mentioned, I'd figured out that we humans have inherited DNA sequences and genes for depression and bipolar disorder from Neanderthals. It seemed clear to me that bipolar disorder was the natural cycle of living for Neanderthals who had to survive Ice Age winters and resume active, productive lives during warmer, sunnier seasons. In 2010, my theorizing was verified when I picked up my copy of *Science* magazine and found that, as I had expected, Neanderthals had interbred with Homo sapiens: Svante Pääbo, Richard Green, David Reich, and their colleagues had sequenced the Neanderthal genome. I immediately communicated with Pääbo and Green, telling them of the EOBD-R theory and urging them to see if genes for depression and bipolar disorder entered the human genome from Neanderthals. Green replied that he was going to San Diego and couldn't pursue the question. Svante Pääbo replied with the single word, "Fantastic." Since then, evidence has emerged that genetic variants influencing depression, mood swings, and chronobiology do come from Neanderthal, providing confirmatory evidence for the EOBD-R theory, and indirectly supporting the importance of the timing and intensity of exposure to light as a crucial factor in human behavior (Dannemann, M. & Kelso, J., 2017; Simonti et al., 2016).

Using my understanding of bipolar disorder's origins, I applied this knowledge to my own circumstances. Treating my depression with BLT not only made sense theoretically, but valid evidence had been published that it works. However, why wasn't it widely used as a first-choice treatment for depression? Could I rely on it? What choice did I have? I took the chance, and by implementing what I had learned about exposure to light and darkness, I've successfully managed my bipolar disorder without taking antidepressants or other psychiatric drugs.

There was a book written years ago that seemed radical at the time. It was entitled *Your Drug May Be Your Problem* (Breggin & Cohen, 1999), and it described my situation. I started with a depression that would have been mildly impairing for a few months until summer, and then it would have gone away. (Moods do go away; that's why they're called moods.) However, because I was put on, and kept on, a heavy drug routine, the drugs made me sick and became my problem. When I abruptly took myself off lithium, a type of manic episode called "rebound" mania occurred. To avoid this, lithium needs to be withdrawn slowly, and I certainly don't recommend that others abruptly quit taking lithium. However, for me, it was the right thing to do. My body had accumulated a toxic mix that was a lethal combination for someone with Charcot-Marie-Tooth disease, and I was having trouble breathing and speaking, a serious sign. I never would have recovered if I had followed psychiatric advice to take medications. Instead, I'd probably be dead. Subsequent research and lawsuits against the pharmaceutical companies strongly support the wisdom of my decision. Psychiatric drugs are much less effective and much more damaging than we've been led to believe. They alter brain function, but often not for the better, and they're not curative in the sense that antibiotics cure infections.

The side effects of the drugs had been profound, and it took years for them to subside. Eventually all the symptoms I described went away: the aching muscles, numbness in both feet, painful feelings in the hands, the extreme weakness, emaciation of the extremities, the hair all over the face, eyelashes all crooked, red spot eruptions on the body, the coldness, the intellectual impairment, and a side effect from the lithium that I didn't realize I had, emotional numbing. One day I went to a movie and laughed. I was so surprised. Then I realized that I had neither laughed nor cried for years. However, some damage was permanent: I still have diabetes; my breathing has been affected, and despite three months of speech therapy, I sometimes stutter. The most crippling side effects were from lithium.

Unfortunately, the long-term adverse effects of lithium continue to be overlooked and underestimated. For example, a study published in *The Journal of Clinical Psychiatry* about lithium's effect on intellectual functioning concluded that lithium treatment was associated with small but significant impairments in verbal learning, memory, and creativity (Wingo et al. 2009). In the studies they reviewed, lithium had been taken for an average of about four years, but I took lithium for sixteen years, and many people take it even longer. Apparently, long-term studies of the effects of lithium have still not been done (A. P. Wingo, personal communication, August 6, 2018). By the time I quit lithium, my cognitive impairment was debilitating, and I was no longer professionally employable, though I was still sort of functional.

Severe mental illnesses and psychiatric drugs remain poorly understood by the public (and professionals). Going off psychiatric medications against medical advice is roundly condemned. People think that the medications are fixing something broken in the brain and that stopping the medications breaks the brain again. Going off the medications has been made to seem morally reprehensible, like willfully making yourself sick. However, going off, or reducing medications, may well be a prudent step for many people. It's best to do this under medical supervision. In any case, the drugs must be withdrawn *slowly.* The blog, "Mad in America," offers information and resources for safely discontinuing psychiatric drugs, but, perhaps, the best route is to find an enlightened psychiatrist who guides patients through the process. It's hard to come off psychiatric drugs, and it may take months. However, it's worth it. For me, it was a life saver.

A true, but dismaying, fact is that psychiatric drugs can induce all the behaviors they were meant to prevent: psychosis, suicide, and violent behavior (Breggin & Cohen, 1999; Moore, Glenmullen, & Furberg, 2010; Whitaker, 2010). It's been suggested that psychiatric drugs have been a factor in mass killings, but information about the exact extent of their role has been hard to come by. We deserve answers. What has been the role of psychiatric drugs in *causing* violent behavior?

There is a powerful zeitgeist in America dictating that depressed and bipolar patients (and other mentally ill individuals) need to be medicated and stay on medications indefinitely. Health care providers think they know what's best, and they thought it was their duty to keep me on medications. They never considered that I might not need drugs. Their mantra was, "If this drug doesn't work, we can try another." There was no appreciation for the fact that the scientific basis for the effectiveness of these drugs is weak. Furthermore, when I objected that I had Charcot-Marie-Tooth disease and the drugs might have adverse effects, I heard this reply: "There is no evidence of adverse effects with Charcot-Marie-Tooth disease." However, that doesn't mean there aren't any adverse effects. It's extremely likely that the possibility was never researched.

NAMI and some mentally ill patients thought that psychiatric medications were another miracle of modern medicine. We wanted to believe, but we were sadly misled as Whitaker documented in his books. And we were not peddled harmless nostrums. The drugs that we, our insurance companies, and the taxpayers are paying for often make us worse, sometimes permanently. We forgot that people used to get along without psychiatric drugs. Abraham Lincoln came out of his depressions. Clifford Beers, founder of the American mental hygiene movement, recovered and was well for years. We thought we were in a new era. Our lives would be better. A non-drug treatment was entirely out of our mindset.

I understand that some people believe that antidepressants are effective. (I thought so, too.) However, realize that the positive response may have been due to the coincidental arrival of summer, or it could have been a placebo effect (Benedetti, 2014). Responding to a placebo doesn't mean your symptoms weren't real, and placebo effects aren't a sign of a weak, suggestible mind; the urge to be well is a normal human response demonstrated throughout history.

The research and marketing of antidepressant drugs has been rotten to the core. Every high school science student appreciates the necessity of controlling relevant variables, but millions of dollars were spent on antidepressant research without controlling the crucial variable of exposure to seasonal light changes. How do we know that improvement in a depression wasn't caused by the onset of summer, not the drug?

Some think that we lack fundamental scientific knowledge about the causes of major depression, bipolar disorder, and other mental illnesses, and, therefore, we are unable to treat mental illnesses in an intelligent, effective way. However, in the case of depression and bipolar disorder, we are ignoring knowledge we already have, mesmerized by the magic pills of fairy tales and the drug industry. Depression can be caused by light deprivation and alleviated by BLT while darkness will dampen mania. Simple? So was the treatment for scurvy. So was the remedy of washing hands to reduce infections. Light and dark therapies may not provide complete treatments, especially for wildly manic states, but these simple, cost effective measures can go a long way to safely manage a troublesome disorder. My own experience is a case in point.

When I stopped taking medications, I used my knowledge of the effects of light to fashion my treatment program. In 1999, there was already clear scientific evidence that BLT is effective in relieving major depression, and there was some evidence that remaining in the dark could reverse mania. Upon these facts, I placed my future, my sanity, and my freedom.

Now, nearly twenty years later, it's obvious that my self-prescribed treatment regime worked, but this is now, and that was then. Then, I couldn't be sure these methods would work. I was scared; terrified might be a better word. Both my brother and sister had serious mental illnesses, and some of the children in the family were getting sick. Would I follow in their footsteps? I lived in a state of apprehension caught between prospects of life in an institution and annihilation of self by drug therapy. The fear of involuntary commitment was real to me and certainly not alleviated by my recent experiences in Minnesota. In my private life, I had known of three women involuntarily committed long term for the financial advantage and convenience of their relatives. A fourth was saved only by the heroic intervention of her sister, a knowledgeable NAMI member. Charlotte Perkins Gilman's story remains relevant. *The Yellow Wallpaper* is still on the wall.

To protect myself, I investigated the constitutional protections provided by affiliation with the Christian Science church. I contacted a civil rights lawyer, and I established a health care power of attorney with a trusted friend who was a NAMI member. Through NAMI, I got help and companionship from members of a depression support group: Mary Jean, Sue, and Teresa.

We met every week for lunch, and they could always be counted on for sensible advice and a sympathetic ear. We remained close friends for years. I was also befriended by Patrick, a big Irishman with bipolar disorder, who allowed me to hike on his property in the Baraboo Hills, an enormously healing activity. It was Patrick who taught me to start each day doing the most difficult thing I had to do. Sadly, I rarely saw any previous friends, acquaintances, or colleagues, and the occasional overt social rejection stung me to the core.

I remained terrified that I would be railroaded into an institution. I wanted a psychiatrist on my side, but it was difficult to find someone. I thought I might be able to work things out with my former psychiatrist, but when I arrived for my appointment, the receptionist began berating me for going off my medications. Immediately offended and alarmed, I left. The next psychiatrist I tried had a dreadful, cold manner. Moreover, a NAMI friend warned me against him. She told me that when she violated a no-suicide contract with her HMO, while she was lying in the intensive care unit, this man callously informed her that the HMO was denying her further care. No, I didn't want to entrust my care to him. The next psychiatrist was a well-recommended young woman who prescribed Zyprexa (olanzapine), a new antipsychotic with side effects that include sudden death. She gave me the prescription. As I was leaving, I asked her if it would be all right if I called her if I had questions. (My next appointment wasn't for a month.) She said, "Only if it's an emergency. I think that's best, don't you?" I didn't take the medication and never returned. The drug is now the subject of thousands of law suits.

I temporarily gave up searching for a psychiatrist and found a psychologist-therapist from the staff of a community treatment program that tries to keep mentally ill individuals living independently in the community. I still struggled with losing things and managing for myself, and I wanted someone to talk to. Besides, I had no idea if I'd improve or get worse. I had every reason to think that I'd have a problem with mood swings. Hadn't America's finest doctors told me I would? However, after a time the therapy interviews began to have a negative effect on me. My therapist seemed to question my improvement, as though he didn't believe me. This triggered an anxiety attack so severe that I backed the car into a cement post upon leaving his office. After a second anxiety attack precipitated by a session with him, I called it quits. "Not being believed" had become a traumatic trigger—from the screaming little girl pinned to the cold cement floor with the Sheriff's gun at her head, to the nightmare of the Mauston case. I'd gone to such lengths to find someone I could rely on, and even he didn't seem to believe me.

During these years, I saw other psychotherapists off and on. I was doing everything reasonable to stay well. I read books on Cognitive Behavioral Therapy (CBT), which is considered an effective treatment for depression. A CBT book that I found helpful was *Feeling Good: The New Mood Therapy* by David Burns (1980). Unfortunately, Burns does not even mention SAD, BLT, or the effects of light on human behavior; however, he does have some useful ideas. CBT teaches the identification and correction of depressive thinking. It emphasizes seeking positive experiences and avoiding the negative. Scheduling is another beneficial CBT concept (Frank, 2005). Setting up and keeping a schedule occupies the mind, which helps prevent depressive thinking. It also helps make sure you get done the things that need to be done or should be done (bills, medical, and dental care). Depressed people find it hard to keep up with the things they should do. Although CBT is useful, the homework required in typical CBT therapy is too intellectually demanding during a severe major depression.

Interpersonal Therapy (IPT) has also been found to be effective in the treatment of depression. A less formal variant of this type of therapy is what I typically used as a therapist. Interpersonal relationships are key to human well-being. As Harvard psychiatrist Peter Breggin wrote, "People are better than drugs—even for the most disturbed patients" (Breggin & Cohen, 1999, p. 39), and I think this is true. Mentally ill individuals who have been in psychotherapy have a lower rate of suicide; a supportive therapist is a counter to the hopelessness and sense of being a useless reject of society.

However, as in the case of antidepressant drugs, the research on the effectiveness of psychotherapies has failed to control for seasonal changes in light. Did the therapy help or did summer come?

About a year after my fateful stay at the Mayo's St. Mary's hospital, I thought I should see a neurologist. I made an appointment with the doctor who had diagnosed the Charcot-Marie-Tooth disease. I was impressed that he made the correct diagnosis, which was missed by a previous neurologist. During my consultation with him, I told him how much better I was since I stopped the psychiatric drugs. I showed him that my watch and rings no longer fell off as evidence of how emaciated my limbs had been.

"The drugs didn't cause that," he stated in a haughty, dismissive tone.

"Yes, they did," I said. "I read about it in a bulletin from the Charcot-Marie-Tooth disease association."

"They don't know anything," he replied.

He refused to credit anything I said. I was so disappointed, taken aback, and crushed that I began to cry. This was a teaching hospital, and there was a young woman resident in the room. I wonder what she was thinking.

"Stop that crying," he said, "or you'll have to leave my office."

I stopped crying. This man might be brilliant, but he was so arrogant that it impaired his judgment. I was certainly glad that I hadn't relied on him. However, I didn't let these experiences set me back; I continued to reach out. I started an email correspondence with Linda Crabtree who was editor of a Charcot-Marie-Tooth disease newsletter. She put me in touch with a fellow clinical psychologist, Dr. Alan Goldberg, and through him I found good medical care.

My health routine is simple. In addition to seasonal BLT and about eight hours of continuous darkness at night, I follow a diet low in simple carbohydrates and rich in protein and vegetables. I do specialized stretches and exercises for Charcot-Marie-Tooth disease, daily early morning walks, and I get weekly massages. For several years, I also meditated twice a day (Benson, 1975). I think all these routines are beneficial, but aside from the light and dark treatments, I doubt that any of them would alter the course of major depression or bipolar disorder.

Three other treatments are part of my routine. However, for one reason or another, I can't wholeheartedly recommend them. Although there is no scientific basis for it, I take acupuncture for Charcot-Marie-Tooth disease, which otherwise has no treatment. I also take estradiol, a form of the female hormone, estrogen. My depression occurred right at menopause, and in my zeal to stay well, despite the medical risks, I take estradiol, which has anti-depressant properties (Carranza-Lira et al., 1999; Ditkott et al., 1991; Schmidt et al., 2000). My decision to take estradiol was guided by the lack of a cancer history in my family and the fact that both my uterus and ovaries had been removed. (I have year-ly breast examinations.) Finally, I take a special formulation of omega-3 fatty acids called Omega-Brite, which has been shown to be effective in the treatment of bipolar disorder (Stoll, 2002), but more research is needed concerning these treatments. Again, I repeat, I am not recommending them.

For me, a routine of about eight hours of continuous darkness at night and seasonal use of BLT manages bipolar disorder with-out the need for psychiatric drugs. I think the regime will work well for most people with bipolar disorder. However, individuals with an active manic problem will need to spend more time in the dark, up to fourteen hours. For more detail about the prac-ticalities of managing depression and bipolar disorder without psychiatric medications, see my online publication, *Depression and Bipolar Disorder: Evidence-based Natural Treatments and a New Theory* (Sherman, 2015).

My recovery and good health have amazed my doctors. My mood and mental state have never been better. Duplicate bridge is a challenging game that requires concentration, memory, planning, good judgment, emotional control, and the ability to get along with a partner. It was a great aid in my recovery, as was my occupation of writing and research on bipolar disorder. Later I began attending and teaching classes for older adults at Plato and the Osher Lifetime Learning Institute (OLLI).

The discovery that managing light and dark can keep me well has been of enormous personal benefit, but the EOBD-R theory has a broader satisfaction. The theory synthesizes ideas about the biological clock and seasonal shifts in mood with theorizing that bipolar disorder descends from a compact, cold-adapted group, Neanderthal. The theory suggests that bipolar behaviors evolved in the northern temperate zone as adaptations to the severe climatic conditions of the Ice Ages. The EOBD-R theory explains and integrates existing scientific observations: Bipolar disorder has the epidemiology of an adaptation; it is correlated with a cold adapted build, and its moods vary according to light and season. Individuals with SAD, which is related to bipolar disorder, have been shown to manifest a biological signal of season change similar to that found in hibernating animals. The involvement of the circadian gene network in the pathophysiology of bipolar disorder has been confirmed. Because selective pressures during the Ice Ages would have been greatest for women of reproductive age, the theory expects that women will manifest winter depression more than males or younger females, which is the case. This sex difference is also found in hibernating mammals. Because the evolution of bipolar disorder took place in the northern temperate zone during the Pleistocene, it was predicted that individuals of African descent, lacking Neanderthal genes, would not manifest circular bipolar I disorder, and the evidence indicates that the incidence of bipolar disorder among them is less. Bipolar disorder and winter depression are essentially behavioral fossils.

A next step in research is to figure out how these genes affecting mental illnesses are regulated and what causes them to be expressed or not expressed. Here, we must look at the effects of light. What effect does erratic and unnatural light exposure have on children? Could a practice, such as lack of seven to eight hours of continuous darkness at night, adversely affect children? Some suggestion that proper chronobiology is beneficial comes from the finding that teenage children whose bedtime was at ten pm or earlier were 24 % less likely to suffer from depression (Gangwisch et al., 2010). Light orders the behavior of all living things, and light can also disorder it. Here is a new frontier for research.

Epilogue

The previous chapter was about discovery, but discovery can be of different kinds. At this late date, I made a new discovery: Dr. Phyllis Chesler's (2002) book, *Woman's Inhumanity to Woman*. I'd sent Phyllis a near-finished, pre-publication copy of this book which ended with the warning: "Unless women stick together, progress will be slow or impossible."

Phyllis wrote back, recommending her book to me. "You'll find it interesting." Indeed, I did.

What was my warning about? I was worried. Would our newly elected female leaders stick together? Or, hungry for long-denied opportunities for power and status, would they knock each other off, jeopardizing progress toward important goals? Many women harbor unexamined sexism, as Chesler (2002) pointed out. My own experiences with women hadn't been promising. At various points in my life story, I alluded to difficulties with other women, but it was a problem with no name. Phyllis's book brought this problem out into the open. However, I had a good laugh when I turned to the front of Phyllis's book and saw the dedication, "Ma—this book is for you." I'd made a similar decision to dedicate this book explicitly to both my father and mother. My mother had made an unprecedented appearance in a dream: She said not a word, but her compressed lips of silent reproach gave me pause. She wasn't lovey-dovey; she was often mean, but she fought for me—fought that I'd have more opportunity than fell to her lot.

However, what about those other women who betrayed me? Some were feminists, colleagues, whose ambitions got the better of their sisterhood. Not that I didn't experience sisterhood. I did, and I treasure it to this day. But what about the well-credentialed women I went to for help? What about the psychiatrist, the chiropractor, and the financial adviser who took advantage of me? Their illegal and unethical treatment was not only disillusioning, but I didn't want to write about it. I felt ashamed for my sex. But, as Chesler wrote, and as I agree, we need to face the truth: We've got to do better.

Look at our history; sisterhood isn't common, but our march for bread during the French Revolution was a pivotal event. Later, we rose up to fight for our civil rights, and we're rising up now, but we've got to work at it. Sisterhood isn't bred into our bones with anything like the intensity of the brotherhood of war. Males have millennia of experience with brotherhood. Bonding to accomplish some group purpose requires leadership, followership, and the subjugation of individual ambitions to the needs of the group cause. Moreover, males have a code of behavior guiding interactions among them. Betrayals are dishonorable. These codes don't exist among women in the same way. Chesler skillfully delineated the indirect hostility of women's actions against each other. You can smell something spoiling, but you don't know where the smell is coming from. A former woman friend exclaimed, "All's fair in love and war." Really?

Loyalty to the leader in disregard for all civility and common sense deserves rebuke not praise, but women underestimate male bonding at their peril. There are a lot of issues here to be thought out, but I doubt they will be resolved without conscious effort. However, the current women's impetus to action, like the march for bread during the French revolution, is broadly based in the need for civility, justice, fairness, equity and a pro-people agenda. This is also the focus of many men. This is not a war on men, but a war against greedy, narrow-minded, and heartless people. Men welcomed the women's march for bread in the 18th century, and many men now also see energized women as a happy addition to the fight to preserve democracy. It's not that we women aren't concerned about our rights. We are, and the push is on to see them written in stone by ratifying the Equal Rights Amendment.

As author of a memoir, I've been asked, "What have you learned about survival?" Avoid psychiatrists? People are no damn good? I never spent time with such extreme, bitter thoughts, but I did learn to be more cautious. My natural impulse was to care about people, to serve some useful purpose, to fulfill the hopes of my mother and father, and the women of the Flora Stone Mather Alumnae Association who raised the money for my full-tuition scholarship. People laugh at idealism, but I am now 85 years old, and I am healthy, happy, with a clear conscience and sense of accomplishment. Idealism has its rewards.

Early on, I rejected drugs and alcohol, which are disastrous for human life. Little did I know that a corrupt and scientifically sloppy medical community was wrecking my body and brain with legally prescribed drugs. Nonetheless, the conscious pursuit of discipline became my obvious path. In my case, it was the path of survival, but for many it is the path to excellence. Do you think George Washington's self-control was natural? What about Ruth Bader Ginsburg? There is a lot to be said for ancient virtues.

It took years, but finally, after torturing myself with thoughts of suicide for nearly fifty years, I realized that voluntarily ending one's life is justifiable only in very special circumstances: I gave up on suicide, and I'm certainly happy that I did. I learned to occupy myself with positive thoughts and activities and gave my highest priority to my personal relationships even though absorbed in my intellectual pursuits.

One final thought that goes along with my inveterate, possibly dysfunctional idealism: Positive change comes from truth, not wishful thinking, and reason and the scientific method are the best ways to sift through to the truth. Women must promote good science and follow its lead.

Hmm, I'd have been more comfortable if I were asked, "What do I hope my readers have learned?" I'll leave you with this final memory: When I was a girl about twelve years old, we lived next door to a family who had a pet beagle hound named Rex (pseudonym). One day I had my pet rabbit in the house, and she was happily hopping about, but my brother thought he would play a trick on me and brought in the neighbor's hound.

The dog quickly took off after my rabbit, and, horrified, I feared for the worst.

Thunk! Bunny thumped Rex squarely on the nose, and, wildly yelping, he streaked out of the house, banging the screen door behind him.

Moral of the story: "Remember Julia Sherman's rabbit."

References

Abrams, Z. (2018) Sexual harassment on campus. *Monitor on Psychology*, *49*, 68-71.

Adam, F., Géonet, M., Day, J., & de Sutter, P. (2015) Mindfulness skills are associated with female orgasm? *Sexual and Relationship Therapy, 30*, 256-267.

American Psychiatric Association. (1994) *Diagnostic and statistical manual of mental disorders.* Washington DC: American Psychiatric Association.

American Psychiatric Association. (2010) *Practice guidelines for the treatment of patients with major depressive disorder* (3rd ed.). http://psychiatryonline.com/pracGuide/ pracGuideTopic_7.aspx.

American Psychiatric Association. (2013) *Diagnostic and statistical manual of mental disorders* (5th ed.). Washington DC: American Psychiatric Association.

Beers, C. (1908/1981) *A mind that found itself.* Pittsburgh, PA: University of Pittsburgh Press.

Benedetti, F. (2014) *Placebo effects* (2nd ed.). Oxford, England: Oxford University Press.

Benson, H. (1975) *The relaxation response.* New York, NY: Harper Collins.

Biggs, M. A., Upadhyay, U. D., McCulloch, C. E., & Foster, D. G. (2017) Women's mental health and well-being 5 years after receiving or being denied an abortion: A perspective, longitudinal cohort study. *JAMA Psychiatry*, *74*, 169-178. doi:10.1001/jamapsychiatry.2016.3478

Boston Women's Health Collective. (2011) *Our bodies, ourselves.* New York, NY: Touchstone.

Boukhris, R., Sheehy, O., Mottron, L. et al. (2016) Antidepressant use during pregnancy and risk of autism spectrum disorder in children. *JAMA Pediatrics*, *270*, 117-124. doi:10.1001/jamapediatrics. 2015.3356

Breda, T., Jouini, E., & Napp, C. (2018) Societal inequalities amplify gender gaps in math. *Science, 359*, 1219.

Breggin, P. R. & Cohen, D. (1999) *Your drug may be your problem: How and why to stop taking psychiatric medications.* New York, NY: Perseus Books.

Brodsky, A., Holroyd, J., Payton, C., Rubinstein, E., Rosenkrantz, P., Sherman, J., & Zell, F. (1975) Report of the Task Force on Sex Bias and Sex-Role Stereotyping in Psychotherapeutic Practice. *American Psychologist, 30*, 1169-1175.

Burns, D. D. (1980) *Feeling good: The new mood therapy.* New York, NY: William Morrow.

Butler, C. A. (1976) New data about female sexual response. *Journal of Sex and Marital Therapy. 2*, 40-46. https://doi.org/10.1080/00926237608407071

Cahill, L., Prins, B., Weber, M., & McGaugh, J. L. (1998) Mechanisms of emotional arousal and lasting declarative memory. *Nature, 371*, 702-704.

Cahill, L., Haier, R. J., White, N. S., Fallon, J., Kilpatrick, L., Lawrence, C., … Alkire, M. T. (2001) Sex-related difference in amygdala activity during emotionally influenced memory storage. *Neurobiology of Learning and Memory, 75*, 1-9.

Caplan, P. J. & Cosgrove, L. (Eds.). (2004) *Bias in psychiatric diagnosis.* New York, NY: Aronson.

Carpenter, T. P., Dossey, J. A., & Koehler, J. L. (Eds.). (2004) *Classics in mathematics education research.* Reston, VA: National Council of Teachers of Mathematics.

Carranza-Lira, S. & Valentino-Figueroa, M. L. (1999) Estrogen therapy for depression in postmenopausal women. *Journal of Gynecology and Obstetrics, 65,* 35-38.

Ceci, S. J. & Williams, M. (Eds.). (2007) *Why aren't more women in science? Top researchers debate the evidence.* Washington, DC: American Psychological Association.

Chernow, R. (2004) *Alexander Hamilton.* New York, NY: Penguin.

Chesler, P. (1972) *Women and madness: When is a woman mad and who is it who decides?* Garden City, NY: Doubleday.

Chesler, P. (2002) *Woman's inhumanity to woman.* New York, NY: Lawrence Hill Books.

Chotai, J., Smedh, K., Johansson, C., Nilsson, L. G., & Adolfsson, R. (2004) An epidemiological study on gender differences in self-reported seasonal changes in mood and behavior in a general population of northern Sweden. *Nordic Journal of Psychiatry, 58,* 429-437.

Clifford, R. E. (1978) Subjective sexual experience in college women. *Archives of Sexual Behavior, 7,*183-197.

Dannemann, M. & Kelso, J. (2017) The contribution of Neanderthals to phenotypic variation in modern humans. *American Journal of Human Genetics, 101,* 578-589. doi.org/10.1016/j.ahg.2017.09.010

Darwin, C. (1859) *On the origin of species.* London, England: John Murray.

Dawood, K., Kirk, K. M., Bailey, J. M., Andrews, P. W., & Martin, N. G. (2005) Genetic and environment influences on the frequency of orgasm in women. *Twin Research and Human Genetics, 8,* 27-33.

de Beauvoir, S. (1949/1952) *The second sex.* New York, NY: Knopf Doubleday.

de Cervantes, Miguel (1615/2003) *Don Quixote.* London, England: Penguin.

Deutsch, H. (1944) *The psychology of women.* New York, NY: Green & Stratton.

Ditkoff, E. C., Crary, W. G., Cristo, M., & Lobo, R. A. (1991) Estrogen improves psychological function in asymptomatic postmenopausal women. *Obstetrics and Gynecology, 78,* 991-995.

Dunn, K. M., Cherkas, L. F., & Spector, T. D. (2005) Genetic influences on variation in female orgasmic function: A twin study. *Biology Letters, 1,* 260-263.

Etaugh, C. & Bridges, J. S. (2013) *A psychological exploration* (4th ed.). New York, NY: Routledge.

Fennema, E. & Sherman, J. A. (1977) Sex-related differences in mathematics achievement, spatial visualization and affective factors. *American Educational Research Journal. 14,* 51-71.

Fieve, R. R. (2006) *Bipolar II: Enhance your highs, boost your creativity, and escape the cycles of recurrent depression—the essential guide to recognize and treat the mood swings of this increasingly common disorder.* Emmaus, PA: Rodale Books.

Fine, C. (2010) *Delusions of gender: How our minds, society, and neurosexism create differences.* New York, NY: Norton.

Fisher, C. (1973) *The female orgasm.* New York, NY: Basic Books.

Fisher, T. D., Davis, C. M., Yarber, W. L., & Davis, S. L. (2010) *Handbook of sexuality-related measures.* New York, NY: Routledge.

Frank, E. (2005) *Treating bipolar disorder: A clinician's guide to interpersonal and social rhythm therapy.* New York, NY: Guilford Press.

Freeman, M. P. & Gelenberg, A. J. (2005) Bipolar disorder in women: Reproductive events and treatment considerations. *Acta Psychiatrica Scandinavica, 112,* 85-96.

Freidan, B. (1963) *Feminine mystique.* New York, NY: Norton.

Freud, S. (1905/1975) *Three essays on the theory of sexuality.* New York, NY: Basic Books.

Freud, S. (1951) *Psychopathology of everyday life.* New York, NY: Mentor.

Freud, S. & Breuer, J. (1895/1955) *Studies on hysteria.* London, England: Hogarth Press.

Fromm-Reichmann, F. (1948) Notes on the development of treatment of schizophrenics by psychoanalytic psychotherapy. *Psychiatry, 11,* 263-273.

Gangwisch, J. E., Babiss, L. A., Malaspina, D., Turner, J. B., Zammit, G. K., & Posner, K. (2010) Earlier parental set bedtimes as a protective factor against depression and suicidal ideation. *Sleep, 33,* 97-106.

Gavron, H. (1966) *The captive wife: Conflicts of housebound mothers.* London, England: Routledge & Kegan Paul.

Ghaemi, N. (2011) *A first-rate madness: Uncovering the link between leadership & mental illness.* New York, NY: Penguin.

Gilman, C. P. (1892/2015) *The yellow wallpaper.* London, England: Penguin.

Gilman, S., King, H., Porter, R., Rousseau, G. S., & Showalter, E. (1993) *Hysteria beyond Freud.* Berkeley, CA: University of California Press.

Glenmullen, J. (2006) *The antidepressant solution: A step-by-step guide to safely overcoming antidepressant withdrawal dependence and addiction.* New York, NY: Simon & Schuster.

Goetzel, R., Pei, X. Tabrizi, M., Henke, R. M., Knowlessar, N., Nelson, C. F., & Metz, R. D. (2012) Ten modifiable health risk factors are linked to more than one-fifth of employer-employee health care spending. *Health Affairs, 31*, 2474-2484. https://doc.org/10.1377/hlthaff.2011.0819

Golden, R. N., Gaynes, B. N., Ekstrom, B. N., Hamer, R. M., Jacobsen, F. M., Suppes, T., ... Nemeroff, C. B. (2005) The efficacy of light therapy in the treatment of mood disorder: A review and meta-analysis of evidence. *American Journal of Psychiatry 162*, 656-662.

Goodwin, F. & Jamison, K. R. (1990) *Manic depressive illness.* New York, NY: Oxford University Press.

Goodwin, J., Bemmann, K., & Zwieg, J. (1994) Physician sexual exploitation: Wisconsin in the 1980s. *Journal of the American Medical Women's Association, 49*, 19-23.

Gottlieb, J. F. & Terman, M. (2012) Outpatient triple chronotherapy for bipolar depression: Case report. *Journal of Psychiatric Practice, 18*, 373-380.

Gräfenberg, E. (1950) The role of the urethra in female orgasm. *International Journal of Sexology, 3*, 145-148.

Green, R. E., Krause, J., Briggs, A.W., Maricic, T., Stenzel, V., Kircher, M., ... Pääbo, S. (2010) A draft sequence of the Neandertal genome. *Science, 328*, 710-722.

Hanisch, C. (1970) Personal is political: The original feminist theory. In S. Firestone & A. Koedt (Eds.), *Notes from the second year: Women's liberation* (pp.76-77). New York, NY: Radical Feminism.

Harris, J. (2001) *Five quarters of the orange.* New York, NY: HarperCollins.

Henriksen, T. E., Skrede, S., Fasmer, O. B, Schoeyen, H., Leskauskaite, I., Bjøke-Bertheussen, J., & Lund, A. (2016)

Blue-blocking glasses as additive treatment for mania: A randomized placebo-controlled trial. *Bipolar Disorders, 18*, 221-232. doi.10.111/bdi.12390

Herbenick, D., Fu, T. C., Arter, J., Sanders, S. A., & Dodge, B. (2018) Women's experiences with genital touching, sexual pleasure, and orgasm: Results from a U.S. probability sample of women ages 18 to 94. *Journal of Sex and Marital Therapy, 44*, 201-212. https://doi.org/10.10 80/0092623X.2017.1346530

Hite, S. (1976/2003) *The Hite report: A national study of female sexuality.* New York, NY: Seven Stories Press.

Huss, M. T. (2009) *Forensic psychology, clinical practice, and applications.* Singapore: Wiley-Blackwell.

Hyde, J. S. & Rosenberg, B. G. (1976) *Half the human experience: The psychology of women.* Lexington, MA: D. C. Heath.

Hyde, J. S., Mezulis, A. H., & Abramson, L. Y. (2008) The ABCs of depression: Integrating affective, biological, and cognitive models to explain the emergence of the gender difference in depression. *Psychological Review, 115*, 291-313. doi:10.1037/0033-295x.115.2.219

Hyde, J. S. & Mertz, J. (2009) Gender, culture, and math. *Proceedings of the National Academy of Sciences, 106*, 8801-8807.

Jamison, K. R. (1993) *Touched with fire: Manic-depressive illness and the artistic temperament.* New York, NY: Simon and Schuster.

Johns Hopkins University. (2016) Depression rates growing among adolescents, particularly girls. https://hub.jhu. educ/2016/adolescent-depressionstudy/.

Kane, J. M. & Lieberman, J. A. (Eds.). (1992) *Adverse effects of psychotropic drugs.* New York, NY: Guilford Press.

Kaplan, A. (1986) The "self-in-relation": Implications for depression in women. *Psychotherapy, Theory, Re-*

search, Practice, Training, 23, 234-242. http://dx.doi.
org/10.1037/h0085603

Kaschak, E. & Tiefer, L. (Eds.) *A new view of women's sexual problems*. Binghamton, NY: Haworth Press.

King, R., Belsky, J., Mah, K., & Binik, Y. (2010) Are there different types of female orgasm? *Archives of Sexual Behavior 40,* 865. https://doi.org/10.1007/s10508-010-9639-7

Kinsey, A. C., Pomeroy, W. D., Martin, C. E., & Gebhardt, P. H. (1953) *Sexual behaviour in the human female*. Philadelphia, PA: W.B. Saunders.

Kirsch, I., Deacon, B. J., Huedo-Medina, T. B., Scoboria, A., Moore, T. J., & Johnson, B. T. (2008) Initial severity and antidepressant benefits: Meta-analysis of data submitted to the food and drug administration. *Plos Medicine, 5*, 260-268. https://doi.org/10.1371/journal.pmed.0050045

Koedt, A. (1970) *The myth of the vaginal orgasm*. Boston, MA: New England Free Press.

Komisaruk, B. R., Beyer-Flores, C., & Whipple, B. (2006) *The science of orgasm*. Baltimore, MD: Johns Hopkins University Press.

Kontula, O. & Miettinen, A. (2016) Determinants of female sexual orgasms. *Socioaffective Neuroscience and Psychology, 6*: doi:10.3402/snp.v6.31624.

Koss, M. P., Gidycz, C. A., & Wisniewski, N. (1987) The scope of rape: Incidence and prevalence of sexual aggression and victimization in a national sample of higher education students. *Journal of Consulting and Clinical Psychology, 55*, 162-170.

Kuperberg, A. & Padgett, J. E. (2016) The role of culture in explaining college students' selection into hookups, dates and long-term romantic relationships. *Journal of*

Social and Personal Relationships, 33, 1070-1096. doi: 10.1177/0265407515616876

Levitan, R. D., Masellis, M., Lam, R. W., Kaplan, A. S., David, C., Tharmalingam, S., ... Kennedy, J. L. (2006) A birth-season/DRD4 gene interaction predicts weight gain and obesity in women with seasonal affective disorder: A seasonal thrifty phenotype hypothesis. *Neuropsychopharmacology, 31*, 2498-2503.

Lewis, K. L., Stout, J. G., Finkelstein, N. D., Pollock, S. J., Miyake, A., Cohen, G. L., & Ito, T. A. (2017) Fitting in to move forward: Belonging, gender, and persistence in the physical sciences, technology, engineering, and mathematics (pSTEM). *Psychology of Women Quarterly, 4*, 420-436.

Lewis, S. (1920) *Main Street.* New York, NY: Harcourt, Brace.

Lloyd, J., Crouch, N. S., Minto, C. L, Liao, L. M., & Creighton, S. M. (2005) Female genital appearance: "Normality" unfolds. *British Journal of Obstetrics and Gynecology, 112*, 643-646.

Loftus, E. F. (2003) Our changeable memories: Legal and practical implications. *Nature Reviews Neuroscience, 4*, 231-234.

Lugo-Candelas, C., Cha, J., Hong, S., Bastidas, V., Weissman, M., Fifer, W. P., ... Monk, C. (2018) Associations between brain structure and connectivity in infants and exposure to selective serotonin reuptake inhibitors during pregnancy. *JAMA Pediatrics, 172*, 525-533.

Lyall, L. M., Wyse, C. A., Celis Morales, C. A., Lyall, D. M., Cullen. B., ... Smith, D. J. (2018) Seasonality of depressive symptoms in women but not in men: A cross-sectional study in the UK Biobank cohort. *Journal of Affective Disorders, 229*, 296-305. doi:10,1016/j.jad.2017.12.106

Maccoby, E. E. (Ed.). (1966a) *The development of sex differences.* Palo Alto, CA: Stanford University Press.

Maccoby, E. E. (1966b) Sex differences in intellectual functioning. In E. E. Maccoby (Ed.), *The development of sex
differences.* Palo Alto, CA: Stanford University Press
(pp. 25-55).

Mackin, W. (2018) *Bring out the dog: Stories.* New York, NY:
Random House.

Mah, K. & Binik, Y. M. (2001) The nature of human orgasm:
A critical review of major trends. *Clinical Psychology
Review, 21*, 823-856.

Mah, K. & Binik, Y. M. (2010) The Orgasm Rating Scale. In
T. D. Fisher, C. M. Davis, W. L. Yarber, & S. L. Davis
(Eds.), *Handbook of sexuality-related measures* (3rd
ed.). New York, NY: Routledge, (pp. 500-502).

Masters, W. H. & Johnson, V. E. (1966) *Human sexual response.* New York, NY: Penguin.

McCarthy, M. M., Arnold, A. P., Ball, G. F., Blaustein, J. D., &
De Vries, G. J. (2012) Sex differences in the brain: The
not so inconvenient truth. *Journal of Neuroscience, 32*,
2241-2247.

McCullough, D. (2001) *John Adams.* New York, NY: Simon
and Schuster.

Millett, K. (1970) *Sexual politics.* New York, NY: Doubleday.

Moncrieff, J. (2009) *The myth of the chemical cure: A critique
of psychiatric drug treatment.* London: Palgrave Macmillan.

Moncrieff, J. (2013) *The bitterest pills: The troubling story of
antipsychotic drugs.* London, England: Palgrave Macmillan.

Moore, T. J., Glenmullen, J., & Furberg, C. D. (2010) Prescription drugs associated with reports of violence toward
others. *PloS One, 5* (12): e15337. https://doi.org/journal.
pone, 0015337

Morrison, J. & Morrison, T. (2001) Psychiatrists disciplined by a state medical board. *American Journal of Psychiatry, 58*, 474-478.

Muehlenhard, C. L. & Shippee, S. K. (2010) Men's and women's reports of pretending orgasm. *Journal of Sex Research, 47*, 552-567.

Novotney, A. (2017) Not your grandfather's psychoanalysis. *Monitor on Psychology, 48*, 41-47.

Oldham, M. A. & Ciraulo, D. A. (2014) Bright light therapy for depression: A review of its effects on chronobiology and the autonomic nervous system. *Chronobiology International, 31*, 305-319.

Olsen, J. (1989) *The rape of the town of Lovell.* New York, NY: Atheneum.

Osen, L. M. (1974) *Women in mathematics.* Cambridge, MA: MIT Press.

Pfaus, J. G., Quintana, G. R., Mac Cionnaith, C., & Parada, M. (2016) The whole versus the sum of some of the parts: Toward resolving the apparent controversy of clitoral versus vaginal orgasms. *Socioaffective Neuroscience and Psychology, 6:1.* doi.org/10.3402/snp.v6.32578.

Phelps, J. (2008) Dark therapy for bipolar disorder using amber lenses for blue light blockade. *Medical Hypotheses, 70*, 224-229.

Previc, F. H. (2009) *The dopaminergic mind in human evolution and history.* Cambridge, MA: Cambridge University Press.

Qui, X. (2004) *When red is black.* New York, NY: Soho Press.

Rethorst, C. D., Wipfli, B. M., & Landers, D. M. (2009) The antidepressant effect of exercise: A meta-analysis of randomized trials. *Sports Medicine, 39*, 491-511.

Rosenthal, N. E., Sack, D. A., Gillin, J. D., Lewy, A. J., Goodwin, F. K., Davenport, Y., … Wehr, T. A. (1984) Seasonal affective disorder: A description of the syndrome and preliminary findings with light therapy. *Archives of General Psychiatry, 41,* 72-80.

Rosenthal, N. E., Genhart, M., Jacobsen, F. M., Skwerer, R. G., & Wehr, T. A. (1987) Disturbances of appetite and weight regulation in seasonal affective disorder. *Annals of New York Academy of Science, 499,* 216-230.

Rosenthal, N. E. (1993/2013) *Winter blues: Everything you need to know to beat seasonal affective disorder* (4ᵗʰ ed.). New York, NY: Guilford Press.

Ruderman, Z. (2018, May 29) 21 women describe what an orgasm feels like to them. Retrieved from https://www. cosmopolitan.com/sex-love/advice/g1551/what-an-or-gasm-feels-like/

Rush, A. J., Modhukar, T., Carmody, T. J., Biggs, M. R., Shores-Wilson, K., Hisham, I., & Crismon, M. L. (2004) One-year clinical outcomes of depressed public sector outpatients. *Biological Psychiatry, 56,* 46-53.

Safron, A. (2016) What is orgasm? A model of sexual trance and climax via rhythmic entrainment. *Socioaffective Neuroscience and Psychology, 6.* doi:10.3402/snp. v6.31763

Sahlem, G. L., Kalivas, B., Fox, J. B., Lamb, K., Roper, A., Williams, E. M., ... Short, E. B. (2014) Adjunctive triple chronotherapy (combined total sleep deprivation, sleep phase advance, and bright light therapy) rapidly improves mood and suicidality in suicidal depressed inpatients: An open label pilot study. *Journal of Psychiatric Research, 59,* 101-107. doi:10.1016/j.jpsy-chires.2014.08.015

Salama, S., Boitrelle, F., Gauquelin, A., Malagrida, L., Thiounn, N., & Desveaux, P. (2015) Nature and origin of squirting in female sexuality. *Journal of Sexual Medicine, 12,* 661-666.

Salisbury, C. M. A. & Fisher, W. A. (2014) A qualitative exploration of gender differences in beliefs, experiences, and concerns regarding female orgasm occurrence during heterosexual sexual interactions. *Journal of Sex Research, 51,* 616-631.

Santmeyer, H. H. (1982) *And ladies of the club.* Columbus, OH: Ohio University Press.

Schmidt, P. J., Nieman, L., Danaceau, M. A., Tobin, M. B., Roca, C. A., Murphy, J. H. & Rubinow, D. R. (2000) Estrogen replacement in perimenopause-related depression: A preliminary report. *American Journal of Obstetrics and Gynecology, 183,* 414-420. http://doi.org/10.1067/mob.2000.106004

Shenk, J. W. (2005) *Lincoln's melancholy: How depression challenged a president and fueled his greatness.* Wilmington, MA: Mariner Books.

Sherman, J. A. (1967) Problem of sex differences in space perception and aspects of intellectual functioning. *Psychological Review, 14,* 290-299.

Sherman, J. A. (1971) *On the psychology of women: A survey of empirical studies.* Springfield, IL: Charles C Thomas.

Sherman, J. A. (1974) Field articulation, sex, spatial visualization, dependency, practice, laterality of the brain and birth order. *Perceptual and Motor Skills, 38,* 1223-1235. https://doi.org/10.2466/pms.1974.38.3c.1223

Sherman, J. A. (1975) The Coatlicue Complex: A source of irrational reactions against women. *Transactional Analysis Journal, 5,* 188-192.

Sherman, J. A. (1976) Social values, femininity, and the development of female competence. *Journal of Social Issues, 32,* 181-198.

Sherman, J. A. (1978) *Sex-related cognitive differences: An essay on theory and evidence.* Springfield, IL: Charles C Thomas.

Sherman, J. A. (1979) Cognitive performance as a function of sex and handedness: An evaluation of the Levy hypothesis. *Psychology of Women Quarterly*, *3*, 378-390.

Sherman, J. A. (2001) Evolutionary origin of bipolar disorder (EOBD) *Psycoloquy:* (028) http://www.cogsci.ecs.soton.ac.uk/cgi/psyc/newpsy?12.028

Sherman, J. A. (2002) Is bipolar disorder a behavioral fossil? Reply to Previc on Sherman on evolution bipolar disorder. *Psycoloquy*: *13* (024) http:www.cogsci.ecs.soton.ac.uk/cgi/psyc/newpsy?13.024

Sherman, J. A. (2012) Evolutionary origin of bipolar disorder-revised: EOBD-R. *Medical Hypotheses*, *78*, 113-122.

Sherman, J. A. (2015) *Depression and bipolar disorder: Evidence-based natural treatments and a new theory.* https://depressionandbipolardisorder.files.wordpress.com

Sherman, J. A. & Beck, E. T. (Eds.). (1980) *The prism of sex: Essays in the sociology of knowledge.* Madison, WI: University of Wisconsin Press.

Sherman, J. A. & Denmark, F. L. (Eds.). (1978) *The psychology of women: Future directions of research.* New York, NY: Psychological Dimensions.

Simonti, C. N., Vernot, B., Bastarache, L., Bottinger, E., Carrell, D. S., Chi, R. L., ... Capra, J. A. (2016) The phenotypic legacy of admixture between modern human and Neanderthals. *Science*, *351*, 737-741.

Slater, L. (2018) *Blue dreams: The science and the story of the drugs that changed our minds.* New York, NY: Little Brown.

Stratton-Porter, G. (1909) *A girl of the Limberlost.* New York, NY: Doubleton Page & Company.

Steinberg, J. R., Laursen, T. M., Adler, N. E., Gasse, C., Agerbo, E., & Munk-Olsen, T. (2018) Examining the association of antidepressant prescriptions with first abortion and first childbirth. *JAMA Psychiatry*. doi:10.1001/jamapsychiatry.0849

Stoll, A. (2002) *The Omega-3 connection: The groundbreaking antidepression diet and brain program.* New York, NY: Free Press.

Styron, W. (1990) *Darkness visible.* New York, NY: Random House.

Taylor, J. A. (1953) A personality scale of manifest anxiety. *The Journal of Abnormal and Social Psychology, 48,* 285-290. http://dx.doi.org/1037/h0056264

Terman, M. & McMahan, I. (2012) *Chronotherapy: Resetting your inner clock to boost mood, alertness and quality sleep.* New York, NY: Avery.

Terman, M. & Terman, J. S. (2005) Light therapy for seasonal and nonseasonal depression: Efficacy, protocol, safety, and side effects. *CNS Spectrums, 10,* 647-663.

Thurston, R. C., Chang, Y., Matthews, K. A., von Känel, R., & Koenen, K. (2018) Association of sexual harassment and assault with midlife women's mental and physical health. *JAMA Internal Medicine, Pub Online* 10/3/18. doi:10.1001.jamaintermed.2018.4886

Tobias, S. (1978) *Overcoming math anxiety.* New York, NY: Norton.

Tóth, G. A., Buda, B. L., & Eiben, O. E. (2003) Contribution to the physique of women with manic-depressive disorder in Hungary. *Collegium Antropologicum, 27,* 581-586.

Travis, C. B. & White, J. W. (Eds.). (2018) *APA handbook of the psychology of women.* Washington, DC: American Psychological Association.

Vaccaro, C. M. (2015) The use of magnetic resonance imaging for studying female sexual function: A review. *Clinical Anatomy, 28,* 324-330. https://doi.org/10.1002/ca22531

Wade, L. (2017) *American hookup: The new culture of sex on campus.* New York, NY: Norton.

Waldinger, M. D., Quinn, P., Dilleen, M., Mundayat, R., Schweitzer, D. H., & Boolell, M. (2005) A multinational population survey of intravaginal ejaculation latency time. *Journal of Sexual Medicine, 2,* 492-497. doi.10.1111/1.1743-6109.2005.0070x

Walker, L. (1979) *The battered woman syndrome.* New York, NY: Springer.

Wallen, K. & Lloyd, E. A. (2011) Female sexual arousal: Genital anatomy and orgasm in intercourse. *Hormones and Behavior, 59,* 780-792.

Wehr, R. A., Turner, E. H., Shimada, J. M., Lowe, E. H., Barker, C., & Leibenluft, E. (1998) Treatment of rapidly cycling bipolar patient by using extended bed rest and darkness to stabilize the timing and duration of sleep. *Biological Psychiatry, 43,* 822-828. https://doi.org/10.1016/50006-3223(97)00542-8

Wehr, T. A., Duncan, W. C., Sher, L., Aeschbach, D., Schwartz, R. J., Turner, F. H., ... Rosenthal, N. E. (2001) A circadian signal of change of season in patients with seasonal affective disorder. *Archives of General Psychiatry, 58,* 1108-1114.

Weissman, M., Bland, R., Camino, G., Faravelli, C., Greenwald, S., Hwu, H., ... Yeh, E. (1996) Cross-national epidemiology of major depression and bipolar disorder. *JAMA, 276,* 293-299.

Wharton, E. (1920) *Age of innocence.* New York, NY: Appleton.

Whitaker, R. (2002) *Mad in America: Bad science, bad medicine, and the enduring mistreatment of the mentally ill.* (Rev.) New York, NY: Perseus.

Whitaker, R. (2010) *Anatomy of an epidemic: Magic bullets, psychiatric drugs, and the astonishing rise of mental illness in America.* New York, NY: Crown Publisher.

Whitaker, R. & Cosgrove, L. (2015) *Psychiatry under the influence: Institutional corruption, social injury, and prescriptions for reform.* New York, NY: Palgrave Macmillan.

Wilson, D. A. (1998) Evolutionary epidemiology and manic depression. *British Journal of Medical Psychology, 71*, 375-395.

Wingo, A. P., Wingo, T. S., Harvey, P. D., Baldessarini, R. J. (2009) Effect of lithium on cognitive performance: A meta-analysis. *Journal of Clinical Psychiatry, 70*, 1588-1591.

Wirz-Justice, A. (2006) Biological rhythm disturbances in mood disorders. *International Clinical Psychopharamocology. 21*, S11-S15. doi.10.1097/01.yic.0000195660.37267.cf

Wirz-Justice, A., Benedetti, F., Berger, M., Lam, R. W., Martini, K., Terman, M., & Wu, T. C. (2005) Chronotherapeutics (light and wake therapy) in affective disorders. *Psychological Medicine, 35*, 939-944.

Wirz-Justice, A., Benedetti, F., & Terman, M. (2013) *Chronotherapeutics for affective disorders: A clinician's manual for light and wake therapy* (2nd rev. ed.). Basel, Switzerland: Karger.

Witkin, H. A., Dyk, R. B., Faterson, H. F., Goodenough, D. R., & Karp, S. A. (1962) *Psychological differentiation.* New York, NY: Wiley & Sons.

About the Author

Born in 1934 in Akron, Ohio, Julia A. Sherman received her PhD from the State University of Iowa in 1957. She is a Fellow of the American Psychological Association and the Association for Psychological Science and has been honored for her pioneering work in the scientific study of the psychology of women. In 1971, she published *On the Psychology of Women: A Survey of Empirical Studies*, and, later, her research on women and mathematics was recognized by the National Council of Teachers of Mathematics as one of the most important contributions of the twentieth century. She served on the APA Committee on Women and as Associate Editor of the nascent *Psychology of Women Quarterly*. Involved in the issue of therapist sexual misconduct as a member of an APA task force, she suffered the whistle blower's fate when she testified against a powerful psychiatrist. Subsequently, recovered from a bout of depression and severe impairment from psychiatric drugs, she used her knowledge to pioneer a new non-drug treatment for depression and bipolar disorder based on chronobiology. One of her most significant contributions is a provocative new theory successfully predicting that genes for depression and mood swings come from Neanderthal.

Index

D

E

H